CHASING

the

RED,

WHITE,

and

BLUE

David Cohen

CREATED AND DEVELOPED IN COLLABORATION
WITH DR. LAWRENCE ABER OF THE JOSEPH L.
MAILMAN SCHOOL OF PUBLIC HEALTH,
COLUMBIA UNIVERSITY

A JOURNEY IN TOCQUEVILLE'S
FOOTSTEPS THROUGH
CONTEMPORARY AMERICA

CHASING

the

RED,

WHITE,

and

BLUE

Picador USA   New York

Picador® is a U.S. registered trademark and is used by St. Martin's Press under license from Pan Books Limited.

www.picadorusa.com

Library of Congress Cataloging-in-Publication Data

Cohen, David.
    Chasing the red, white, and blue : a journey in Tocqueville's footsteps through contemporary America / David Cohen—1st ed.
        p. cm.
    Includes bibliographical references p. 293
    ISBN 0-312-26154-3
        1. United States—Description and travel.   2. United States—Social conditions—1980-   3. United States—Biography.   4. Cohen, David—Journeys—United States.   5. Tocqueville, Alexis de, 1805–1859—Journeys—United States.   6. National characteristics, American.   I. Title.

E169.04.C646 2001
917.304'929—dc21   2001036350

First Edition: November 2001

10   9   8   7   6   5   4   3   2   1

FOR MY WIFE, PAMELA,

MY CHILDREN,

JESSIE AND KAYLA,

AND MY PARENTS,

MAURICE AND JEANETTE

CONTENTS

Introduction   ix

1: NEW YORK, NEW YORK
A City of Two Tales   1

2: THE RUST BELT
The American Dream in Retreat   52

3: THE OHIO RIVER VALLEY
Hard Work and the American Dream   81

4: THE MISSISSIPPI DELTA
"Luck Available One Mile"   131

5: ON THROUGH THE DEEP SOUTH
The Battle for the Soul of America   163

6: CALIFORNIA
The America Tocqueville Never Knew   218

7: WASHINGTON, D.C.
The Sum of the Parts   266

Notes   293
Acknowledgments   309

INTRODUCTION

In 1831, when the United States of America was barely born—a child, crawling, stumbling, just beginning to discover itself—a twenty-six-year-old Frenchman by the name of Alexis de Tocqueville came to pay a visit to see what his country and Europe could learn from their energetic young cousin. Today, the United States of America has grown to more than double its physical size and has matured into the richest and most powerful member in the family of nations. A foreign journalist of dual British and South African nationality, I find myself the recipient of a rare gift, a fellowship whose brief is not unlike Tocqueville's: to roam, to explore, and to see what we can learn from this success story in whose image the United Kingdom, Europe, and much of the world is being fashioned and transformed. This fellowship—the Harkness[1]—is the same one that once brought foreign journalists such as Alistair Cooke and Harold Evans to America. Both had grown to love the United States, adopted the country as their own, and, with the fresh eye of an outsider, described it for others. But no single foreigner has had a more profound impact on the world's view of the United States than Tocqueville, whose classic text, *Democracy in America,* laid out the deep structure of what this country was about. His distillation of its essential character—its passions and its prejudices—is widely regarded, by Americans and foreigners alike, as perhaps the most insightful ever written, true even to this day. But is it? Is what Tocqueville said still an accurate portrayal of contemporary America?

I fly into Newark Airport in midsummer—hot, sweaty, tired, and with a new tune reverberating through my head. As I move through baggage claim and customs into America itself, I become aware of a vibrant, but muffled, beat that appears to be following me around, but which in my jet-lagged state it seems only I can hear. Nothing like travel to put a magical new song in your heart, a new cadence in your step, between negotiating the snap logistical decisions that have to be made on arrival in a new country. But after a few minutes of this catchy tune that I can neither place nor shake, I begin to wonder where it is coming from, and how it planted itself on my person.

Then I click. It is not, alas, a singing soul that I have, but a singing suitcase. The portable radio I had carefully packed in with my jeans and T-shirts appears to have switched itself on and is now finely tuned to 97.9 FM, the Latino station. It belts out a high-energy diet of salsa and merengue while a disc jockey does continuity, hardly a word in English.

"*Oro Sólido! Oro Sólido! Oro Sólido—El Poder de New York!*" The disc jockey repeats, raplike, the chorus lyrics from what I discern to be the hit song by the group Oro Sólido: "*Domini-cana! Ba Puerto Rico! Ba-ra Colombia! Okay-okay-okay-okay-okay. Yesssss-suh!*"

Yessss-suh!

It is an exuberant introduction to the ethnic diversity of America, a diversity that Tocqueville marveled at too, and which led him to pose his first important question. "Picture to yourself if you can, my dear friend, a society formed of all the nations of the earth: English, French, German . . . all people having different languages, beliefs, and opinions: in a word a society without roots, without memories, without prejudices, without habits, without common ideas, without national character; a hundred times happier than ours . . . There's the starting point. What serves as a tie to these diverse elements? What makes of them a people?"[2]

The common cause that bonded Americans, Tocqueville noted in his diary, was not the pursuit of life, liberty, or happiness; no, it was none of these lofty but abstract ideals. It was, quite transparently, the pursuit of wealth. "As one digs further into the national character of the Americans, one sees that they have sought the value of all things in this world only in the answer to this one question: how much money will it bring in?" In America, "the passion to get rich leads and dominates all the others."[3]

The detail with which Tocqueville went on to describe this egalitarian—if somewhat rampant—pursuit of wealth marks, perhaps, the very earliest rendering of an ideal we today call the American Dream. Some historians say that it was Tocqueville who first coined the phrase "the American Dream." Others argue that the credit should go to nineteenth-century novelist Horatio Alger, while a third view maintains that the exact origins of the phrase are lost in time, dating back to Jefferson and the founding fathers.

It is immediately clear to me, as a foreigner newly arrived on these shores, just how powerful this idea still is.

The American Dream is the electricity of the nation. Its current moves everywhere, energizing visitors, would-be-immigrants and residents alike. From the moment I arrive, I can taste it, I can feel it, I can smell its intoxicating burn in the air. It invites you, the individual, to realize your potential, to shine like a thousand-watt bulb and be the best you possibly can. And it celebrates its success stories along the way—hoisting them above the fray and illuminating them as proof of its magnificent existence.

If the American Dream seems almost sacred, then it is matched by the American's belief in God, for nowhere in the West, aside perhaps from Ireland, does one find a more religious nation. Tocqueville noted this too. Religion, he said, was the filter that purified the morals of Americans as they exercised their primary passion, the pursuit of wealth: "Never have I been so conscious of the influence of religion on the morals and social and political state of a people as since my arrival in America."[4]

This dual loyalty is written even into the content and design of the dollar bill. "One Dollar," it says on one side; "In God We Trust," on the other, above large unifying capitals that proclaim "ONE," as if to emphasize that here in America, the spiritual and material pursuits of man are in perfect harmony. The American Dream, the pursuit of the dollar, has God's byline.

So these two alternating currents that Tocqueville observed—religion and materialism—I see them too, still playing dominant roles in American society.

But then I begin to notice some other things. Things that make me wonder: is the linchpin—the founding premise—on which Tocqueville built his entire analysis of American society still valid? *Democracy in America* begins with the celebrated lines:

> No novelty in the United States struck me more vividly during my stay there than the *equality of conditions*. It was easy to see the immense influence of this basic fact on the whole course of society. It gives a particular turn to public opinion, and a particular twist to the laws, new maxims to those who govern and particular habits to the governed. I soon realized that the influence of this fact extends far beyond political mores and laws, exercising dominion over civil society as much as over the government; it creates opinions, gives birth to feelings, suggests customs, and modifies whatever it does not create. So the more I studied American society, the more clearly I saw equality of conditions as the creative element from which each particular fact derived, and all my observations constantly returned to this nodal point.[5]

(Some historians say that the English title given to Tocqueville's book is actually a mistranslation and that a more accurate title would have been *Concerning Equality in America*.)[6]

Tocqueville painted a picture of America as a nation with greater equality of material wealth, and of opportunity, than any country in Europe, with the gap between rich and poor becoming ever narrower. People in America tended to be moderately wealthy and more middle-class, he said, and you didn't find the huge disparities between rich and poor so evident in England and France.

But he didn't stop there. It was the trend toward equality, he said, that had had a profound social and psychological impact on the American character, for it had made Americans into an extraordinarily gentle, empathetic, and compassionate people. "There are several causes which can concur in making a nation's mores less rough, but I think that the most potent of them all is equality of conditions,"[7] he wrote. "Equality which makes men feel their freedom, also shows them their weakness,"[8] creating "an empathy" between them. In short, it was equality of conditions that made Americans "extremely open to compassion."

But what if inequality of conditions—and not equality of conditions—has become the defining "creative element" of contemporary American society? To what laws, customs, opinions, feelings, and habits might such a society then give birth? How would such a society unravel?

There are three disturbing facts that I discover on my arrival in the late 1990s—facts that I struggle to square with the egalitarian, compassionate image of the country that Tocqueville had so eloquently described.

1. Almost one in five American children under the age of six is living in poverty, and an astounding 40 percent are living in poverty or near poverty. America, moreover, has a child poverty rate that is substantially higher—often two-to-three times higher than that of most other major Western industrialized nations.[9]

2. Inequality is dramatically on the rise in America. Between the late 1970s and the mid-1990s, the average income of the richest fifth of families increased by 30 percent, after adjusting for inflation, whereas the real incomes of the poorest fifth of families fell by 21 percent.[10]

3. Unprecedented budget surpluses at both state and federal levels make it appear as if Americans have the economic means to help the least-well-off members of their society, but not the will to do so.[11]

How does one make sense of these apparent contradictions?

On the one hand, I am encouraged by some middle-class Americans to dismiss the experience of millions of their fellow countrymen with a single sentence: "You know, our poor are really quite rich."[12] They have color televisions, VCRs, stereo systems, cars, food to eat, a roof over their heads.

On the other hand, there are those who tell me that the poor in America are doubly troubled. They experience the physical stress of insufficient resources (absolute poverty) *and* the psychological stress of struggling to make ends meet in the midst of ballooning abundance (relative poverty). The research shows, they say, that relative poverty—inequality—is almost as damaging to the human spirit as absolute poverty. America, they add, is a country with the Western world's richest and the Western world's poorest children. In other words, although the picture of poverty in America cannot compete with the images of deprivation coming out of the Third World, poor families in America are poorer than poor families in France, Germany, Italy, the United Kingdom. And the gap between them and the rich families is wider.

What would a modern Tocqueville discover if he were to retrace his original route today?

He might find that in retrospect, America was always this way, and it was just that back then, the have-nots were called slaves, and everyone else shared in an egalitarian society. Tocqueville described the conditions of slaves in the South, and discrimination against black people by custom in the North, yet these observations were treated as an aside when he formulated his general egalitarian proposition about American society.

Alternatively he might find that in the last thirty years, there has been a seismic shift in America's economic structure, a shift that has led to a new inequality and provoked a fundamental change in the national character. This would be consistent with the Frenchman's theory, for Tocqueville described a direct connection between equality of material conditions and the level of compassion that courses through a society.

Recent American history appears to support this relationship. In the Great Depression of the 1930s, for example, Americans felt they were poor together and compassionate New Deal legislation was the result. From World War II to the early 1970s, Americans up and down the income spectrum prospered, not equally, but at the same rate of progress, and in this time poverty legislation made it to the top of the agenda with Lyndon Johnson's War on Poverty. In the last three decades, as the tectonic plates of the American economy have cracked and realigned—the industrial economy giving way to both a low-end service and high-end information-age economy—the gap between rich and poor appears to have widened dramatically. With that gap, attitudes to the poor seem to have hardened. Perhaps there is a threshold beyond which a rising inequality leads to a tear in the social fabric, and a perversion of the relationship between the haves and the have-nots.

A third possibility is that my use of macro statistics leads me astray, and that the majority of Americans really do hold caring attitudes towards the poor. Maybe the compassionate heart and egalitarian society that Tocqueville described is alive and well, but you have to travel to the individual cities and states—to the micronation—to find it.

There is only one way to know for sure.

You have to hit the road.

To divine the rhythm of this country's beating heart, you have to navigate its arteries and tiny pulsing capillaries. As Tocqueville himself declared, to comprehend the whole of America, you have to first explore the many parts.[13]

And so it is that I spread before me a copy of an old map of the original 1831 route that Tocqueville followed. The mode of transport he used, the people he interviewed, the physical descriptions of the places he visited, and the evolution of his thinking are tucked away, not in *Democracy in America,* but in his lesser-known journals. These journals—in the form of fourteen handmade pocket diaries and nearly two dozen letters which have since been translated into English and published[14]—show that in nine months, Tocqueville and his traveling companion, Gustave Beaumont, visited seventeen of the country's then twenty-four states. They covered 7,384 miles, traveling by horse, stagecoach, steamship, and occasionally on foot. Theirs was an epic intellectual and physical adventure, ranging the length and breadth of Jacksonian America. Of course, America was a smaller place then: the entire population was 12.8 million,[15] as compared with 270 million today, and it extended only about as far west as the Mississippi River. Cities like New Orleans were compact enough for Tocqueville to attempt to meet "all the celebrated men, legislators, publicists, lawyers, poets and orators" in twenty-four hours. And he still had time, between calls, to "insert visits to . . . beautiful women" ("solely for the purpose of resting ourselves, I swear"), catch the evening play, then the ball, and return to his lodgings at midnight to organize his notes.[16]

I scribble down an itinerary, an edited version of the Frenchman's route:

- New York City
- Flint, Michigan
- The Ohio River Valley
- The Mississippi Delta
- The Deep South
- Washington, D.C.

I make one addition—California—the new frontier and command center of the information age.

Then, with Tocqueville in my rearview mirror, the road stretching before me, I tune my car radio to the Latino music station (of which I have grown unexpectedly fond) and set out to find America.

CHASING

the

RED,

WHITE,

and

BLUE

1

NEW YORK, NEW YORK

A City of Two Tales

I approach Manhattan from the George Washington Bridge shortly after dawn. At that hour, with the sun backlighting the city low and to the east, it appears as if a carton of milk has been emptied over its cardboard-cutout skyline, dousing it in a creamy, soft-focus halo. In that half-moment, Manhattan looks as intimate as a village. If I just reach out far enough, I can scoop it up and hold it in my hands.

But as the sun rises in the sky, the halo evaporates, and Manhattan emerges, a sharp-angled metropolis, its windows glinting and shimmering, a thousand cut diamonds in the morning sun.

"Come, come, come seek your fortune," it seems to beckon. A giddy, one-track monologue begins pounding in my head.

I find myself sharing my innermost thoughts with a bridge toll collector.

"How are you today, sir?" she inquires, breezily.

"Actually," I confess, "I'm feeling a little discombobulated."

"Huh?"

"See, I've just arrived from London," I continue, "and suddenly I find that I can't stop thinking about making money. I mean *rrreal* money, ma'am. And . . . well, since in your line of work you meet a lot of people coming into the city, ma'am, I was just wondering if you could tell me whether . . . whether this is normal."

She laughs. "That'll be four dollars, sir."

Then *whoosh!* I'm off, hurtling over the bridge that spans the Hudson River and into the long and thin of it, into the island twelve miles long and three wide with the shape of an exclamation mark and an energy to match—an energy so condensed and all-consuming that I really do struggle to hold on to a sense of self. There is something about Manhattan that is primal, provoking stirrings of outrageous ambition and, yes—greed.

This feeling only intensifies in the ensuing weeks as I carom through Wall Street, imbibe the ubiquitous coffee-shop phrases "feeding frenzy" and "sealed bids," and join in the three topics of conversation beloved of New Yorkers: real estate, real estate, and . . . you got it. It is a conversation that never wanes, because the first challenge for every new arrival is finding a place to live, but mostly because real estate in this town is booming in a way that makes the roaring eighties seem like a *miaowww*.

I stop. Pause. Breathe. Center myself.

And then, ears pricked, I try to decipher what the conversation is really about. Of course, there are many conversations in this city of conversations—one thing New Yorkers know how to do is *talk*, and they do it loud, fast, and with relish. But it doesn't take a Freudian to realize that all the fuss over real estate is a segue into something deeper.

If where one lives and the price of one's property really do preoccupy the minds of New Yorkers, what does that reveal about what New York has become?

One of the first New Yorkers I meet is Freddie Williams, a former Golden Gloves boxer, who happens to have stopped for a shoe shine and occupies the seat beside mine. His muscular frame threatens to burst the seams of his pinstriped suit at any moment, but there is no doubting the quality of his leather boots, which, as the shoe-shine man suggests, are "to kill for." Winning pendant dangling around his thick neck, Williams recounts how he won the Golden Gloves as a welterweight back in 1959, became the number-three contender of the world light-heavyweight division, and was a regular sparring partner of Muhammad Ali's at the New Garden Gym. When I explain what I am doing in New York, he tells me that he is, as it happens, on his way from his apartment in Harlem to sign the papers on a new home that he is buying outside of the city. Feeling expansive, he tells me how much he loves

America and that he and his wife have finally, finally been able to afford the home of their dreams. "Even if it is outside the city," he adds.

But when I congratulate him, and ask what the secret of his success has been, he turns away. He reaches up as if to pull something from inside his face, turns back toward me and holds it up like a trophy. I cannot stop myself recoiling in horror. There is a hideous fleshy void where his right eye should have been. In his hand he holds a glass eye. I hear him say something about a detached retina . . . how doctors advised him to quit . . . how he needed the money . . . fought one fight too many.

And then he prompts me: "Here, hold it. *Feel* my eye."

"Ugh . . . you sure?" I mumble. He hands me a smooth, marble-like object.

But I can't stop staring, totally transfixed, at the dumb, expressionless folds of skin where once that eye had been.

"This is a tough town—and the truth isn't always pretty," he says. Sometimes you lose body parts in the battle to survive.

There are layers to this reality, he seems to be telling me, hidden costs beneath the gloss of success.

What you see depends on the angle whence you look. Even that perspective may change with the light and time of day. New York is a place of fleeting, shifting, partial comprehension. And yet, illusion and hype are integral to the allure of this city, home to more than seven million people.

I might need help to peel away the layers, preferably from intermediaries at the hub of the conversation and with intimate knowledge of the city.

THE VIEW FROM MADISON AVENUE

The Corcoran Group is the highest profile real estate firm in New York City. Barbara Corcoran, the owner and founder of the group, and a cult figure in real estate circles, has agreed to see me, and while I wait for her to emerge from a meeting, her assistant, Scott Durkin, takes me on a whirlwind tour of their Madison Avenue offices. He leads me through their tastefully appointed blond-wood reception area, with a drinks cabinet offering free supplies of Arizona Green Tea, and walls inscribed in fancy script with quotable quotes like:

"The only credential the city asked was the boldness to dream."

Beyond the reception area, the place is a warren of cubicles crammed with brokers and their assistants frenetically working the phones. An onsite masseuse kneads the neck of a flopped-out, depleted broker, while another waits for her turn to be rejuvenated. I catch fragments of disconnected, animated conversation as I pass— "ya, ya, ya, vision and direction" . . . "oh yes, it's got *great* feng shui" . . . "the co-op board want to see a photo of your dog before they accept you, and if your dog dies, they say you can't buy a replacement." When I remark that the place has the buzz of money laced with a workaholic, almost cutthroat edge, Durkin explains that each broker must pull in at least $110,000 in commission (half of which is then paid over to the Corcoran Group) if they are to keep their cubicle and their job. By the year-end, he says, 10 percent of them typically won't have done the business and will be shown the door.

Barbara Corcoran, fifty, sweeps into the conference room, dressed in her trademark red power suit (she owns twelve of them), blond hair cropped short, face sans makeup but lit by a vivacious smile. "Don't be deceived, I hail from humble beginnings," she immediately assures me. She recounts how she grew up in Edgewater, New Jersey, which is a strip "one mile long, two blocks wide" situated almost directly below the George Washington Bridge on the "wrong side" of the Hudson River but with a tantalizing view of the Manhattan skyline. Corcoran, I soon discover, manages the double act of being charmingly self-deprecating and super-confident while talking at a mile a minute and performing three tasks at the same time. Between test-tasting a batch of cookies to be sent to clients—"The cookies suck!" she shouts to Durkin— she tells me how she built herself up the hard way, from scratch, and that after twenty-six years in the business, she knows this town like the back of her hand. Between them, her four hundred brokers handle one-fifth of all residential sales in Manhattan, and there is neither a nook nor a cranny on this space-constrained island that has escaped her attention.

"Who lives here, Barbara?" I ask.

"It is clear to me that Manhattan has changed," she says. "When I started in this business in the early 1970s, and for a long time thereafter, the typical buyer was young and middle class. Today the typical buyer is simply wealthy. I don't even meet middle-class people anymore. Or rather, I meet them coming to work in Manhattan, but I don't meet them *living* in Manhattan. This town has changed from a middle-class town to a town for the rich."

But the best way to grasp "what's going on out there," she says, is to witness it firsthand. She has generously arranged for me to spend time on the town with "her girls"—Emilie, Wendy, Carrie, and Sharon—to help me understand "who's selling, who's buying, and what you get for your dollar." I'm to start at the top end and work down. "Those four are my star brokers and each has their unique style," she says. "Emilie is a socialite. She knows everybody, has access to all the right circles, and is fabulously confident in her delivery. Wendy is New Age and becomes involved with her customers on a spiritual level. She prods her way into their soul." While I contemplate the novel thought of a real estate broker rooting around in her client's soul, Durkin whisks me off to meet Sharon, who, like Carrie, earned more than $2 million last year and is "redefining how much money can be earned in this business."

Sharon Baum is known for driving her clients around in a Rolls-Royce Silver Spur II hung with the license plate "SOLD 1." I catch up with her just as she returns from closing on an $8 million apartment, which has just earned her—gulp!—a $480,000 commission.

"For that price," I ask, "was it special?"

"Oh, it was a beautiful prewar apartment on Fifth Avenue in the eighties, three bedrooms and a library, sold to an entrepreneur in his fifties, but it didn't—" she starts to chuckle—"it didn't even have direct Central Park views. Come to think of it," she remarks to her assistant, "we often sell eight-million-dollar apartments without views."

"That other one we sold," adds her assistant, "that was eight million—and that looked at walls!" They double over laughing. "Eight million for a view of a wall. It's wild," says Baum.

Later I have an opportunity to view a top-end apartment myself. Emilie O'Sullivan has the exclusive on a Fifth Avenue penthouse, and this one does have magnificent views of Central Park and the Jackie Onassis Reservoir. "It's going for six something," she tells me. The "something," which she dangles like loose change at the end of the six (million), turns out to be an additional $800,000. The apartment has a pleasant aroma, having been spruced with an urn of azaleas ("an old trick—fragrance works on the unconscious," comments O'Sullivan), and classical music wafts elegantly in the background. Little touches leave clues as to the proclivities of the owner: a score—of Haydn's "Little Dance in F"—lies open on the Steinway piano, copies of *Yale Alumni Magazine, Opera News,* and a program of Tennessee William's *Not About Nightingales* adorn the coffee table. The shock to the buyer is that for this price, you get a lot of view but not much else: an impressive living room and view, yes, but only one bedroom, a tiny kitchen, no dining room.

"For seven million you don't get much living space," I remark.

"It's a penthouse with"—dramatic pause—"a terrace," she explains. "The last terrace apartment with views of Central Park that came on the market was bought by Robert Redford two years ago, and there was one other where my client was overbid by Bette Midler. They come up very rarely."

O'Sullivan talks to me in hushed tones. It's open-house day for the brokers from other agencies to preview the property, after which they decide whether to bring along their high-end clients, and so she stands in attendance ready to be accessible and to answer any questions. Dozens of brokers in high heels and power suits squeeze out of the private elevator and offer quick comments as they zip through within seconds.

"Emilie, it's absolutely gorgeous, dear."

"Spectacular—you feel you could almost dive into that reservoir."

"We all want to stay, Emilie."

"Someone's going to pay for that view."

Zip, zip, zip, zip, zip.

O'Sullivan, in her bleach-blond fifties, is from a well-connected family—her father was a property developer, she says, who owned and developed most of Bethesda, Maryland, just outside Washington, D.C. "Who cares what they think? This will go within weeks," she says airily. "I know smaller apartments without these views that are quite frankly yuck-poo and they're asking six."

I compliment her on her outfit, impeccably put together. "It's a Michael Kors coat-and-dress ensemble in the tradition of the classic sleeveless look which Jackie Onassis made famous," she explains when pushed.

"And the scarf?" I ask. "Cashmere?"

"Pashmani, I believe, made from the hair of the chin of a goat."

"The hair of a goat, huh."

"The hair of *the chin* of a goat," she corrects me. "Costs five hundred dollars." She swats the air dramatically. "Oh, I'm such an East Side girl. Done to the nines twenty-four hours a day, even when I'm sleeping." She breaks into gales of laughter. "Gosh, I'm known for being discreet. I'll lose all my clients talking this way."

I recount how Carrie Chiang, Corcoran's *most* successful broker, had told me she spends "forty thousand dollars a season" on her personal wardrobe. O'Sullivan is finished. "She told you that! Oh, I'm so amused. I would never! . . . Did she tell you about Puff Daddy? This guy walks into her office one day and he says he's looking for a place, he's Puff Daddy. Carrie has no idea he's famous, so she says to him: "Puff Daddy, huh. So do I call you Puff, or do I call you Daddy?" She shrieks. "Can you imagine?"

Celebrity stories aside (and she has them on RuPaul, Billy Joel, Michael J. Fox), the point O'Sullivan underscores is that the people who can afford Manhattan these days are the stars of the entertainment industry and Wall Street types. "Wall Street is driving the real estate market in a more direct way than ever before," she tells me over lunch at Circo with a client, a thirty-three-year-old venture capitalist who has just bought a loft in TriBeCa for "four something." "My client base is ninety-nine percent Wall Street, ninety-nine percent white. Rarely do I even see a doctor."

The next day I accompany broker Wendy Sarasohn (tanned, slim, skintight suede trousers) and her client, Cindy, on an apartment-hunting spree. Cindy's husband has just sold his company, and now that his children are grown up, they have moved from Long Island back to the city, where they are renting for $12,000 a month. She wants to buy something, ideally for $800,000, she says, $2 million tops. You would think that Cindy would feel full of the joys of life, having such a generous budget at her disposal. But considerable as Sarasohn's skills are—and she is quite the most charming, unpushy, soulful realtor one can hope to encounter—she is unable to prevent Cindy looking depressed by the end of the day. "I'm frightened," admits Cindy. "I'm frightened that if we don't buy something, things will continue to go up and we'll be priced out of the market. I'm frightened that if we do buy something, the market will crash. My husband is on a contract for $400,000 a year. In this place, that's peanuts."

There is nothing like the Manhattan real estate market to make even the rich feel poor.

"In today's New York," Barbara Corcoran later tells me, "a family of four earning less than $250,000 is living in poverty. And a single adult earning less than $100,000—I'm sorry, unless they find a rent-stabilized apartment, they're not moving to Manhattan."

"You know that the official poverty line for a family of four is about $16,500?" I say.

"Wait. You mean if somebody earns more than sixteen, they're not considered poverty-stricken? I can't imagine!" (Sixteen thousand, she quickly calculates, is the average broker fee for the sale of an apartment in Manhattan.)

Corcoran's world is high-end, so I expect her perceptions to be a little skewed. Yet what I discover, after speaking to brokers in other firms, is that if she is exaggerating the wealth requirements, it is not by much. You only have to glance at the numbers to see why. According to industry-wide statistics, the average sales price of an apartment in Manhattan south of West 116th Street and East 96th Street is an astronomical $734,000. The average price for a two-bedroom condominium is $958,000, or $760,000 for a two-bedroom co-op. In London, by comparison, the average price of a property is way down at $230,000.[1]

"Even at the bottom end," Corcoran runs her finger down the list of once modestly priced neighborhoods—Gramercy Park, Chelsea, Murray Hill, TriBeCa, the Village, SoHo, Flatiron, the Upper West Side—"there is practically nothing for a family to buy under $400,000."

Of course, the New York Corcoran refers to is Manhattan below Harlem.

"That is what people *mean* when they talk about 'New York,' " she says matter-of-factly. "They're not thinking the ghetto or the four outer boroughs" (Brooklyn, Queens, Staten Island, and the Bronx). "Manhattan has put a huge padlock on the door, one that only the rich can open."

THE VIEW FROM WHITE PLAINS ROAD, THE BRONX

But this image of Manhattan, and by extension New York, being a city for the rich while the middle classes (those earning $50,000 to $100,000) are ineluctably squeezed out is only half the story.

There is another side to the city—one that falls beyond the line of vision of the Corcoran brokers, and one curiously absent from the image I held in my mind when, pulse pounding, I first crossed the bridge into Manhattan.

The facts are that one-quarter of New York City's population lives below the official poverty line, and as much as 44 percent earn less than $30,000 a year. Moreover, the poverty rate for Manhattan tracks almost exactly the poverty rate for New York City as a whole.[2]

Where can these people possibly afford to live?

I put the question to Sandra Silverman, a veteran broker in

perhaps the cheapest part of New York—the Bronx. Her office abuts "Ping Pong Nails" in a quiet street off Pelham Parkway. "What have you got for a family of four earning $16,000 a year?" I ask her.

She pulls a sour face. "I don't work with people like that," she says. "Honestly, I don't know where people who earn sixteen thousand live! There was a time when they could get an apartment in the city [public housing] projects, but today the wait to get in is maybe ten years. The lowest Bronx rental that I have for a two-bedroom is $850. To afford that, you need to be earning at least $35,000 a year." She explains that as a rule of thumb, landlords will expect their tenant's annual salary to be four times their annual rental before they will agree to let to them, which means that somebody on $16,000 couldn't really afford more than $4,000 a year, or $333 a month, $400 tops. "Landlords nowadays are very particular," she says.

So what advice would she offer a family earning less than $35,000? "Rob a bank, call your relatives, get a better job, get a life!" she retorts. And then she catches herself. "Oh, don't quote that . . . I feel sorry for people like that. I have a compassionate side."

It occurs to me that Silverman might be high-end Bronx. After all, there are gentrified parts—like Riverdale and Throgs Neck—which my stereotyped preconception of the Bronx had failed to appreciate.

What I really need is to seek out the hustling, semilegal brokers who flog the rentals in the cheapest part of the borough.

Danny Rivera is a sweet-faced Puerto Rican who works out of an office on a strip of White Plains Road where most of the Bronx brokerages, with their garish yellow and pink storefront canopies, have congregated. Rivera, thirty, has yet to take his real estate exams and so does not have the license that would allow him to legitimately show apartments. It is a legal nicety he is happy to ignore, however, and for this reason I must also confess that Danny Rivera is not his real name.

"Six seventy-five is the lowest price two-bedroom we have. I tell truth to people. I don't like lie," he tells me in halting English and lights up a Marlboro. "I also don't smoke," he says winking. "Actually I smoke only when I nervous, or when lot of clients come in at once."

He grabs the keys of a 1990 Pontiac Bonneville and proceeds to charm me with his candor on the drive over.

"I make mistake. Apartment $725, not $675," he starts out unpromisingly.

"Can you describe it for me?" I ask.

"Big, big bedrooms, nice apartment."

"And the area?"

"West Tremont. Deep in the South Bronx."

"What's that like?"

"If somebody needs an apartment very very soon, then it is nice. But for me, I not like the area."

"What's wrong with it?"

"Nice inside, but you need a bullet-proof vest to step outside. There is a lot of drug dealing. In that neighborhood you get cheap rental, but maybe you pay with your life."

The apartment is all Rivera has cracked it up to be, and a little more besides. For example, you have to walk up six flights of stairs because the elevator shaft is just a black hole, the hallways are strewn with litter and covered wall-to-wall with graffiti, and the apartment has such a steeply sloping bathroom floor that the toilet is practically *in* the bath. But—the rooms are airy, with pleasant views of the Harlem River.

The next apartment he shows me is a converted basement with zero natural light and ceilings so low that you have to walk bent over. "That one's going for $650. Incredible price. Be gone by the end of the week to some very short people," he assures me.

"Would you move into any of these apartments?" I ask him.

"Are you crazy?" he says.

"But what option do you have?" I persist. Rivera, who has two children, had told me that he earns $1,000 a month, as does his wife, which puts them on $24,000 a year before taxes.

"You have three choices," he explains. "You can try and get

into subsidized public housing and live in a building where every-one is unemployed. Or you can go for the cheapest private rentals in the worst areas where you are always anxious because your children may not be safe. Or you can pay more rent than you can afford. We pay half our [after-tax] family income, $850 a month, for a two-bedroom in an area where we hope we won't get killed. We have money for rent, but no money for life."

According to the 1996 Housing and Vacancy Survey, one-quarter of all renters in New York City (525,736 households) have "severe rent burdens," which is officially defined as having to fork out—as Rivera does—over half their household income in rent.[3]

New York, New York! It seems apt they named it twice, for it is indeed a city of two tales. The one boasts a cast of characters who are affluent and predominantly white; the other is economically teetering on the edge and multicultural—African-American, Asian, and Hispanic. The New York for those who have money could hardly be more different from the New York for those who have not.

There is a third story—that of the ordinary middle classes, who, excluded from the first New York and wanting no part of the latter, are increasingly priced out of Manhattan. They move to New Jersey, or to the suburbs beyond the city limits, or to select ethnic enclaves in the outer boroughs. But as the middle layer is squeezed out, the gap between the first New York and the second New York, between rich and poor, becomes ever more severe.

The burgeoning inequality is reflected in census statistics. Whereas the richest tenth of Manhattan's families earned 39 times that of the poorest tenth in 1970, this had climbed to 48 times by 1980, and to 66 times by 1990. At this exponential rate of increase, the earnings ratio of richest to poorest is projected to approach 100 to 1 in the year 2000 census. Manhattan's widening income gap is not an exception. Rather, it mirrors the broader trend of the city and of the state. Moreover, it is not the case that the rich have got richer at a faster rate than the poor have got richer, but rather that the poor have actually got poorer. Between the late 1970s and the

NEW YORK, NEW YORK | 13

late 1990s, the average income of the bottom fifth of families in New York State fell by 21 percent in real terms, whereas the average income of the top fifth of families grew by 42 percent.[4]

Yet it was in Manhattan that Tocqueville first glimpsed the image of a world trending, as he put it, "irresistibly towards greater and greater equality."

What did Tocqueville observe? And how did we get from there to here?

THE VIEW FROM BROADWAY: THE YEAR 1831

"So here we are in New-York," Tocqueville wrote in a letter to his mother at the end of his third day. "One sees neither dome, nor bell tower, nor great edifice, with the result that one has the constant impression of being in a suburb. In its center the city is built of brick, which gives it a most monotonous appearance. The houses have neither cornices nor balustrades . . . the streets are very badly paved."[5] Paris was always going to be a hard act to follow, and Manhattan's aesthetics clearly did not excite the Frenchman. So after docking at the base of Manhattan where the South Street Seaport now stands on the morning of May 11, 1831, he and Beaumont checked into a pension on Broadway and promptly went to sleep, exhausted after their five weeks at sea.

But the very next day, as news of arrival of the emissaries of the French government circulated in the New York press, the Frenchmen were inundated with invitations and their American adventure was off to a flying start. In 1831 it was still possible to meet, as they did, most of the important officials of the city within a week of arrival, care of a red-carpeted courtesy tour the likes of which would flatter a visiting prime minister today. "We have been presented to the Governor of the State of New York, to the Mayor of the city, to the Recorder, to the Aldermen, and to nearly all the magistrates,"[6] Beaumont noted, just eight days into their stay. Evenings they went out into society to meet the most esteemed New Yorkers: Peter Schermerhorn, who owned the land that is today the South Street Seaport; Nathaniel Prime, a banker and "the richest businessman in New-York"; Julia Fulton, daughter of Robert Fulton, inventor of the steamship, and the man after whom Fulton Street in Lower Manhattan is named; and so on.[7]

New York City *was* Manhattan then, and just the tip at that, its population of 220,000 crammed into the densely settled area south of Canal Street. It seems hard to imagine, but Midtown was farm country then, Harlem still a thick forest, and Broadway a cobblestone road that extended from the Battery in the south to Fourteenth Street before dwindling into a muddy lane. The minutes of the Common Council (the equivalent of today's City Council) dated two days before Tocqueville's arrival reveal the geographical limits and order of business of the time:

"Resolved that Eighth Street be paved from Broadway to the Sixth Avenue.

"Resolved that Ninth Street be paved from Broadway to the Sixth Avenue."

Petitions for "a well and a pump" on Ninth Street near Sixth Avenue granted, the minutes record.[8]

If Tocqueville was unmoved by the physical dimensions of the place, he was immediately engaged by the human spectacle it offered—its ethnic diversity, the thirst for riches, and the apparent equality between its citizens. This ethnic diversity seems risible when you compare New York then—98 percent white and of Northern European origin—to the city today, where 150 languages are spoken and where whites (43 percent) are outnumbered by a combined population of African-Americans (26 percent), Hispanics (13 percent), Asians (7 percent) and ethnic others.

But what impressed Tocqueville above all else was how equal the immigrants stood to one another. "The equality is very great. Nobody is very rich; fortunes are limited," he observed.

"What seems clear to me," he wrote in a diary entry, "is that this country shows the attainment of outward perfection by the middle classes, or rather the whole society seems to have melted into a middle class. No one seems to have the elegant manners and the refined courtesy of the high classes in Europe. But at the same time no one is what in France one might call ill bred. All the Americans whom we have encountered, even to the simplest shop salesman, seem to have received, or wish to appear to have received, a good education . . . All the customs of life show this mingling of the two classes which in Europe take so much trouble to keep apart."⁹

Tocqueville had originally come to America—his trip funded privately by his own aristocratic family, but officially sanctioned by the French government—to study the United States prison system. He was to report back on the then-novel idea that criminals might be returned to society as reformed men after serving time in a penitentiary. But after spending nearly two months in New York and surrounds, undertaking intensive interviews and investigations, he had already stumbled across the proposition that was to form the spine of his great commentary on America.

This proposition, which he articulates in a letter written shortly after leaving New York, was that the outstanding feature that dominated every facet of American life was its equality. Historians have criticized Tocqueville for often using the two words "democracy" and "equality" interchangeably, for a lack of precision. But in his New York notes he makes clear that he was impressed by the equality of the people in the broadest sense: political equality in the democratic self-government of the people; civil equality in the unrestricted access of the ordinary person to seek public office; legal equality before the courts; social equality in the way Americans regarded each other; and economic equality in the unlimited business opportunities and in the broad distribution of wealth.¹⁰

Even the city's small black population, then only about 4,000 strong, was making progress, he thought. A law had decreed that from July 4, 1799, all children born of slave parents should be free, so that by 1830, there were only 75 slaves left out of 45,000 "colored persons" in the whole of New York State.¹¹

But Tocqueville's thinking had a directional component that went further. He concluded that this social and economic leveling tendency was not a chance or a static condition, but *an irresistible trend* almost in the form of "a natural law" that would sweep across Western civilization. Such thinking spools its way directly from his New York journals into his introduction to *Democracy in America,* where he states almost triumphantly: "The gradual progress of equality is something fated. The main features of this progress are the following: it is universal and permanent, it is daily passing beyond human control, and every event and every man helps it along." It was a trend, he declared, most advanced in America but also evident in Europe, that worked to "impoverish the rich and enrich the poor" and against which it was "useless to resist."[12]

On what had Tocqueville based such a sweeping and prophetic idea?

Yale historian George Wilson Pierson, the translator of Tocqueville's diaries into English, points out in his 1938 book, *Tocqueville and Beaumont in America,* that the Frenchman had made an acutely embarrassing error. He had come to regard the new U.S. inheritance laws as the key to explaining the trend toward equality, but in so doing had misunderstood how the inheritance laws actually operated. It is unclear how Tocqueville, who usually checked his information from at least two sources, made such a mistake, but he had come to believe that on the death of an American, it was compulsory for the property of the deceased to be distributed equally among all the heirs. This would lead to a forced subdivision of land on death, he calculated, breaking up concentrations of wealth and reducing even rich families to the level of small property holders.

The truth was that only the property of Americans dying intestate (without a will), a small minority among those who had wealth to pass on, were likely to be affected in this way. But as his letters show, Tocqueville was completely enamored by this law and its potential impact on society: "Do you know what in the way of politics strikes me most in this country?" he wrote. "The effects of the inheritance laws . . . We are ourselves going, my dear friend, toward an equality without limits. I don't say that it is a good thing, what I see in this country convinces me on the contrary that France will ill stomach it; but we are going there pushed by an irresistible force. All the efforts that will be made to arrest the movement will only procure temporary halts; since the human force does not exist which can change the inheritance law, our families will disappear, the goods will pass into other hands, wealth will tend more and more to be equalized, the high class to melt into the middle . . ."[13]

These thoughts were carried forward into *Democracy in America,*
where Tocqueville referred directly to the effect of the laws of
inheritance on the gradual equalizing of wealth, and on the "fact"
that "poverty as well as wealth ceases to be hereditary."

"It was the law of inheritance which caused the final advance
of equality," he wrote:

> I am surprised that ancient and modern writers have not attrib-
> uted greater importance to the laws of inheritance and their ef-
> fect on the progress of human affairs. They should head the list
> of all political institutions, for they have an unbelievable influ-
> ence on the social state of the peoples. Moreover, their way of
> influencing society is both sure and uniform; in some sense they
> lay hands on each generation before it is born. When the law-
> giver has once fixed the law of inheritance, he can rest for cen-
> turies . . . the mechanism works by its own power and
> apparently spontaneously aims at the goal indicated beforehand.
> If it has been drafted a certain way, it assembles, concentrates,
> and piles up property, and soon power too, in the hands of one
> man; in a sense it makes aristocracy leap forth from the ground.
> Guided by other principles and directed towards other goals, its
> effect is even quicker; it divides, shares, and spreads property and
> power . . . It grinds up or smashes everything that stands in its
> way; with the continual rise and fall of its hammer strokes,
> everything is reduced to a fine, impalpable dust, and that dust is
> the foundation for democracy."[14]

"When the law of inheritance ordains the equal sharing of a
father's property among his children," continued Tocqueville, "the
results are of two sorts . . . The death of each owner causes a revolution in property; not only do possessions change hands, but their
very nature is altered, as they are continually broken up into smaller
fractions . . . But the rule of equal shares does not only affect the
fate of the property; it also affects the very soul of the landowner
and brings his passions into play . . . The law of equal shares pro-
gresses along two paths: by acting upon things, it affects persons;
by acting on persons, it has its effect on things."[15]

It is astonishing to discover that one of the most significant strands of Tocqueville's famous commentary is based on a mistake that few people other than Tocqueville scholars are aware of. In trying to trace the root of the Frenchman's error, Pierson suggests that Tocqueville was "in the grip of a preconceived idea" imported from France. The idea in question had been advanced by an influential French academic whose lectures Tocqueville had attended—a Professor Guizot—and who had argued that "history was governed by certain inexorable laws." Foremost among these laws, he claimed, was the law of "progress" and of "the gradual, inevitable forward march of society through the slow growth and rise to power of the Middle Class." Tocqueville saw the embodiment of this idea in the United States and lapsed into an "unconscious desire" to "fit the facts" to a conviction he already held.[16]

It was a huge error with far-reaching consequences. For it meant that, contrary to Tocqueville's theory, there was nothing "natural" about the tendency to equality after all. Instead, the economic equality that so impressed him in 1831 would have to be fought for by every succeeding generation.

And yet, despite his mistake, Tocqueville had also drawn his conclusions from broader observations of New York life. For as Pierson notes, Tocqueville had "unwittingly come to the United States at the very moment when a great humanitarian movement was just gathering way." People were advocating the abolition of imprisonment for debt; free education through tax-supported public schools was on the agenda; a savings bank was created to encourage the poor to develop habits of thrift; prison reform was in vogue. Tocqueville had absorbed an attitude. "Unquestionably," Pierson argues, "the conscience of America was awake; philanthropy was in the air."

THE INTERVENING YEARS: FROM TOCQUEVILLE'S TIME UNTIL TODAY

You could argue that New York's egalitarianism is embedded in its geography, in the very vision with which the city was laid out. In 1806, when the city appointed commissioners to draw up a plan for the development of Manhattan, a simple rectilinear grid of streets was marked out between 14th Street and 155th Street, later to be extended over the whole island. Unlike other great cities—such as Paris, London, and Rome—there were no grand circles, ovals, squares, piazzas, or larger lots designed to create focal points or afford distinctive vistas. Instead, the city was broken down into small, regular, straight-sided, right-angled lots, each lot more or less equal in size and prominence to the others. Broadway, which wandered on a diagonal from east to west, was the only nonconformist street to survive the plan. The commissioners could have opted for a more ostentatious European design, but their simple grid system reflected a popular mindset that sought to include the working-class artisan in the real estate market and encourage economic development on a broad base. In the year Tocqueville arrived, for example, it was common for *New York Evening Post* editorials to rail against New Yorkers who displayed their egregious wealth by "adding granite pillars to brick facades" or "building with white marble and in a different style to their neighbors."[17]

But already by the 1840s, class differences were beginning to assert themselves on top of the pre-existing race differences, most notably in the form of a cultural divide between Broadway and the Bowery. The well-off, who tended to live in the Wall Street area and on lower Fifth Avenue, frequented the theaters on fashionable Broadway for their entertainment; the poor, who lived in overcrowded East Side slums such as Five Points, took their amusements in the bawdy saloons, brothels, and theaters on the Bowery.

A story: On the evening of May 10, 1849, the tension between the haves and the have-nots boiled over with tragic consequences. A throng of working-class young men made their way up the Bowery to the Astor Place Opera House—situated midway between Broadway and the Bowery—and tried to smash their way into the theater. They began pelting the theater with rocks and tried to halt the evening performance of *Macbeth*. On the face of it, the reason for their anger seemed bizarre—they had come to protest against the choice of an aristocratic English Shakespearean actor, William

Macready, in the lead role, ahead of their working-class local hero, Edwin Forrest. The protest ended when the militia were called out and fired indiscriminately into the crowd, killing twenty-three people and wounding one hundred. It marked the first time American troops had ever fired on Americans, and it provoked enormous soul-searching in the city. New Yorkers interpreted the Astor Place Riot, as it became known, as evidence of a bottled-up anger at the growing inequality in society, and of an antipathy that had not found an appropriate outlet. "The terrible tragedy is a lesson to us all," one commentator wrote at the time. "We are all responsible, all guilty. For we make a pact with society that has permitted thousands of its members to grow up in poverty and ignorance . . . The mob is but a symptom of our social condition, and it points out a disease to which we should lose no time in applying a proper remedy."[18]

Contrary to Tocqueville's prognosis, the divide between the haves and the have-nots widened as the nineteenth century progressed. Later came the 1863 draft riots, which included a murderous race riot in which hundreds of African-Americans were chased through the city by marauding whites. At least fifty "colored persons" were caught, beaten, and killed and fifty more maimed for life.

But just as notable as this pulling apart was the extent to which healing the divide occupied the minds of New Yorkers and rose on the public agenda. When Central Park was laid out in 1859, for example, Frederick Law Olmsted, its co-designer, described two functions for the park. The first was as a place for the contemplation of nature; the second was to create a social mixing bowl where the haves and the have-nots could rub shoulders with one another and where the have-nots might be inspired to do better.[19] It was an inspiring vision of what a great democratic city could be.

This concern for the least-well-off members of society was to find its most vivid expression in New York's housing reform movement. It was to lead to its public housing becoming, not just the first, not just the biggest, but for a long time, the finest in the nation.

Tocqueville would have wanted to know: what allowed this

humanitarian streak—so often found only on the margins of society—to become mainstream and politically actualized?

Of all the problems the city faced at the turn of the twentieth century, the overcrowded tenement slum was considered the most intractable. The tenements were originally built as five-story single-family dwellings, but a second wave of immigration between 1880 and 1924—this time from Eastern and Southern Europe and primarily composed of Jews and Italians—led to an acute housing shortage and resulted in tenements being occupied by up to four families per floor. By 1900, there were 42,700 tenement houses in Manhattan, housing 1,585,000 people—an average of 37 people per tenement—and this comprised, according to the 1900 census, half the entire population of New York City.[20] Up to twenty families squeezed into what had been single-family homes in conditions that rapidly became less than sanitary.

In those pre-vaccination days, however, there was one compelling reason for the wealthy and the middle class to care about the living conditions of the poor: public health. The tenements were breeding grounds for infectious diseases that tended to be incubated in conditions of poverty. These diseases—such as tuberculosis, typhoid, and cholera—were potentially fatal and could be transmitted through air or water with frightening speed to the rest of the population. In the earlier horse-drawn-coach era, the wealthy had been able to insulate themselves from interaction with the poor, but the opening of the "el" (elevated line) in 1871, followed by the first subway in 1904, resulted in a mass-transportation system that led to a chaotic mixing of the classes.

Housing reformers cleverly played on the self-interest of the broader population and used public health concerns to force the agenda of social change. In the late nineteenth century, housing reform had taken the form of imposing restrictive regulations on landlords to improve the sanitation, light, and safety of their tenements. But by the 1920s, most reformers had come to realize that restrictive legislation could only go so far: it could only control what was already built. To alleviate overcrowding and to make an appreciable difference in the lives of poor people, they needed to build new public housing. That would take public will and public money.

"A great ideological battle was fought," says Frank Braconi, an urban economist and the executive director of the Citizens Housing and Planning Council, a New York–based research and advocacy group. "On the one hand, many people saw the provision of public housing as socialism. And in many ways it was. On the other, it was an oddly moralistic period and there was a lot of compassion for poor people and a fierce will to improve their lot. Compassion won some people over. But to sell an idea in American politics, there is always a 'what's in it for me?' that has to be negotiated to win over the mainstream." That's where public health came in. Reformers were able to hitch their liberal and ethical concerns to the wagon of public health and, to a lesser extent, to the belief in some circles that social problems like vice, crime, and prostitution were also outgrowths of the tenement slums.

The reformers won a great victory, and in the early 1930s, the first public housing project in the Unites States was unveiled in New York, funded by city bonds and overseen by Mayor Fiorello La Guardia. Within a few years, as the Great Depression cast a shadow across America, the city reformers received a dramatic boost when Roosevelt's New Deal legislation took on the federal funding of public housing as a means to create thousands of jobs and kick-start the U.S. economy. From then on, public housing became subsumed under a federal program using federal money.

Over the next fifty years, New York City built 180,000 low-rental apartments, housing 600,000 people, in 344 high-rise public housing projects scattered throughout the five boroughs. It was a massive investment in social welfare, the equivalent of building ac-commodation to house the population of a medium-sized city. (The second-largest public housing stock in America is in Chicago and is only a quarter of the size.) But even more impressive than the sheer scale of the investment was the reputation it developed as the best-quality public housing with the best-quality tenants in the nation.

Two factors were critical to its success. First, the projects were built in and among New York's existing neighborhoods. This meant that children living in the projects went to the same neighborhood public schools as everyone else and were integrated into the community. This was in stark contrast to other American cities like Chicago, which built its public housing in geographically remote areas, out of sight, out of mind, and cut off from easy access to public transport, jobs, schools, shops, and entertainment.

Second, the New York City Housing Authority adopted the philosophy of fostering a mixed-income public housing population. Working families were given preference over families on welfare; and later, war veterans were given priority status, adding to the mix. The last thing they wanted was for the projects to turn into vertical slums.

"The best families were selected from the tenements," says J. Phillip Thompson, associate professor of political science at Columbia University. "Moving to public housing was considered a step up, not a step down. There was a rigorous selection process. Housing advocates, including people like Eleanor Roosevelt, wanted to demonstrate the kind of lives poor people could lead when they were housed decently and given a chance. It was with that kind of thought and commitment that public housing began in New York City. It was regarded as real quality."

By the early 1970s, New York City was a middle-class town. Manhattan was too. By and large, apart from some rough, poverty-impacted neighborhoods, the poor lived in and among the middle class; the middle class were spread throughout the city, many in apartments that were rent stabilized; and the wealthy perched on the Upper East Side. Most of the very wealthy had moved to the suburbs of Westchester, Connecticut, and Long Island. "In those days people who really 'made it' left. It was the losers who remained," says Corcoran.

So despite Tocqueville's error, despite there being no guarantee of an inevitable trending toward equality, the outstanding feature of middle-classness observed by the Frenchman had remained remarkably robust.

But starting in the late 1970s, the city began bifurcating in a way that Tocqueville would not have recognized, but which led directly

to the two New Yorks I journey through today. The private residential market, which had been almost exclusively a rental market,
began to shake off the shackles of rent stabilization, and real estate
prices, left to find their own level on the free market, took off. At
the other end of the spectrum, public housing went into a downward dive.

The context was that following the 1973 oil shock, New York
City, like the rest of the country, was hit by a series of economic
disasters—but had, in addition, a few extra problems unique to
itself. The first was the overnight abandonment of 100,000 tenement apartments by private landlords, who, as the recession took
hold, found it cheaper to abandon their assets than to maintain
them. The second was a new wave of immigration, this time of
blacks and Hispanics fleeing economically depressed Third World
countries. The third was a spiraling homeless population. And later,
into the 1980s came an AIDS epidemic, a crack epidemic, and a
spiraling crime rate. To make matters worse, the city was on the
brink of bankruptcy and simply did not have the funds to spend its
way out of trouble. The city's request for a federal bail-out was
met by a blunt rebuttal, captured in a famous *Daily News* headline:
FORD TO CITY: DROP DEAD.[21] Finally, as Ronald Reagan took the
presidency, his administration's determination to cut back the welfare state meant that almost no new housing stock would be built
to accommodate the flood of new immigrants.

Successive mayors, Ed Koch and David Dinkins, tried to use the
existing public housing stock to solve the city's social ills, including
the soaring homeless problem. They did this by tilting public housing preferences toward families on welfare and by setting aside one-
quarter of their vacancies for homeless families. This left limited
room in the mix for working families. Between 1980 and 1995,
working families as a proportion of the public housing population
fell from 53 percent to 33 percent, and with it, the reputation of
the projects went into free fall. At the same time, the racial mix of
the projects changed radically. Up until the 1960s, public housing
residents were mainly working-class white ethnics. But by the end
of the nineties, only 7 percent of public housing tenants were

white, 52 percent were African-American, and 30 percent Hispanic (predominantly Puerto Rican).[22]

Today's tenants are overwhelmingly poor—54 percent of public housing households earn less than $10,000 a year, 75 percent earn less than $20,000, and 88 percent earn less than $30,000 a year.[23] What had begun with high hopes and served as a mixed-income flagship to the nation has become ghettoized in a manner little different than the failed projects of other large American cities.[24]

The private residential market, on the other hand, took off in exactly the opposite direction. There the trend was luxury, luxury, luxury. It began in the late 1970s when private landlords, seeking a market return on their investment, turned thousands of rent-stabilized apartments into real estate that could be bought and sold by converting their buildings into co-ops or condominiums. Suddenly prices that had been artificially held down became subject to the forces of demand and supply on the open market.

Demand escalated for a number of reasons. The city's economy changed from a light manufacturing economy—paying solid but unspectacular wages—to a two-headed service economy. At the bottom end—the minimum-wage sector—the pay was (and remains) too meager for the workers to be players in the private housing market. But at the top end—Wall Street—white-collar professionals used their prodigious purchasing power to bid up property prices in Manhattan, and it had a ripple effect throughout the city. There was also the Donald Trump factor. Trump built luxury residential skyscrapers that displayed a faith in the future of Manhattan at a time when its reputation was still "murder capital of the world." Trump is a love-to-hate character for many New Yorkers, as are his gleaming high-rise creations, but property developers and brokers give him credit for his visionary approach and the impact he had on changing the perception and potential of the city.

Crime continued to plague the city throughout the 1980s, but in the 1990s, Mayor Rudolph Giuliani used the New York Police Department to aggressively, and somewhat controversially, "clean up" the city. The result of their zero-tolerance policies, as well as

of other demographic and social shifts—such as an abatement of
the crack epidemic and the broader economic recovery—is that
New York begins the new millennium with a violent-crime rate
that ranks it, quite remarkably, among America's safest cities, on a
par with Boise, Idaho.

New York has once again become a destination of choice, a
place where people *want* to live. Empty-nesters who no longer need
large family homes, and who can afford it, have begun moving back
to the city as they find the aesthetic of suburban life dull compared
to the cultural life of Manhattan. Foreign businessmen buy apartments in Manhattan as status symbols. Demand is booming, but
supply is relatively static, and under those conditions, prices move
in one direction only.[25]

At the turn of the twenty-first century, then, public housing has
become the repository for the poorest of the poor, while the private
residential market has become increasingly high-end. The middle
classes who arrive hoping to settle in Manhattan find that they
cannot afford to buy there, or to rent, unless they can somehow
find themselves one of the cheaper "gold dust" rent-stabilized
apartments, whose number, though still significant, diminishes
every year. "The contrast between the two New Yorks could not
be greater than if we were talking about the U.S. and Bangladesh,"
says Columbia University's J. Phillip Thompson.

But another analogy strikes me when I visit a public housing
tower block on the Upper West Side of Manhattan. The building,
on West 93rd Street, is twenty-two stories high but is serviced by
only two horrendously slow elevators. Reach your apartment and
you will be safe inside, say the tenants, but waiting, waiting, waiting
the ten to fifteen minutes for that elevator to arrive, you are a
captive and prime target for muggers. While you wait you can kick
around the rubbish on the floor, wonder about the bloodstains on
the wall too large to be squashed mosquitoes, or read graffiti that
bluntly says, "FuCK yOu." The tenants here are overwhelmingly
African-American and Hispanic. Of those who are employed, most
have menial jobs. They cannot afford to move out, even if they
want to, because they cannot afford more than these highly subsi-

dized (and hence highly sought-after) $300-a-month rentals. (There is a ten-year waiting list.)

The life stories of the residents I interview are horrific. They tend to involve drug addiction, divorce, prison, drug rehabilitation, poverty, and arson. I have never been to Bangladesh, but I did grow up in apartheid South Africa in the 1970s, and the feeling of being in this project transports me back to a reality I did not expect to find in America. In certain aspects, the projects bear the same relationship to Manhattan as Soweto does to Johannesburg. Obviously, the quality of housing in the projects is far superior to most of the housing you find in Soweto; but I am struck by the analogy of the one being black and poor, and the other being white and rich, and their relationship to each other being that the former's occupants are employed in low-paid menial jobs—like cleaners— to service the latter. Actually, even this analogy is not quite apt, because Soweto is physically separated from Johannesburg, whereas many of the projects exist in and among New York's affluent neighborhoods. In this respect, the projects seem akin to the Jo-hannesburg backyard, where domestic maids and gardeners have their "rent-subsidized" living quarters, and whose salary, education, and training was never enough under apartheid, and is still insufficient today, to afford them the economic freedom to leave.

And yet, and yet . . . Setting aside for now the long-term implications of social exclusion, one cannot help thinking that this historical narrative should not surprise us, and that if we are to assess modern New York by modern American standards, we ought to move the goalposts. For the equality of wealth that impressed Tocqueville was always likely to be a fleeting phenomenon in a country that embraced an unfettered strain of capitalism. Many of today's New Yorkers do not even begin to judge their society by its ability to create equality of income. That, they scoff, is the aim of socialism. What they are about, they say, is "equality of opportunity," because that is what affords upward social mobility and access to the American Dream. And social mobility, they will tell you (and if they don't tell you, they will think it), is the difference between being poor in America and being poor in Europe. In

America, so the argument goes, you can easily rise out of your class, whereas in Europe, in the United Kingdom, upward mobility is much more the exception than the rule.

But at the same time, New Yorkers also recognize a powerful relationship between the neighborhood they live in—"location, location, location"—and their prospects of upward mobility. This unique and complex relationship, this "neighborhood effect," which everyone recognizes but few talk about directly, has such profound consequences for "equality of opportunity" that Tocqueville would have wanted to investigate its nuances wherever he traveled—in the big cities of the East Coast, in the smaller cities of the Midwest, and in the agrarian and the high-tech communities on the West Coast.

For now, I simply open a line of inquiry. I seek the perspective of a small sample of New Yorkers from across the neighborhood spectrum. How do their personal testimonies help us to understand the impact of "neighborhood" on "equality of opportunity" in New York City and, by proxy, big-city America? How much bounce is there to this widely trumpeted American ideal of upward mobility?

THE LOWEST-PAID EMPLOYEE ON WALL STREET

Tocqueville's address in Manhattan was 66 Broadway, right around the corner from Wall Street. From there he stepped out and met the first people that shaped his perception of America. Whom would he meet were he to step out from that same location today? I ponder this question as I journey one morning to the heart of the financial district, my object being to proceed from the exact spot that the Frenchman would have daily departed from in May and June of 1831.

Physically, of course, it is another place. The twin towers of the World Trade Center hedge the skyline and the narrow street is cooled, despite the beating summer sun, by the slanting shadows of wall-to-wall skyscrapers. Only the Gothic-revival Trinity Church, which stands at the confluence of Wall Street and Broadway, offers a glimpse of the past: its blackened gravestones, among which workers take their lunch under the dappled shade of maples, date back to the early 1800s. (Alexander Hamilton is buried there.) The *pension* where Tocqueville stayed has long since been torn down. Now the Bank of New York Building rises on the spot and takes up the whole block. I plant myself in front of the bank and contemplate how to proceed.

Across the street are two signs. The one, a large white banner, advertises 19TH CENTURY LUXURY RESIDENCES SMART-WIRED TO THE 21ST CENTURY. Rentals start at $3,400 a month. The other sign says INTERNATIONAL HAIRCUTTERS. I decide to take my chances.

The shop is staffed by four hairdressers—from Colombia, El Salvador, Uzbekistan, and Italy. Only Aida from El Salvador says she speaks "some English."

"Okay, sit down," she says rather forcefully.

"I would like a trim, please," I say.

"What is 'trim'?" she asks.

"You know, cut it just a little . . ."

"You like razor?" she says, pulling one out and holding it aloft, her eyes lighting up triumphantly. "You want all off?"

"No like razor!" I gulp.

"Scissors?" she tries, looking disappointed.

While Aida snips away—and while I try to figure out how to broach the subtle subject of *style* of cut—we scrape together a conversation of sorts. Among them, they explain to me that on their pay—$200 a week, no benefits—none of them can afford to live in Manhattan. They all live in Queens, except for the Russian-Jewish woman, who lives in Borough Park, Brooklyn.

Earlier I had made a mental note of the incredible diversity you encounter as you walk down Broadway: every color, hue, and language. There are religious Jews in yarmulkes and beards, Asians in traditional garb, Hispanics, African-Americans, and whites. Here is the storied image of Manhattan as melting pot. But this happy cliché conceals a deeper truth—for although these people work in Manhattan, they cannot afford to live here anymore. Unless they live in public housing, or a rent-stabilized apartment, home for most of them is the outer boroughs—Brooklyn, Queens, Staten Island, or the Bronx.

The first English-fluent person I meet after my haircut is Carlos Reyes. He is standing on the corner of Wall Street and Broadway, blue-eyed and smiling, with arms powerful enough to throttle a bull (or a bear). He is an ex-marine, forty-five years old, and he has, he tells me, "the lowest-paying full-time job on Wall Street."

"My job is to stand in this heat, smile, be vigilant, be polite, direct tourists, and protect the ass of big-shot executives," he begins, when we adjourn to a nearby coffee shop after his shift is done. He is paid $8 an hour to be a security guard/courtesy officer, $2.85 above minimum wage, a rate of pay that makes him feel "used and undervalued," he says. "The people who I guard make in one day what I take home in a year. There is something sick about that."

Despite his low pay, Reyes, who calls himself a Nuyorican (a Puerto Rican born and bred in New York), nevertheless considers himself to be someone who has achieved both upward mobility and the American Dream. The reason is simple: he bought his own home, something his father was never able to do. His father worked his whole life in a picture-frame factory, and although he actually earned, back in the seventies, more than Carlos earns as a security guard today, he never owned his own home. When the city and several community regeneration groups got together to build low-income housing on some unused lots of land in the South Bronx at the beginning of the 1990s, Reyes saw his opportunity. Together with his mother-in-law and two sisters-in-law, they pooled their resources and paid $130,000 for a five-bedroom house. "We were pioneers," he says. "The house itself was wonderful—more real estate than we ever thought we'd be able to afford."

But if Reyes had known then what he knows now, he would never have bought in the South Bronx, he says. His wife had just given birth to the first of their two children, and they hadn't begun to think about education.

"The area we live in . . . there are all these newspaper reports that say it's coming back, but to be honest, it's a dead area. We are what they call working poor, but we are surrounded by such poverty that to our neighbors . . . they think we're *rich*. You have kids having kids, drug dealers, and they have children who end up at school with your children.

"My seven-year-old son is in the second grade at the local public school. It's ninety-nine percent Hispanic, completely underfunded and lacking resources, and most of the kids are from teenage mothers with fathers in jail. His teacher just wants to survive the day. When I was at school, at least they taught me to read and write and do arithmetic. My son won't even learn that unless I teach him. What he will learn about, though, is sex and drugs, because he sees it all around him. My son asks me: 'Daddy, why that girl's mother wear her skirt so tight she can hardly breathe? Daddy, it's so short, she might as well wear nothing. Daddy, if she sneezed it would pop.' I explain: 'Don't judge, son, look past what they wear and what they do. That prostitute might do a bad thing, but she might be a good person.' But I also teach him: don't trust these people an inch. It's not an education my child is getting; it's a guide to survival."

It is tempting to regard Reyes's take on his child's educational prospects as unique to his particular neighborhood, but the demographics show that public schools in New York have, by and large, become places where the city's poor are educated. In 1997, 73 percent of the city's 1.1 million public school students were receiving free school lunches, compared with only 37 percent in New York State, which means that three-quarters of the students come from families living in poverty or near-poverty. (The 25 percent who are not poor tend to be clumped in the high-performing public schools that exist in affluent areas like Manhattan's Upper East Side.) The demographics also show that just 16 percent of the total enrollment is white.[26] The overwhelming majority of nonpoor and white New Yorkers send their children to parochial (religious) or private schools.

Recent test results bear out how low standards of achievement have sunk. Two-thirds of city public-school fourth-graders (nine-year-olds) failed the state reading and writing test in 1999. In grades 3, 5, 6, and 7, the number of students reading and writing on grade level is less than 50 percent.[27]

But instead of the city administration pumping more money into the system to help the children in public schools compete, the opposite has occurred. In the eight years from 1990 to 1998, despite a 10 percent increase in total student enrollment, the New York City budget for public schools was cut by $2.7 billion. This amounted to cuts of $2,520 per child, or $75,000 per class. The amount spent, moreover, is $1,819 less per student than in upstate public schools, where the enrollment is whiter and wealthier.[28] Prior to 1984, it used to be the other way around, with expenditure per city public-school student exceeding expenditure per state public-school student.

As if to rub salt in the wound, at the same time that the city administration enacted these cuts in the school budget, it gave tax breaks to the wealthy estimated at $10 billion over five years (1999 to 2003).[29]

How do education experts explain what has happened?

The themes they emphasize, it turns out, are similar to that which afflicted public housing. Prior to the 1970s, they explain, the city's poor were educated in and among the middle class in mixed-race public schools. In those days, there was a high drop-out rate, but if you were smart and applied yourself, you were headed for college. When the wave of immigration from Third World countries hit in the late 1970s, the white middle class—fearing they would be swamped by people of color, many of whom could not speak fluent English—abandoned the public schools in droves. They did so reluctantly and gradually at first, then not so gradually, and they haven't been back since.

The defection of the white middle class was followed by a sharp decline in per-pupil funding. Noreen Connell, the executive director of the Educational Priorities Panel (an advocacy group for better-quality public schooling in New York City), says that "plain racism might best explain the decline in per-pupil funding. Prior to the 1970s, public-school students were majority white, but the perception today is that the public schools are serving the immigrant population, which is mainly African-American and Hispanic. It's a narrower base from which to draw financial support. As the white middle class withdraw their children from public schools, they vote against increased taxes to raise spending on a public education system they no longer feel serves them. Many people believe this is the reason why the city administration did not mount a real rescue effort. Of course, money isn't everything, and there are other reasons for the decline in standards—like poor teachers and poor teaching methods. But overall, what we have in New York City today is a segregated education system. And of course, separate is never equal in the United States."

It is interesting, and not a little disconcerting, to note that most senior City Council officials and Board of Education members—across the political spectrum—have opted to send their children to private or parochial schools, where annual tuitions range from $5,000 to $20,000, rather than negotiate the troubled public school system. According to the *Daily News*,[30] prominent New Yorkers in public office who send (or have sent) their children to private or parochial schools include Mayor Rudolph Giuliani, Public Advocate Mark Green, Interim Schools Chancellor Harold Levy, City Council Speaker Peter Vallone, State Controller Carl McCall, and Attorney General Elliot Spitzer. "If they attended public schools, Giuliani's and Green's children would go to Manhattan's Public School 151 on East 91st Street, where only 52 percent of the children read at grade level," notes the *Daily News* report. Only two of the seven Board of Education members send their children to public schools, the report adds.

What might Tocqueville have made of this "segregated" education system?

Judging from his journals, he would have regarded it as a total anathema to the values he believed Americans stood for. For it was, ironically, in New York that Tocqueville believed that he had discovered the two "moral safeguards" that would guarantee the future of equality and democracy in America: religion was one, education the other. Universal public education would make democracy work, he argued.[31] The American system of universal public education was a symbol of the "enlightenment" of American society because it managed to advance equality of opportunity and hence both the good of the individual and the good of society at the same time.[32]

But if education was seen as important to life opportunities in the nineteenth century, and even back in the 1970s, it is absolutely critical today. Kristin Morse, a deputy director of the NYC Partnership, a not-for-profit advocacy group working in the areas of education and economic development, notes that "what has changed even more than the quality of the schools is simply the importance of being educated. In the 1960s, an eighth-grade education got you a job on which you could raise a family, such as a police officer or other civil servant, whereas today you have to finish twelfth grade and have some college behind you. The bar has been raised as the job market has changed."

Dr. Henry Adam, a professor of pediatrics at the Albert Einstein College of Medicine, speaks to me "as a parent and a citizen" when he says: "Most parents who live in New York City feel totally different about their lives if they are empowered to send their children to a private or parochial school.

"I would say that being able to afford this choice is the *real dividing line* between the haves and the have-nots in New York City today."

It is a dividing line that is causing acute anxiety among thousands of service employees in the city. When the trade union that represents workers like Carlos Reyes recently polled their 150,000-strong membership, they found that their top worry was "the education and future of their children." Gerry Hudson, the executive vice-president of the Health and Hospital Workers Union (part of the Service Employees International Union, whose members include a range of skilled and unskilled workers, from doormen to nurses), tells me that these New Yorkers say they feel "deeply insecure about their children's future." "Our members' average salary is $35,000 a year and they regard themselves as middle-class—but they aren't rich enough to afford private schools," he says. "They are stuck with the public school system, but what they see are poorly performing schools, violence in their schools, kids not gaining the computer literacy they will need to compete in the job market. And they see their kids falling behind the kids of their employers." The result is a searing sense of frustration.

Reyes believes that his children have been put in a position where they will not be able to compete. "They don't have a chance," he says. "I wish I had the money to move to a better area or to send them private, but I don't. I'm up at four A.M. every day to go to work in a job I hate; every day I go stand out there in all weather; the last vacation I had was never, and even that was to visit my relatives in New Jersey. And I can't even say to myself it's worth it because my children will get the kind of education that will allow them to do better than me.

"How do you think that makes me feel? Trapped. Without hope. That the American Dream ended with my generation."

THE PRISON OFFICER WHOSE SCHOOLMATES ARE NOW HIS INMATES

Harry Miller (not his real name) grew up in a public housing project in Brooklyn. He moved there with his mother when he was six years old, the year his parents split up, and for the next thirteen years it was his whole world. When he was nineteen, he escaped from the projects, he says, and he adds that in his neighborhood, he was one of the lucky few who "got out a free man." Miller likes to make bold statements and, by his own admission, he can be a bit of a showman, but on this count he is simply articulating what for him is an everyday lived reality. For the past dozen years, Miller has been a prison officer at Sing Sing Correctional Facility— the grim New York state penitentiary situated on the east bank of the Hudson some thirty miles upriver from New York City, a prison that Tocqueville visited. During that time, he claims, most of his former schoolmates and peers have passed through the prison, including his childhood best friend, currently serving a life sentence for murder.

Miller, who is African-American and in his early thirties, is re-luctant to use his real name for this interview because, according to prison regulations, he is supposed to notify the authorities every time a new prisoner arrives whom he knows personally. But they come at such a rapid rate, he says, that strict compliance is simply impractical. Besides, he says, he would feel bad because they would have to be transferred to another prison, further away from their parents. "How could I do that and look their mothers and fathers in the eye, many of whom I know personally?"

These days, when Miller does his rounds to check in on the inmates under his watch, he sometimes gets the eerie feeling that he is back in the old neighborhood.

"Yo! Homeboy from down the way!" they call out.

"Pass us a cigarette, brother."

"Can you get a message to my mother?"

They often use Miller's nickname, known only to those who knew him in the 'hood, a nickname that refers to the quicksilver, stylish way he played basketball. "The way you play," they had told him, "is the best show we gonna see for free." Miller, they were convinced, was headed for stardom. He sometimes reminisces how he could have turned pro, been a contender. But then he stops: "I *have* made it," he likes to remind himself. "I grew up in the projects and I don't have a criminal record."

After speaking to me a few times over the phone, Miller arranges to meet me at his studio apartment in Ossining. He opens the door for our ten A.M. interview still in his sleeping shorts, wearing no shirt, and bleary-eyed after two hours' sleep.

"Night shift again," he mumbles.

He offers me a seat on his living-room carpet (there is no furniture), next to six stuffed bulldogs he won for his four-year-old son at Coney Island. Earlier his wife had tiptoed out while he slept to take their son to day care. Now he fixes us some coffee, turns up the radio, and begins to dance while he talks—he's working on some new moves, he says—his physique cut and toned like a lightweight boxer's.

Miller grew up in a small apartment on the first floor of an eight-story tower block, one of twelve tower blocks that made up their public housing development. He lived there with his mother and two sisters, one of fifty-seven families in their building alone. In the late 1970s, as New York City buckled under recession, and

Miller entered his teen years, the atmosphere in the projects began to change. "Jobs were scarce, and some of the adult males in the neighborhood, including my father, turned to crime," he says. "They called my dad 'the Wolf Man of Harlem' because of his wild Afro mane and because he made his living holding up Harlem drug dealers. I remember how he walked around dressed in a ridiculous long coat that he wore even on the hottest summer days, and under it he kept a sawn-off shotgun strapped to his shoulder with telephone wire. He was my role model. He was all of our role models. My dad really wasn't that unusual."

Miller and his friends started their own racket at the age of eleven. There was a factory-warehouse directly across the road from their project, called Cascades, which he says is still there today. Miller used to break in at night and steal sheets and pillowcases, which he sold on the street: "two sheets for five dollars." Later they realized that on the second and third floors were finer pickings, such as adding machines and computers. "We'd take them up to the roof and throw them off because we were not strong enough to carry them with us down the drainpipes," he recalls. "When we got down we found that maybe two or three were still working and we'd sell them to the local neighborhood store."

At seventeen, Miller's friends began graduating to more serious crimes, like auto theft and muggings, and their vices deteriorated from cheap beer to reefer, and then to cocaine, glue sniffing, and mainlining. Miller sensed that he was at a personal crossroads. In retrospect, a unique combination of personal attributes and chance events caused him to take a different path from his peers, he says, though at the time he saw no way out of the fog that had descended on his life.

First, his father was killed. He was shot dead, he says, on the corner of 123rd Street and Lenox in Harlem, and the pain of losing a father just as he was getting to know him set off a ping inside his head that he might be headed the same way. Second, Miller was extremely close to his mother, and the thought of someone mugging her and stealing her pocketbook with all her hard-earned wages inside sickened him to the core. "She worked two, sometimes three, jobs to provide for us, and so she had little idea of the trouble I had got into. I was a mama's boy and she was the center of my universe. She taught me morals, she taught me to respect myself, she taught me to achieve by setting goals—she had high hopes that I would do something worthwhile with my life. It bothered me to disappoint her."

Miller was also a gifted athlete. Every weekend, he would journey into Manhattan to play basketball with the pro-amateurs at the famous Fourth Street courts, known as "the Cage." There he would mix it with playground legends like Herman Helicopter ("his arms were everywhere"), and occasionally pros would come down in the off-season. It was a culture within a culture where you brought your game and hoped some talent spotter would offer you a contract. But hoop dreams aside, Miller also found that the sport performed a social and psychological function. "That court was my haven from the projects in Brooklyn. I could take out my frustration on the court," he says. "The game is what saved me. It taught me humility. As talented as I was, I had to learn to deal with defeat. That, more than anything, made me grow up. Some of my friends, they didn't have that outlet."

Finally, Miller was academically bright. He got A's and B's whereas most of his peers in the local public school were simply failing, he says. It gave him more options than his peers of finding decent-paying work and earning a living the honest way.

But before he could make the change to a straight lifestyle, he had to do a radical thing, he says. "I had to leave my neighborhood. I realized that I couldn't change my friends, but that maybe, maybe I could change me. As someone I knew liked to say—you go into the barbershop enough times, eventually you going to get a haircut."

So he took a bunch of civil-service tests, was offered training as a New York State corrections officer, and moved to a studio apartment thirty-five miles north of the city in suburban Ossining. At first he couldn't get used to how quiet it was compared to the siren-wailing streets of Brooklyn.

"When's it going to happen?" he asked his neighbor.

"When's what going to happen?" his neighbor replied.

"When do the police arrive? When does the shooting start?"

Miller thought he had severed ties with his past. He was totally unprepared for what would follow.

"The day I started my job at Sing Sing, there were all these people I recognized and they were calling me by my name," he says. "It was horrible. They were shouting through the bars: "Yo! Homeboy from down the way!" I thought to myself: Is this where all my old friends have ended up? My whole neighborhood in Sing Sing?"

Twelve years later, Miller still feels torn. On the one hand, he wrestles with the idea that his former friends have brought ill fortune upon themselves. "If you are prepared to get your degree, to work hard, there are more opportunities to make it in America than anywhere in the world," he says. On the other hand, he empathizes with them. "I see the link between the person who spent their childhood in poverty and the person who spends their adult life in prison. Ninety percent of the prisoners in Sing Sing are African-American and Hispanic. Ninety percent! Figure that. I know the odds are stacked against a kid making it out of the projects. I know that unless you have the type of mother I had . . . where you grow up plays a big, big role."

We talk for a few hours, and then it is time for Miller to dress for his three P.M. shift. He sprinkles baby powder on his feet, slides on his polished black boots, buttons up his shirt, which says NEW YORK STATE CORRECTIONS OFFICER, and checks the cartridge of his 9-millimeter handgun.

"Shit!" he exclaims, examining the barrel. "It's got cheese all over it! I must have had it in my bag with my son's lunch."

I laugh at the juxtaposition of the gun and the cheese sandwich. "Where did you learn to shoot?" I ask him. "Sing Sing?"

"Naaa," he says, "my friend's backyard in Brooklyn."

On the drive over to Sing Sing, Miller delineates the chain of command in state prisons, starting at the top with the governor of the state, and descending through half a dozen white-collar tiers, mainly filled by whites, to the twenty thousand New York State corrections officers.[33]

"Who is below you in the organizational structure?" I ask.

"Just the prisoners," he says.

And then, almost to himself, barely audibly, he adds, "Still *just* the prisoners."

We drive on in silence. The forbidding walls of Sing Sing loom up ahead. If Miller had been alive in 1831, he might well have been interviewed by Tocqueville. The Frenchman spent nine days at Sing Sing, then a new penitentiary, interviewing the prison guards, the Harry Millers of yesteryear. On seeing the prison for myself, I am struck, as was Tocqueville, by what a monumentally grim place it appears to be. "One cannot see the prison of Sing-Sing . . . without being struck by astonishment and fear,"[34] he wrote. Tocqueville's statistical notes show that in 1831, one third of the prisoners were either "Negro" or "Irishman."[35] The original four-story cellblock that was built in 1826 no longer houses prisoners, but it still stands alongside the present fortress.

I voice my gut response to Miller. "It is hard to comprehend that you actually *choose* to spend your life inside this place when you are in fact a free man," I say.

Miller looks impassively ahead. "When I think back," he says, "I realize that I was trained for it. The stress of living in the ghetto actually prepares you for the stress of a life in jail. I am my brother's keeper. Where I come from, this is about as good as it gets."

"TWENTY MILLION AND I'LL WALK"

Adam Hart Diamond, twenty-seven, can afford to live in Manhattan. He would have it no other way. Diamond is a realtor who nurtures a reputation as a "killer closer." A year ago, he decided to use his reputation, his aggression, and his razor-sharp edge to start making money for himself instead of lining the pockets of others, and so he resigned his job at another realty firm in order to start one of his own. He called it Hart Diamond Real Estate and opened up in the Flatiron District, just a few blocks from where he rents a modest one-bedroom apartment in Gramercy Park. Success has been swift, he says. He has eighteen brokers working for him, is already "very profitable," and has, he claims, "one of the fastest-growing" brokerages in the city.

You would think that Diamond, who is half Spanish European (his mother) and half Jewish (his father), might be pleased with his speedy progress, but he is not smiling when I catch up with him at his office one balmy summer afternoon.

"Am I happy? You want to know, am I happy? Listen! I am trying to survive. Plenty of time in later life to find out what will make me happy."

On his message board, he has written a single instruction for his brokers. It reads: "E5 Str—ATTACK!!!"

"So the East Village is hot?" I ask him.

"Huh! I wrote that last week. The East Village is yesterday's news. The hot new area as far as I'm concerned is Harlem. It's the only place you can still get cheap rentals. Where else can people go? I haven't sold anything there yet, but it's going to happen. People are buying whole buildings there."

Diamond counts cash under his desk while we talk: people's deposits that need to be checked, part of the job, he claims. He wears a blue cotton shirt over a white T-shirt, and wears his hair plastered back. He counts fast: "20 - 40 - 60 - 80 - 100; 20 - 40 - 60 - 80 - 200; 20 - 40 - 60 - 80 - 300; 20 - 40 - 60 - 80 - 400; 20 - 40 - 60 - 80 - 500; 20 - 40 - 60 - 80 - 600; 20 - 40 - 60 - 80 - 700; 20 - 40 - 60 - 80 - 800; 20 - 40 - 60 - 80 - 900; 20 - 40 - 60 - 80 - . . . (slight pause to catch his breath) . . . One thousand. 20 - 40 - 60 - 80 - 100; 20 - 40 - 60 - 80 - 200; 20 - 40 - 60 - 80 - 300; 20 - 40 - 60 - 80 - 400; 20 - 40 - 60 - 80 - 500; 20 - 40 - 60 - 80 - 600; 20 - 40 - 60 - 80 - 700; 20 - 40 - 60 - 80 - 800; 20 - 40 - 60 - 80 - 900; 20 - 40 - 60 - 80 - . . . Two thousand. 20 - 40 - 60 - 80 - 100; 20 - 40 - 60 - 80 - 200; 20 - 40 - 60 - 80 - 300; 20 - 40 - 60 - 80 - 400; 20 - 40 - 60 - 80 - 500; 20 - 40 - 60 - 80 - 600; 20 - 40 - 60 - 80 - 700; 20 - 40 - 60 - 80 - 800; 20 - 40 - 60 - 80 - 900; 20 - 40 - 60 - 80 - . . . Three thousand. 20 - 40 - 60 - 80 - 100; 20 - 40 - 60 - 80 - 200; 20 - 40 - 60 - 80 - 300; 20 - 40 - 60 - 80 - 400; 20 - 40 - 60 - 80 - 500; 20 - 40 - 60 - 80 - 600; 20 - 40 - 60 - 80 - 700; 20 -

40 – 60 – 80 – 800; 20 – 40 – 60 – 80 – 900; 20 – 40 – 60 – 80 – . . .
Four thousand. 20 – 40 – 60 – 80 – 100; 20 – 40 – 60 – 80 – 200;
20 – 40 – 60 – 80 – 300; 20 – 40 – 60 – 80 – 400; 20 – 40 – 60 –
80 – 500; 20 – 40 – 60 – 80 – 600; 20 – 40 – 60 – 80 – 700; 20 –
40 – 60 – 80 – 800; 20 – 40 – 60 – 80 – 900; 20 – 40 – 60 – 80 – . . .
Five." He wraps the wad of bills in an elastic band and stuffs them
into his top pocket.

"You were saying?" he goes, lighting up a Camel.

"I was just wondering," I begin, "what drives Adam Diamond."

"Not having," he shoots back. "Not having money scares the
shit out of me."

"How much do you make?" I ask.

"I'd say a couple of hundred thousand this year so far, but that's
not money, really," he says.

"How much do you need to feel secure?"

"I dunno," he says. He rests his head on his desk, then looks
up. "Twenty million? Twenty million and I'll walk."

"Twenty million?" I laugh.

"That'll do it," he says, scowling.

"Why do you need so much?"

"It's not so much. I don't think you're considered rich with $20
million. That's not rich, that's—"

He breaks off momentarily to shout to one of his brokers who
is trying, apparently unsuccessfully, to close a deal over the telephone. "Bring her here!" he bellows, rising from his chair. "I'll
finish her off!" The broker rebuffs his offer, raising his hand in a
"have patience—not yet" halt signal, and Diamond reluctantly sits
down. He doesn't show apartments anymore, he says. "My job is
to help people close. I do whatever it takes to get the job done."

He continues where we left off. "You need to make a lot of
money if you want to live in Manhattan. It's a greedy city. Rentals
are overpriced. Why do I do it? Because it's the best place in the
world to live. The energy here is incredible."

"That energy," I enthuse, "I feel it too. What gives this city its
energy?"

"Money," he says. "The opportunity to make a shitload of
money."

Diamond is relentlessly forward-looking and not at all the kind of person to dwell on his past, but he does say that the particular experience he had growing up in Manhattan has irrevocably shaped his worldview. He is, he tells me, the only child of a single mother who moved with him to Greenwich Village in 1980, when he was eight years old. (His father, from whom he was estranged, died when he was ten.) His mother opened a garment factory and built up a small chain of fifteen factories making "better dresses." But it all unraveled, he says, when America signed the NAFTA treaty, creating free trade with countries like Mexico. "NAFTA was the end for us," he says. "My mother couldn't compete with the cheap labor costs in the Third World countries. By the early nineties, she was bankrupt. We tried to sell her factories. In the end we couldn't give them away."

"It wasn't fun," Diamond continues, shaking his head. "Nobody gave a shit. Nobody gave a helping hand. Not the city, not the state, not the country, not friends, not family—no one gave us a penny. I learned then what this city is about.

"This is the greatest city in the world, but I learned that if you don't have money, you are no one, and nobody will care about you. So there you have it—that is why I am focused on making money. I get up at seven A.M., I go for a swim, then I come to the office and work until nine or ten P.M. I have no time for women in my life. I've been without a girlfriend for two years now." He grimaces, then (almost) smiles. "Boy, I just met a real cutie today. She just walked into my office. She's hot. She's gorgeous. She's wild. And she's hungry to meet somebody. I got to be careful, though. You can't approach a client. It is called sexual harassment . . ." He trails off. "You know, I tell you that story about my past, but sometimes I think I was just born angry. There's a fire in me. I know that money won't make me happy. But I don't know what will. And until I find out . . . money, money, money"—he snaps his fingers three times. "The only thing that makes me feel safe in this town is money."

Does Diamond suffer from an extreme case of affluenza? Or is this really a town where even the rich can't sleep easy?

I take these questions to Murray Nossel, a clinical psychologist, cultural anthropologist, and filmmaker who lives on Manhattan's Upper West Side. I have not yet begun to recount the details of my conversation with Diamond when Nossel, thirty-nine, volunteers a story about a "daymare" of his own.

"I don't know if it is just me," he begins, "but I find myself increasingly consumed by a fear of falling, a fear I will be left without any means of survival in this city. I say to myself: 'Hello? You have six university degrees, two of them from Ivy League universities, what's your worry?'

"When I analyze it, I think it's because every time I go to a Manhattan dinner party, all I hear about is Internet billionaires and Wall Street stock offers. The cumulative force of this one-track conversation is such that I can't help feeling that I am being progressively shut out of the city. One response I have is to try to grab my share of the wealth being generated. I think, it's so close, if I just reach out it can be mine. Even though I define success in my life in terms other than money, I find myself stuck in an internal conversation in which the terms are set by Wall Street, and I have to manage both my envy and my sense of how much money I need simply to survive. It's crazy, but the more affluent the city becomes, the more survival is redefined upwards. It's a scary position to be in. Because what has also returned, with a vengeance, is the idea that people are wholly responsible for their own destinies. I have no sense, living here, that the community will take care of me. It's all up to the individual. And yet, what this city does offer me is an incredible opportunity to find my niche and to express myself. There is an ambivalence built into living here that takes a lot of internal strength to manage."

Paul Wachtel is a professor of psychology at City College and the author of *The Poverty of Affluence: A Psychological Portrait of the American Way of Life.*[36] Wachtel's book analyzed the greed of the eighties and had argued that Americans got caught in a vicious circle of earning and spending. The more they earned, the more they spent, the more they needed to earn, the harder they worked, the less time they had for themselves and their relationships. This cycle did not lead to greater happiness—in fact, quite the contrary.

"Our frenzied commitment to consumption was in fact a desperate attempt to replace the sense of community that our very growth had torn apart," he thought.

But the 1990s, he now thinks, are a whole new game. "If the eighties were about conspicuous consumption, the nineties have gone beyond wanting money as a means to access the good life. Money has become an end in itself," he tells me. "It is the easy way to keep score. Money is about self-worth."

Later he modifies this slightly. There are defining sectors of Manhattan—the arts, parts of the media, philanthropy, and academia, for example—where satisfaction is derived from the job, and where money is secondary and not the primary measure of self-esteem, he says. "But compared to other cities, Manhattan also has a disproportionately large number of people working in the world of finance, insurance, and real estate, and these people tend to have a frighteningly direct relationship between their self-esteem and the size of their salary. The culture of scorekeeping and envy trickles down and makes it harder for everyone to be content with what they have. I have clients who earn a million a year but feel unhappy because the people they work with earn more."

This scorekeeping, he suggests, has two effects. It means that people are unable to feel the happiness and the satisfaction that goes with having more. And it means that they don't have empathy for the people who really *do* have less.

WHERE IS MANHATTAN HEADED?

Is Manhattan really destined to become an island of the rich? Or are rumors of the death of the middle class much exaggerated?

In December 1997, the New York City Council published a report entitled "Hollow in the Middle: The Rise and Fall of New York City's Middle Class."[37]

The single most troubling finding, the report notes, is the decline of the city's middle class. The report goes on to quantify the shrinkage in the middle class and to assess the cause and effect. "In 1989," it explains, "over 35% of all New York City residents lived in middle-class families. By 1996, only 29% of all residents were still in the middle class." (It defines the middle class as a family whose total income falls between 100% and 200% of the city's median income: for example, $34,000 to $68,000 for a single person; $49,000 to $98,000 for a family of four.) This decline in the middle class "may be permanent," it warns. "Rather than an outcome of the business cycle, we may be witnessing a fundamental change in the local distribution of income" caused by "changes in the occupational and industrial distribution within the New York City labor market." In other words, the city has fewer jobs that pay middle-level wages, and more jobs that pay lower- and upper-level wages. Over the last seven years the economic and social structure of the city has become increasingly 'hollow in the middle,' " it says.

On the release of the report, City Council Speaker Peter F. Vallone went on the record to say: "Our research shows without question that New York is headed in the wrong direction. When we lose the middle class, we lose our tax base, our social fabric, and our history. I cannot imagine what will happen to us if we let the middle class disappear. The middle class is and always has been our economic engine. The rich getting richer and the poor getting poorer is a dynamic we cannot afford."

But despite Vallone's rallying cry, City Hall has yet to come up with a realistic solution.

Larian Angelo, one of the authors of the report and deputy director of the Finance Division of the New York City Council, admits that "it is going to be difficult to arrest this trend, which is why you haven't seen a stream of what-to-do-about-it reports." When I visit her in her office on Broadway across the street from City Hall, Angelo tells me that although their report did not run the numbers for each borough separately, the decline of the middle class in Manhattan is known to be even more pronounced than in New York City as a whole. "The structural changes in the labor market are even more severe in Manhattan, with more people in both upper and lower income categories, and fewer in the middle," she says.

The best hope for the middle class, argues Angelo, is retaining the city's rent stabilization laws. "Rent stabilization keeps rents mod-

erate. It is the strip of Velcro to which the middle class cling."
The Housing and Vacancy Survey shows that one-third of all
housing units in New York City are rent stabilized, and that in
Manhattan itself, half of all housing units are rent stabilized. Of
course, not all such tenants are middle class: 56 percent of rent-
stabilized tenants are working poor, earning less than $30,000;
only 40 percent of tenants earn incomes that would be considered middle-class.[38] But even the rent-stabilization laws—
instituted during World War II as an emergency "temporary"
measure and subsequently regarded almost as a birthright by many
New Yorkers—cannot be taken for granted, warns Angelo.
"Their renewal has to be fought for at the state level every two
years, and with some people in high places having the attitude
that it is archaic, regressive, and leading to a gross misallocation
of resources, its future must be considered seriously under threat.
If rent stabilization went, the impact on Manhattan and on the
middle class would be extraordinary," she says.

In the past, the city has helped to promote affordable housing
and stable neighborhoods by building subsidized middle-income
units—known as Mitchell-Lama housing—and more than 120,000
such units exist throughout the city today. But there have been no
major city-subsidized constructions of this type for years now. Instead, the city offers a myriad of programs that promote private and
productive partnerships. Commissioner Richard T. Roberts, who
heads up the city's Department of Housing Preservation and Development, tells me in an interview that he has put together a
coalition for the construction of another 3,500 units for middle-
income families. "We recognize that the market doesn't respond to
the middle class, so we're trying to assist the market by making a
commitment to affordable housing." He asserts, though, that "if the
commitment to affordable housing is to be sustainable, the long-
term player has got to be private capital."

But J. Phillip Thompson, the Columbia University political science professor, insists that there are public solutions at hand, and
that a great opportunity is being missed. "New York City has just
gone through an unparalleled period of economic prosperity. Taxes
could have been increased marginally to fund housing, social and

education improvements to benefit the vulnerable members of the city's population. Instead, what did they do? They supported tax breaks for the wealthy," he says.

In the early part of the twentieth century, public-health worries could be used by reformers to drive issues like neighborhood regeneration to the top of the city's political agenda. Not today. In today's hypervaccination age, the kind of diseases you might get from living in poor neighborhoods—increased susceptibility to asthma, for example—are not contagious and hence unlikely to be of great concern to nonpoor population groups. The fact that exposure to cockroach feces, mold, dust, cigarette smoke, poor ventilation, and overcrowding leads to quite shocking increases in asthma hospitalization rates is not something that the majority of the broader population either knows or worries about. (A study by the Mount Sinai School of Medicine, to assess the relationship between asthma hospitalization rates and socioeconomic factors, reports that the hospitalization rate of children in East Harlem is 222 per 10,000 residents, whereas the rate in high-income zip codes—such as Battery Park City and Greenwich Village—is almost zero.)[39] It is harder to make the case today that the early housing reformers did—that economic regeneration of marginal areas helps everyone—because the chain of causality is longer, more complicated, and, hence, less persuasive.

Urban economist Frank Braconi takes a different tack. "I don't think you can stop Manhattan becoming an island for the rich and I don't know if you would want to," he muses. "Manhattan has morphed from a place of pockets of affluence into an affluent place. That's not necessarily a problem. The rich will always seek out the best places to live.

"The real question is this: Can we use the prosperity of Manhattan to make New York's marginal neighborhoods desirable? Can we encourage the middle-income people who cannot afford Manhattan to move into and gentrify other parts of the city? If so, we are sitting on a potential for the revitalization of marginal areas. If the middle class simply displace poor people, we won't have achieved much, but if it happens gently—and we're already seeing the gradual gentrification of parts of Brooklyn, Queens, and the Bronx—then you have to be optimistic about prospects for the city. We are then looking at the potential for creating in the boroughs the mixed-income, mixed-race neighborhoods that once characterized Manhattan. For example, most of Queens today is lower-middle-class: lots of blue-collar and civil-service workers, but still very few entrepreneurs, very few people connected to the advanced sectors of the economy. If we have learned anything, it is that you cannot regenerate neighborhoods if they are uniformly poverty-impacted. You have to have a middle-class base."

Will the middle class go for it? Will they really move into places like the South Bronx and Harlem?

There are some signs that things are moving—albeit slowly—in the right direction. Karen Phillips, CEO of the Abyssinian Development Corporation, the neighborhood revitalization arm of the Abyssinian Baptist Church under Reverend Calvin Butts in Harlem, maintains that with a fair wind, we could be looking at a second Harlem Renaissance. "Harlem is one of the last places where the ordinary person can afford to buy or rent in Manhattan," she says. So far, two hundred brownstones have been renovated using city programs. The families who are moving in are solidly middle-class, earning about $70,000 a year, she says. "It's still overwhelmingly an African-American influx, it's still very few whites, and it's still got a ways to go, but give us another ten years of economic growth and hopefully we'll have made enough progress for this change to be sustainable through the next economic downturn."

In the meantime, Manhattan south of Harlem—the Manhattan that people think about when they think about Manhattan—threatens to become a different type of city with a different ambiance and temperament from that which it once had.

E. B. White was clear about what made Manhattan great. "There are roughly three New Yorks," he wrote (though really he, too, was talking about Manhattan):

There is first the New York of the man or woman who was born here, who takes the city for granted and accepts its size and turbulence as natural and inevitable. Second, there is the New York of the commuter—the city that is devoured by locusts each day and spat out each night. Third, there is the New York of the person who was born somewhere else and came to New York in quest of something. Of these three trembling cities the greatest is the last—the city of final destination, that city that is a goal. It is the third city that accounts for New York's high-strung disposition, its poetical deportment, its dedication to the arts, and its incomparable achievements. Commuters give the city its tidal restlessness; natives give it solidity and continuity; but the settlers give it passion. And whether it is a farmer arriving from Italy to set up a small grocery store in a slum, or a young girl arriving from a small town in Mississippi to escape the in-dignity of being observed by her neighbors, or a boy arriving from the cornbelt with a manuscript in his suitcase and a pain in his heart, it makes no difference; each embraces New York with the intense excitement of first love, each absorbs New York with the fresh eyes of an adventurer, each generates heat and light to dwarf the Consolidated Edison Company.[40]

Manhattan used to be about people arriving from all over Amer-ica and around the world, finding their niche, and attempting to make it. That's what made it such a vibrant, versatile place. That's what made it the financial, media, and cultural capital of America. That's what gave the place its passion and made it great. But today, with ten-year waiting lists on public housing, with vacant rent-stabilized apartments a rare, rare thing, and with almost all other housing—whether rental or for sale—beyond the ordinary person's budget, pretty much the only people who can afford to move to Manhattan are people who work in the financial sector, or those who have *already* made it.

Economists have a word for the phenomenon when one factor in a mix becomes so powerful that it obliterates the others. They call it "crowding out."

On current trends, the city is set to become a narrower place—

full of lawyers, accountants, brokers, entrepreneurs, and bankers. As the farmer from Italy, the young girl from Mississippi, and the boy "with a manuscript in his suitcase and a pain in his heart" no longer find Manhattan accessible to them, so the ambiance of the city will alter. As money and the pursuit of wealth becomes the only game in town, crowding out more refined pursuits, so Manhattan threatens to become more like Monte Carlo: a richer city but a poorer place.

But that is all in the future. In the all-encompassing present, we cannot help but hold on to the myth that the city is still accessible, that if we can make enough money, we can pick it up and hold it, and mold it, in our hands.

I leave the city by the same route as I arrived. The George Washington Bridge shimmers in the early-evening darkness. Behind me, the yellow flickering lights of Manhattan sprinkle the city in a layer of gold dust. As I exit the bridge, I feel as if I am leaving the most powerful magnetic field on earth. There is a magical allure to the city, an amnesiac spell that it casts—it makes you forget everything untoward about it in an instant. It tilts your ambition toward you and prompts: "Now hit it out of the park, baby!"

My mind flits back to my meeting with Adam Diamond, who is attempting to do just that. But superimposed on Diamond's driven demeanor, I see another image—a chimera of the boxer holding up his glass eye.

Today, the price of not making enough money has become simply this: you are locked out of the city, you cannot live in Manhattan. You must go live in "unfashionable" New Jersey or the outer boroughs, or the upstate suburbs, or (gulp! for most whites) Harlem. The New Yorkers' preoccupation with "real estate, real estate, real estate" reveals a deeper truth about this otherwise great city, a truth that is not apparent to the naked eye, but which, at its core, is about a fear we all have.

It is the fear of being excluded.

2

THE RUST BELT

The American Dream in Retreat

I fly from New York City to Milwaukee and board a twin-propeller plane for the forty-five-minute hop to Flint, Michigan. Inside the tiny eighteen-seater, which is like a zip-up cylindrical pencil case, the passengers hunker down, cramped into seats on either side of the lead-thin aisle, and break open their sandwiches, using newspapers for napkins.

PIAZZA CASHES IN: $91 MILLION DEAL is the day's headline. The New York Mets catcher Mike Piazza has just become the highest earner in U.S. baseball history, with a seven-year deal averaging $13 million a year. While I try to imagine what a single person can usefully do with such an extraordinary amount of money, I attempt to digest Rust Belt demographics: an incredible 60 percent of children under age six in Detroit, 56 percent in Flint, are living in poverty.[1]

I am headed for Michigan with one mission in mind: to understand the impact on the Americans of deindustrialization. What do the cities that put America on wheels look like now that the party is over? Have relations between the haves and have-nots altered as the sun sets on the manufacturing age? If we are to grasp the full complexity of the American character, it seems that an essential piece of the puzzle must be filled in here in Michigan, the nation's eighth-most-populous state with a population of 9.6 million.

Far below me, Lake Michigan stretches like a ruffled blue duvet. And then we're roaring over farmland, a brown-and-green patch-work quilt, totally cultivated as far as the eye can see.

When Tocqueville rode into Flint on July 24, 1831, inland Michigan was the very limit of the frontier: untamed, uncultivated, mile after mile of untouched pine forest. Tocqueville and Beaumont had rented horses in Detroit—which then had a population of "two or three thousand souls"—and rode three days and two nights, without rest, regular meals, or shelter. They passed through "silent forests of tall trees" and "small silver lakes" lit by the moon.[2] They encountered the occasional white settler along the way, but otherwise Michigan was wigwam territory, home to seven dozen Native American Indian tribes, the Ojibwa, the Odawa, and the Potawatomi the principals among them.

There were no roads then, no signposts to guide their way, no gas, board, and lodging, no motor vehicles and no whirring flying machines to disturb the solitude. The 1830 census,[3] then the fifth census of the United States, records the population of Michigan as 31,639, 100 percent rural and, since Native Americans tended to be excluded from census counts, almost entirely white.

Tocqueville's hunch was that the country's vast unexplored lands—as symbolized by the frontier—had a profound psychological impact on Americans. He wanted to travel to the frontier to understand this for himself, and to see what internal force drove the pioneer on. "Having purchased a compass as well as munitions, we set out, gun on shoulder, as carefree and lighthearted as two students leaving school," he wrote in his journal.[4]

In traversing upstate New York en route to Michigan, Tocqueville had already witnessed how quickly white Americans were transforming the wilderness. With "astonishing speed" and by their agency, "the forests fall, the swamps dry up," he wrote. "Lakes as large as seas, immense rivers, vainly oppose its triumphal progress. The wildernesses become villages; the villages, towns. A daily witness of these marvels, the American sees nothing astonishing in them. This unbelievable destruction, this still more surprising growth seem to him the usual procedure of the events of this world."[5]

The rapid planing of the frontier had, Tocqueville believed, made Americans into the world's greatest optimists. Fifty years of unrelenting progress and success had instilled in Americans a confidence in their ability to overcome nature and an incredible belief in themselves. There is not a country in the world where men are so confident of their future or so certain of their ability to master the forces of nature, he wrote in his diaries.

This enduring character trait—this off-the-leash optimism—is immediately evident as I fly into the Flint of today. The city's Bishop International Airport was expanded in the early 1990s, at a cost of several million dollars, to accommodate an anticipated glut of visitors. But our little aircraft is the only one on the vast gray tarmac. By the time I enter the newly remodeled terminal building, all five of my fellow passengers have disappeared, and since there are no planes slated for take-off, I have the novel experience of having the entire airport to myself. The arrivals hall— a huge, steel-framed box—hums with disembodied chamber music, augmented by the lower-pitched *mmmm* of automatic slide doors occasionally opening and closing. At one end of the foyer, past a shiny Buick Ultra on display by General Motors, officials of the car-rental agencies—Avis, Budget, National, Hertz—stand like stick soldiers behind their counters. In the distance, I make out a suitcase going round and round on the rotunda. I know it is mine. It is the only one.

The Riverfront Hotel on South Saginaw Street is an impressive sixteen-story building, one of four high-rises in downtown Flint. I arrive early evening but find the foyer lights out, a piano at which no one plays, no staff members in sight (not even a receptionist), and no sound save for the arthritic rattling of slightly out-of-condition escalators. The gift and confectionery shop on the ground floor carries a natty slogan engraved on its window which says: FLINT—OUR SPARK WILL SURPRISE YOU. The shop is shut. I head for the restaurant, Bleachers, which, judging by the three people at the bar, appears to be open for business.

"Hello," I venture. "Hello?"

After a few minutes, a woman emerges from the half-lit gloom, seats me, and takes my order of chicken soup. It is brought by a disheveled dishwasher, his apron hanging alarmingly loose—almost around his knees—who keeps mumbling "dead meat" to no one in particular. After a while of wondering whether this is his way of inviting me to enjoy the soup, I discern what he is saying: "I'm dead meat if I lose this job."

The Riverfront is about the last hotel left in downtown Flint, all the others having been closed or converted into flophouses for the homeless. It was built in the eighties as the Hyatt Regency, part of a $200 million plan to revitalize the downtown after the city's troubles began. Across the road, they erected Autoworld, an indoor amusement park that cost the city and its sponsors $90 million. "The best hope for Flint's economic diversification lies in the tourism industry and the money spent here to attract it will be worth it eventually," Flint's then-Mayor, James Rutherford, said in 1982. But the grandiose plan to save Flint was as ill conceived as it was over-optimistic, and it failed dismally: Autoworld closed within two years, the Hyatt was sold for a pittance and became the Radisson, which too was sold and became the Riverfront, which limps on today, occupancy barely 20 percent.

From my room on the thirteenth floor, I look out over north Flint, a hodgepodge of concrete car parks, low-rise office blocks, and domestic housing. Directly below, the Flint River winds like a spindly canal between concrete banks marking the spot of what, two decades ago, was a bustling city center. Uncle Bob's Diner, Thompson's Chinese Restaurant, the movie houses, the Coney Island hot-dog store, the ornate Capitol Theater Building—all have long since been shut, boarded up or abandoned. The graffiti I come across later makes the point: EVERYTHING'S GONE, it says.

Really, I have booked in here to keep my appointment with history. The hotel is said to rise on the exact spot as the tavern that Tocqueville stayed in back in 1831. What's more, Tocqueville's hosts, John and Polly Todd, are recorded as having been the first white settlers in Flint, arriving just months prior to the Frenchmen. By eating and sleeping on the same site, I imagine that I can reach back and touch hands with Tocqueville, and also with the beginning of history as Flint knows it.

"We finally caught sight of a clearing, two or three cabins and, what pleased us even more, a light," wrote Tocqueville:

> The river, which stretched like a violet thread at the end of the valley, convinced us that we had arrived at Flint River. Soon . . . we found ourselves before a log house, separated from it by a single barrier. As we were preparing to cross it, the moon showed us on the other side a great black bear which, standing upright on its hind feet and drawing its chain in, showed as clearly as it could its intention to give us a fraternal accolade. What a devlish country is this, said I, where they have bears for watchdogs. We'll have to call, answered my companion; if we tried to cross the fence we should have difficulty making the porter understand.
>
> We shouted, then, at the top of our lungs and so well that a man finally put his head out the window. After having examined us in the moonlight,—Enter gentlemen, said he. Trink, go lie down! To your kennel, I say, these are not thieves. The bear retreated waddling, and we entered . . . There was only one bed in the house; the toss having given it to Beaumont, I pulled my mantle about me and, stretching out on the floor, slept as profoundly as becomes a man who has just done fifteen leagues on horseback.[6]

At around seven A.M., I am roused from my sleep in my hotel room by the demented pounding of a jackhammer: *Bababababababa! Babababababa!* I open my door and peer gingerly outside to find every room door thrown wide open and the hallway alive with construction workers breaking up the bathroom masonry, tossing whole baths and basins into the passage with abandon. I close my door and am contemplating my next move when, without knocking, a man brandishing a mallet bursts into my room and, not having seen me, heads for the bathroom, where he begins to take apart the washbasin. *Bang! Bang!*

I too am finding my host full of surprises.

"What are you doing?" I protest, rushing in, feeling somewhat underdressed in my sleeping shorts. The worker is startled to see me, but quickly he regains his composure and indicates in crude sign language that I should leave. The more I protest, the more he just stands there making hand signals, like a deaf man. After a while it dawns on me: he *is* a deaf man.

Dave, the wheelchair-bound front desk manager, shakes his head in apology. "Sorry, we forgot to tell them you were there. They weren't supposed to get to your floor until next week," he says. "The Riverfront has been bought by the Ramada," he goes on to explain, "and they're spending millions to refurbish most of the four hundred rooms to bring the place up to a four-star level."

"But why?" I ask. "Why spend millions refurbishing when you can't attract enough visitors to even fill twenty rooms? It's not like the competition down the road has better rooms. There *is* no competition."

Dave shrugs. "I suppose you gotta believe that *this time* it will be different," he says.

So, Flint's premier hotel gets to celebrate its third "Grand Re-Opening!" You would think three failures were enough. In most small cities with a depressed population of less than 150,000 people, you won't find a state-of-the-art international airport or a 400-room hotel. A 200-room hotel—now, that might flourish. But Flint insists on building a structure for itself that it simply cannot fill.

A recurring theme in Flint's attempt to reinvent itself has been its stubborn, almost willfully stupid denial of reality. Perhaps this is the flip side of the sunny optimism that Tocqueville so admired, and which seems, over generations, to have taken hold as an archetypal American character trait.

But if Flint struggles to adjust to being just another small, seemingly irrelevant postindustrial city, this is partly because its recent history has been so disproportionately grand. For as anyone from Flint will tell you, the story of Flint showcases the American Dream. It is the story of the automobile-centered industrialization, and deindustrialization, of America, a story that bookends the dawn and dusk of the twentieth century.

The wild and fragrant forested Michigan that Tocqueville rode through in 1831 was tamed within decades, as the Frenchman anticipated, by the lumbering industry. Within forty years, almost the entire state had been reduced to miles and miles of tree stumps as the timber mill, the first significant manufacturing enterprise, led Michigan out of the pioneer age and into the industrial age. Thereafter, with no more pine to cut down, and the climate, quality of soil, and flatness of the land well disposed to farming, Michigan became an unremarkable agricultural state, not unlike many other midwestern states.

It wasn't until mass production of the automobile started in Flint and Detroit in the early twentieth century that Michigan began to evolve the identity it has today. In 1903, a visionary by the name of Henry Ford launched Ford Motor Company in Detroit, employing the revolutionary concept of the production line to mass-produce automobiles—the Model T—for the first time. It is often assumed that Henry Ford invented the production line and the first automobile; in fact he invented neither. Both were already in existence; Ford's genius was to bring the two together. In Flint, another visionary by the name of William Durant, who had the most successful carriage-building company in America, realized that the future of his product line lay in automobiles and founded General Motors in 1908.

General Motors became the biggest automobile manufacturer in the world, then the biggest company in the world, and Flint went along for the ride. In the twenties, its population skyrocketed from 20,000 to 100,000. After the war, in the fifties and sixties, large numbers of young Americans migrated from the South to work in the GM factories. They came from Mississippi, Oklahoma, Arkansas, Kentucky, South Carolina, Alabama—black and white. They came any way they could—in cars, buses, tractors. Some even walked.

These young Americans left behind their friends and families to pursue the American Dream. Auto factory jobs were plentiful and paid well. A famous victory by the fledgling United Auto Workers union (UAW) over GM management in 1937—which history records as "the sitdown strike"—had opened the door to middle-class earnings for blue-collar workers, black and white. Factory workers without so much as a high-school education could, and did, make a decent middle-class living. The downside was that assembly-line work was boring, repetitive, and demeaning to the spirit. Workers were well paid but also simply a cog in the machine. In such an environment, there was little intrinsic job satisfaction, and the focus of workers shifted to the material rewards a paycheck could offer. Conspicuous consumption came to the working classes. As early as 1924, a *Flint Journal* editorial commented on this phenomenon: "The American citizen's first importance to his country is no longer that of citizen but that of consumer. Consumption is the new necessity."

By the early 1970s, an incredible three out of four Flint workers—some 80,000 people—were employed by GM. If you lived in Flint, it was just assumed that you worked in the shop. You'd be out somewhere, say Flint old-timers, and people talked to you as if you were at the factory—they never thought to ask where you worked, they just knew. Every family was related to GM, and through GM to each other. Entire communities sprang up, and with them shops, schools, and churches to support the workforce of GM. There were parades through the downtown honoring something or someone every few weeks. The atmosphere was carnival-like. Flint citizens enjoyed a standard of living that put them on top of the economic heap. Throughout the fifties, sixties, and seventies, year on year, median household income in Flint easily exceeded the national average. In some years, it was the highest in the nation. This was despite burgeoning white flight to the new satellite suburbs that were being erected beyond the Flint city limits. The city was voted one of America's best places to live and bring up kids. "The happiest town in America," one commentator called it. Buicks, Pontiacs, Chevrolets, Oldsmobiles—they rolled off the production line as Americans embraced the automobile with a passion. An iron arc was built to span the main road in Flint:

VEHICLE CITY, it announced. The city's motto became "What's good for GM is good for Flint." And for a long time it was.

The 1973 oil crisis changed everything. Fuel prices soared and suddenly "the big three," GM, Ford, and Chrysler, with their clunky cars, were unable to compete with the smaller, fuel-efficient Japanese imports. GM's profits nosedived; Ford and Chrysler nearly went bankrupt. In order to survive, the three motor giants drastically slimmed down their operations. There were mass layoffs and plant closures. The UAW tried vainly to stem the tide. Signs warning NO JAPANESE CARS went up in the Union Hall parking lot. If you owned a Japanese vehicle and you parked it there, it got beat up bad.

But the oil shock was merely the first of several shocks to rock Flint and Detroit. In the 1980s, with large companies having to compete as global corporations in a global marketplace, manufacturers began to realize they could slash labor costs by moving factories to cheap-wage countries. It made no sense to pay American autoworkers $19.97 an hour when you could pay Mexican workers just across the border 70 cents an hour, they argued. Trade treaties with Mexico helped pave the way, and motor assembly plants went up in Mexico like Lego kits. It did not help Flint's case that its highly unionized workforce was regarded as one of the most militant in the country, or that the U.S. environmental laws were much tougher than in Mexico. Neither did widely circulating rumors of sloppy American workmanship: one theory had it that you didn't want to buy U.S. cars made on Mondays because the workers were hung over. Such stories were given juice by tales of strange rattling noises that sometimes emanated from the Monday models, caused—so it was claimed—by empty whiskey bottles left inside the door mechanism. At the time, GM management insisted such stories were apocryphal. Today, GM workers tell you they were true.

The era of deindustrialization on U.S. soil had begun in earnest. In Flint and Detroit, factories were physically torn down or left derelict. They left gaping holes, physically and economically, in the city infrastructure. The phrase "the rust belt" emerged for the first time. In the twenty years between 1978 and 1998, the GM workforce in Flint fell by more than half, from 80,000 to 30,000.[7] Another 15,000 jobs are due to go within the next decade as GM withdraws, inexorably, from its birthplace.

The paternalistic social contract that existed between the employer and the city has been shredded. Whereas GM's former owner-directors, like C. S. Mott, felt a loyalty to Flint, rubbing shoulders with workers over lunch sandwiches at the local five and dime, GM's contemporary board of directors look to Wall Street, whose customers in Stockholm, London, and Miami may not know, much less care, that a place called Flint even exists.

The pursuit of wealth had brought Americans flocking to Flint and fashioned it into a fabulous boomtown, a microcosm of the beating heart of industrial America. Now that same instinct had left it languishing in its wake.

I arrive in Flint in the early fall and set about traversing the city and surrounding suburbs. I pull reports on its demographics and interview its people: rich and poor; young and old; white and black; community leaders, philanthropists, journalists, activists, and other commentators.

Tocqueville's method of investigation was first to ascertain the hard facts—those physically striking to his naked eye as well as those hidden within papers and press cuttings. He would typically begin his day at a library or buried in research reports. "We breakfast at eight, according to custom. We then go to the Athenaeum, which is a sort of public library, where French, English, and American newspapers are to be found . . . We pass as much time as we can there making statistical investigations on the state of the population, on the public institutions, and on all the political questions which occupy us."[8] Tocqueville wrote this entry in New York, but his journals show that he practiced this technique, where circumstances permitted, throughout his American journey. Having rounded up a set of objective facts, he set himself questions and problems to solve, which he then tackled with zeal by interviewing as many Americans as he could. From this greater pool of knowledge, he built his real understanding. But Tocqueville didn't stop there. He now began to make interpretations. What he was after was to understand the origins of these facts and observations, their points of contrast and similarity, their significance beyond themselves, and to this end he would analyze them using rational techniques of induction and deduction, all the while trying to breathe into them their deeper meaning.

Sometimes Tocqueville made great play of the most self-evident fact of all. He begins *Democracy in America,* for example, with a chapter entitled the "Physical Configuration of North America," in which he describes the physical layout of the country, or as he puts it, the "striking geographical features which can be appreciated at first glance."[9] This point of departure was not accidental, nor was it simply for the European reader to be able to form a vivid mental image of America at a time when few enjoyed the luxury of foreign travel. Rather, Tocqueville believed that the physical configuration of a country had a profound impact on the peculiar nature of its social mores, opinions, and attitudes.

In Flint, and in the suburbs beyond the city limit that comprise metropolitan Flint, two facts are immediately striking to my naked eye: the one is the urban geography of the place, the physical configuration of the living arrangements between the haves and have-nots; the other concerns the city's economic arrangements. A disturbing attitudinal shift coils around both like a double helix.

Economically, Flint has coped with GM's departure by replacing the 50,000 manufacturing jobs lost since 1979 mainly with new service-sector jobs. So far, so good: total employment in metropolitan Flint has held steady at 180,000 jobs. The catch is as follows: the majority of the jobs that were lost paid $40,000 to $60,000 a year, whereas the majority of the jobs that replace them pay $8,000 to $12,000 a year. These are the high-turnover, low-respect $5.15-an-hour minimum-wage jobs on fast-food production lines at places like McDonald's, Wendy's, Burger King, and Dunkin' Donuts, though in truth there are dozens of such employers, including garages and car-rental shops and low-cost hotels. They populate the neon strip malls that encase Flint and bisect its surrounding suburbs.

There are, I am told, thirty McDonald's franchises within the Flint city limits alone.

The people most hurt by this are not the GM workers who took early retirement or got laid off on 95 percent of full pay, but the younger generation, who never made it into the factory in the first place. Not only have they lost their shot at the middle-class lifestyle of their parents; but, as minimum wage has failed to keep pace with inflation, many find that being in work doesn't necessarily translate into being out of poverty.

The result of this new economy is that Flint's working poor population has ballooned. In 1998, almost one-third of the city's population lives below the poverty threshold. The poverty rate for its children under six is a mind-numbing 56 percent. Aggregately, the economy rolls on; individually, there is much pain, and the income gap between the haves and have-nots becomes ever wider.

But the separation between the haves and the have-nots is not just economic. There is a mighty geographic divide—a divide that can be drawn in black and white. For in Flint, poverty, neighborhood, and race are superimposed. The third of the population who have become poor are almost entirely the African-American population, and by and large they all live in one place: the north end of Flint. When the GM plants closed, the African-American workers were the hardest hit, it is claimed, because they tended to have the lowest seniority and so were the first to be laid off. It was a case of "last in, first out," and perhaps a little racism thrown in to boot. Even more importantly, their children, more so than the whites', had come to rely disproportionately on GM.

As unemployment soared, and crime became a serious factor in Flint, the whites abandoned the city to the blacks. It used to be that Flint's ethnic composition reflected that of Michigan: 80 percent white, 20 percent African-American and other minorities. But the white flight that had begun back in the 1960s became a flood in the 1980s and 1990s. Today the city is half black, half white. The whites that remain within the city limits tend to be concentrated in affluent, semi-gated communities, like Miller Road in southwest Flint. The rest fled to the townships beyond the city limits in surrounding Genesee County, to satellite self-contained suburbs like Grand Blanc and Flushing, and they took their businesses and tax base with them. So whereas the population of the city of Flint has fallen from 190,000 in 1960 to 140,000 in 1998, that of Genesee County grew from 375,000 to 430,000.

The contrast between where the haves and have-nots live is dramatic to the eye. The city is in an appalling state of disrepair: many houses are abandoned; there is no shopping, business, or entertainment; the schools are run-down, the depression is tangible. It is a black hole in the middle of the proverbial doughnut, a hollowed-out core.

But cross over into Miller Road and suddenly you're driving down verdant, tree-lined boulevards, all oaks, elms, and birches, past mansions (they are too grand to be called houses) with Greek pillars, ornate arches and domes, and set well back from the street on sumptuous grounds striated with the lines of a well-mowed lawn. Now the people in the street are all white. You see signs that say PATROLLED AREA. You see hedgerows and tennis courts and a manicured golf course. And you start to see bulldozers—doing road repairs, enlarging houses.

The brick-and-mortar statistics tell a story: there have been more than one thousand home starts in Grand Blanc in the last ten years; there have been just three in the entire city of Flint.

Tocqueville understood that the physical configuration of a nation impacted its political and social systems, its mores and attitudes. Earlier, in New York City, I had begun to explore and write about the effects of social geography on the ideal of "equality of opportunity." In Flint, the social geography is even more extreme. In Flint, the physical separation between the haves and the have-nots has become calcified and absolute: they live in separate neighborhoods, send their children to different schools, pay their taxes to distinct governing bodies.

Tocqueville would have wanted to know: What has been the impact of this physical separation on the hearts and minds, feelings and attitudes, of the people?

THE YOUNG HAVES

Scott Swedorski is a kid millionaire. He is twenty-eight years old and part of the new wave making their fortune through the information revolution.

On the day I visit him in his office, situated a few hundred yards beyond the Flint city limits, he has just returned from a vacation in Hawaii. His scuba-diving kit is propped against the wall and he wears one of those trademark short-sleeve florid Hawaiian shirts, showing off his newly acquired suntan. He is still a kid at heart, he says. He drinks pop, keeps buckets of candy in the office pantry, and there's a bulbous pumpkin on his desk for Halloween. I find him modest about his financial success, frank about his social attitudes.

"I never give poor people a second thought," he says. "I guess you could call it selfish. I guess you could call it tunnel vision. But I bet that everybody who works here feels the same way, that I am typical of my generation.

"To be honest, I avoid poor people. It is easy to do. I just give Flint city—where the black people live—an extremely wide berth. I would drive miles out of my way not to travel through downtown Flint," he says.

Swedorski has even stopped saying that he lives in Flint. Recently, when he was vacationing in Australia, someone asked him where he was from. When he replied "Flint," the person said: "Oh! That's the place where the poor are so starving, they eat rabbits!"— an allusion to the Michael Moore film *Roger and Me,* in which a poor Flint woman takes to breeding and apparently eating her own rabbits in order to keep her hunger at bay. Swedorski has never seen the film, nor does he intend to, but now when people ask him where he lives, he says "Flushing." Nobody's ever heard of Flushing, but he'd rather be anonymous than in any way associated with the rabbit eaters of Flint.

Like almost everyone who grew up in Flint, Swedorski comes from a family of autoworkers. His father, his father's father, his uncles—all of them worked "in the shop" at General Motors, in the giant Buick City plant. He grew up in the white, middle-class neighborhood of Flushing, which is outside the Flint city limits, and he had all the material comforts—their house had a swimming pool, his parents bought him a car when he was fifteen, and they put him through college. He never entertained the idea of following his dad into the shop, he says. He lived a suburban life and never got to know or interact with poor people.

If his views on poor people are difficult to distinguish from his views on black people, it is because in his mind the two are the same. "It was understood," he says. "Whites here, blacks there. There was no interracial mixing. The talk was that the city of Flint had fallen because black people moved in, and they, you know, bred like . . . like rabbits. This is not my personal view, I am not a bigot, but this is what I heard growing up, and a person is not immune to such attitudes. Some members of my extended family feel a lot more racial hatred than I do because they experienced personally what the arrival of black people did to their property values. My in-laws had a house on Delmar [Avenue], a beautiful area. But when black people moved in, the area dived and in the end they took $10,000 for the house and got the hell out of there. Now they say there are crack houses, shootings, that it's very dangerous there. But I glided by oblivious to all this. I never saw that stuff in Flushing. It was like, yeah, they're over there, and yeah, we're over here."

Swedorski studied computer science at Mott Community College in downtown Flint, where he got his associate's degree and met his wife, Victoria. After college, he drifted into a job as a cybrarian for the Flint Area Library Online Network, a position he was thrilled to get, paying $25,000 with full benefits. It was 1991, people were just beginning to discover the Internet, and as a hobby, working at home and at night, he decided to build a Web site where one could browse and download software. He called it TU-COWS (pronounced "two cows"), which stands for "The Ultimate Collection Of Winsock Software." Swedorski tested the software and rated programs on a sliding scale using his cow theme: five cows for good, one for bad. He did it for fun, and never expected to make a bean, he says, but within three years tucows.com had become one of the most popular sites on the Web. Suddenly, as

advertisers hooked on to the commercial potential of the medium—
they were willing to pay good money to place their banner on the
most popular Web sites, where it would be seen by hundreds of
thousands of cyberspace browsers—the hobby took on grander proportions.

Overnight Swedorski became a millionaire. By 1998, tucows.com
was rated the sixteenth-most-popular site on the World Wide Web,
with an average of 1.4 million hits a day. He had 579 mirror Web
sites around the world, employed 27 people, and his company was
valued at $20 million.

The challenge, he says, is not to let the money go to his head,
to still be the same, fun-loving, down-to-earth Scott he always
was—and to get his Cessna pilot's license so that he can fly north
to gamble in the casinos and not have to endure "the boring three-
hour drive." Another thing: now that he's worth millions, he's
realized, he says, how little it is. "A few million doesn't go a long
way today. You have to think about putting it away for your retirement, for your kids' private schooling and college," he says.

Swedorski attributes his success to being an early adopter of information technology. Indeed, in a small way, Swedorski has displayed the type of vision that once made the automakers of Flint
rich and famous: they saw the automobile as the coming thing and
profited; Swedorski saw the World Wide Web as the coming thing
and he is profiting too. But that is where the similarity ends. Unlike
the automaker visionaries who created philanthropic foundations—
such as the Ford Foundation and the Mott Foundation—to give
back to their communities and to society, Swedorski feels that the
less fortunate do not deserve a moment of his time or a dollar out
of his burgeoning bank account.

"I don't see why I should help them," he says. "I made everything I have from scratch. If I can do it, so can they. Okay, you
might say that I had a good starting point, given my education and
background, but I still think people can make it if they just try.
There are plenty of jobs these days. McDonald's always has a sign
that says 'Help Wanted.'"

He blames the United Automobile Workers union for the
downfall of Flint. "The union has a 'you owe me' mentality. They

have been overaggressive and this has pushed GM to go elsewhere. I've formed these views after seeing my father in the union, and after seeing for myself how hard it is to run a successful business," he says.

I ask him what he thinks it must be like to raise a family on $16,000 a year. "I don't know how they survive," he says. "And I don't want to know. You know, some poor people are poor because they have nineteen kids. They should exercise self-control. If you can't afford children, don't have them. That's what I say. I do not see any connection between myself and these people. America is supposed to be a melting pot, one happy family, the same culture, but it's nothing like that. There is just us and them; whites and blacks; haves and have-nots. My generation is much more selfish than prior generations. We don't care about anything other than our own self-preservation. Our grandparents went through unifying things, like the world wars, but we are the yuppie generation. We have tunnel vision and no guilt! In local politics I vote Republican, because they offer me lower property taxes, which saves me money. I view politics through my own self-interest."

Tocqueville would have been surprised by Swedorski's narrowly self-serving attitude. He would have called it un-American. In a chapter called "How the Americans Combat Individualism by the Doctrine of Self-Interest Properly Understood,"[10] he wrote: "Every American has the sense to sacrifice some of his private self interests to save the rest. We (on the other hand) want to keep, and often lose, the lot." Tocqueville argued that the principle of self-interest properly understood was so "universally accepted" among Americans that it was raised to the level of a doctrine. This doctrine was popular up and down the income spectrum: "You hear it as much from the poor as from the rich," he said.

"The Americans," he wrote, "enjoy explaining almost every act of their lives on the principle of self-interest properly understood. It gives them pleasure to point out how an enlightened self-love continually leads them to help one another and disposes them freely to give part of their time and wealth for the good of the state . . .

The doctrine of self-interest properly understood does not inspire great sacrifices, but every day it prompts some small ones."

Blind sacrifice, on the other hand, was rarely found in America. "In the United States there is hardly any talk of the beauty of virtue," he wrote. "But they maintain that virtue is useful and prove it every day. American moralists do not pretend that one must sacrifice himself for his fellows because it is a fine thing to do. But they boldly assert that such sacrifice is as necessary for the man who makes it as for the beneficiaries."

In 1831, Tocqueville was saying, Americans really understood the utility of enlightened self-interest. It was, he thought, an important part of what made them into a wise, generous, compassionate, and peaceful nation. It was a simple but profound concept: by helping the less fortunate, you ended up helping, in both material and spiritual ways, yourself.

But self-interest properly understood is a foreign concept to Scott Swedorski. He cannot imagine how his private interest is served by helping others. Downtown Flint is only five miles down the road, but to Swedorski it is another country. "I never have to see the poor people who live in that hole," he says, "and so I don't."

THE COMFORTABLE

Thomas Downer has worked for General Motors for thirty-four years. He has done pretty well out of it: he has three houses, five cars, a cabin on the lake up north, a boat, and he earns $80,000 a year including overtime. He likes to tell the story of the college professor who once worked alongside him on the assembly line.

"Why the hell you here?" he asked the professor one day above the din.

"The money," he said. "I can't get anything like it at the university."

Downer savors this story, though in the same breath he wants you to know how "damn hard" he's worked. Some of his colleagues work so much overtime that they make $100,000. "But then you live in the shop, and you never get to see your wife and children," he says.

Like the college professor, Downer also joined GM for the money. "I hate the production line, doing the same thing over and over, for eight hours a day, five days a week, fifty weeks a year, year in and year out," he says. "It's so monotonous it drives you crazy." But the job has afforded him a middle-class lifestyle and allowed him to indulge his passion for buying and restoring old cars. He has a 1960 white Corvette, a 1960 blue Corvette, a 1978 Buick Regal, a 1994 Corvette, and a 1998 Chevy Silverado. The latter, which is for his everyday use, is a shiny red, top-of-the-line, $35,000 pickup truck with a fluffy red carpet.

Downer has offered to drive me around GM's Buick City complex, the largest GM factory left in Flint, where they roll out the Pontiac Bonnevilles and the Buick LeSabres around the clock. The sheer size of Buick City is thrilling—it is two and a half miles long, comprises twenty-five plants, and looks like a giant beached whale. It is so large that it has its own police and fire departments. "As far as you can see . . . Buick City!" says Downer expansively. "This here is Paint (Division), that is Engineering, the building we just drove by used to be Headquarters before the top brass moved to Detroit, that one is the Assembly Plant." He stops. "It closes in a few months, with the loss of twenty-five hundred jobs," he adds.

At Union Hall, some of Downer's colleagues—sporting big-buckle belts, tattoos, T-shirts with rolled-up sleeves, and *Easy Rider* cool—have a lot to say about the upcoming closure, but they are powerless to stop it. The rules are that you cannot legally strike over plant closures, only line speed-ups and health and safety violations. GM is moving the Buick LeSabre and Pontiac Bonneville assembly operations to Detroit and Lake Orion, thirty miles to the south, because they say they want to rationalize their south Michigan assembly plants onto two sites. As Flint's is the least modern—built at the beginning of the century—it's the one to close. But as Downer and his colleagues know, once the assembly plant is gone, the parts factories, and everything else, soon follow.

"This town," says Downer, "was General Motors' town: the schools, the churches, the railroad, the grocer shops, the hotels, the airport—the whole community was built around, became dependent on, GM. I can understand why GM want to move their plants to Mexico, where they can get away with paying their Mexican workers seventy cents an hour—but I never dreamed GM would, could, abandon the city they built the way it has."

As Downer drives, he points out how the city has been devastated. "These open fields used to be houses," he says. "This barren land used to be a GM factory and parking lot. The part of town they call the North End—" he points to the other side of Saginaw Street, which runs south to north and bisects Flint—"it used to be prosperous, now it's dirt poor and dangerous. At night you hear gunshots and see fires. I won't even drive through. Believe me, you don't want to be in that part of town. Unless you want to be knifed or shot."

The part of town Downer is referring to is not just a few streets; it is the whole northwest quadrant of Flint, which used to be 80 percent white, but now is a ghetto where the majority of the city's 70,000 blacks live. A house there costs $25,000, maybe less, because nobody's buying.

Downer used to interact with the black people who lived there when they still worked at GM. But with each passing year they became more detached from his world and their difficulties began to slip from his imagination.

This is despite watching his own son, Ryan Downer, a twenty-seven-year-old father of three, become poor. "My son has an associate's degree in electronics, but his job is to collect garbage for twelve dollars an hour. On that he has to feed five mouths. And it's a hazardous job: he got hit by a car jumping from the truck and punctured a lung and broke his ribs. It's our children who suffer. The decent-paying jobs aren't there for them to go into," he says.

He hurts for his son. But his understanding does not extend to the African-American folk on the North End. "Those people who have a lesser life have often *chosen* a lesser life," he says. "My advice to them is: *just do it*. Don't be afraid to take the next step. If you're afraid to try, you will never succeed. And do whatever makes you happy. It's all in what you want to be and where you want to go."

I ask him: what does he think is the challenge of life on $16,000 a year?

"For me . . . $16,000? That's what I buy a car for," he says.

THE HAVE-NOTS

Anthony Harris lives in the part of town Swedorski and Downer won't set foot in. He is thirty-one, a machinist by trade, and African-American. Last year, he earned $11,000 but took home $6,000 after paying child support for his two children, which puts him below the poverty line whichever way you calculate it. For him, life is about survival. "You get paid on Friday, you're broke by Wednesday, you eat cheap, sometimes you don't eat at all," he says. And last year was a relatively good year. Since then he's been downwardly mobile.

Harris's father migrated here from Georgia when he was seventeen to get a job with General Motors, and worked there for thirty-three years in the same plant as Swedorski's dad, though they probably never knew each other, he surmises. Growing up, the Harrises always had enough—enough food, enough new clothes, plenty of toys, bikes for Christmas. There were picnics and barbecues. Harris watched his older brothers and their friends graduate from high school and go to work in the shop. Pretty soon they had brand-new cars, nice homes too. Harris had it in his head he would do the same, but when he was in junior high, GM started closing factories and he began to realize he couldn't rely on GM. He finished school and went to technical college in Grand Rapids, Michigan, where he learned to operate an extruder, a machine that makes plastic moldings from plastic pellets, like tabletop trims, he explains. Unfortunately it was not a well-paying trade, and he got caught in a cycle of intermittent unemployment and low-paying jobs. Of the last ten years, he has been unemployed for four. His last job was operating an extruder for six dollars an hour. "They had promised me a raise within two weeks and another after two months," he says. "But two months went by and nothing. I said,

"If you don't want to pay me a living wage, I don't want to work for you anymore."

On the day I meet him, Harris has been unemployed and homeless for one month. He sleeps in the Carriage Town Mission in downtown Flint in a tiny cell, eight feet by twelve feet, which has room only for a bed. He wears an old, soiled tracksuit top, the hood pulled up and over his head. He struggles to make eye contact, his personal hygiene has deteriorated, his self-esteem seems to be hanging by a thread. He is also hungry and totally broke. "It's hell to be homeless," he says softly. But he is homeless, he emphasizes, because he chooses to be. He could live with his parents, but their attitude towards him is too hard to swallow on a daily basis.

Harris says that his father despises him for not having made it. "When I was your age, I had a house, a car, I made a decent living," his father admonishes him, he says. "He looks down on me, tells me I'm a nobody, because—and it's true—if you don't have money in America you're a nobody. It used to make me mad to listen to my own father put me down like that. I'd tell him that he doesn't know how it is, that in his day there were decent-paying jobs. But now I just let him talk, I let him say whatever he wants . . ."

As Harris speaks, his tone shifts from indignant to resigned. "And I agree," he says softly. "It's all on me. I don't blame society. I blame me. I made my bed, I got to lie in it."

Harris says his father's attitude is so difficult to resist because it's not just his father's. "It's all around. Anyone who's fifty or older in Flint has that attitude towards our generation," he says. You can resist it for so long, then it gets inside you. Harris doesn't need his dad to get down on him, he says, because now he does a good enough job getting down on himself. He gets overwhelmed with feelings of depression and self-hatred. He tries to counter these feelings by reminding himself that he has done better than some: his school friends, for example, who are either dead or in jail. "I'm not going to rob, steal, or kill for a dollar. I'll work for it first," he says.

But Harris has become convinced that the only way of working himself out of poverty is to leave Flint. "This is Dead-End City. There are no decent-paying jobs. Just the five-dollars-an-hour minimum wage jobs. That don't cut it. Working for places like McDonald's is a joke. Fast food is a joke. Me, I have skills, I'm an extruder operator. But I'll take any job that pays properly; I will even shovel doo-doo."

"Where will you go?" I ask him.

"Detroit."

"What's in Detroit?"

"I guess by being so big, Detroit probably has more better-paying jobs," he says. "All I need is a starting salary of eight dollars an hour and I'll be okay. I'll be in Detroit before the year is over. It's a twelve-dollar bus fare to Detroit. I'll make it. I can do plumbing, roofing, though I prefer extrusion work. I'm down, but not out. Something will come up. Something will come up."

The African-American children of the GM workers who did get college degrees have tended to sprint from Flint, behaving just like the whites, taking their skills and earning power with them and leaving those who are left behind trapped even deeper in poverty.

James Dover is an African-American GM retiree who lives in the North End, and whose three children all got college degrees. His one son is a computer analyst for IBM, his daughter is a lawyer for the Justice Department in Washington, D.C., and his eldest son is a supervisor in GM's Delphi Plant. All three of them left the North End and exhort their father, aged seventy, to do the same. But Dover is a stubborn old mule. He believes in community. He believes that "America is supposed to be all of us heading in the same direction, not two societies, one white, one black; one affluent, one poor; one educated, one not." And he insists: "If I won't stay, who will? Life has been decent to me; now is my time to give back."

He says this despite the fact that his house has been broken into so many times of late that he now keeps a double-barreled, twelve-gauge shotgun and a Colt .45 pistol for his protection. His response has been to become active—to create neighborhood block clubs and to coordinate community programs like after-school clubs to expose kids to computers—and he says he is busier now than before he retired from his job as a salaried supervisor to forty workers in GM's exhaust department. ("By the end of it, I was truly exhausted," he says, smiling at his pun.)

Do African-Americans who have made it attempt to help their compatriots who have not? I ask Dover when I visit his home. He is spry and lithe, wears sports socks, no shoes, and rotates a Titleist cap (golf is his hobby) about his head as he ponders my question. "When a black person who has lived here a length of time manages to get out, he leaves running," he says. "He turns his back. He leaves his relatives behind and starts a whole new life with new neighbors, new friends. It's just like leaving a nightmare. He doesn't want to touch it anymore; he doesn't even want to think about it."

Ironically, this attitude began when barriers to integration came down in the 1960s and blacks, like whites, started "to jump over each other to attain their place in the sun," he says. "Before then, in the bad old days of segregation, blacks helped each other out. Now nobody wants to stay and help, and everybody just wants to make it, then leave. They have the same attitude as whites. They say: 'If I made it, you can too.' " The result is an underclass increasingly detached from the rest of society.

"I have never seen it as bad as I do today," continues Dover. "I happened to know Old Man Mott [one of GM's founders]. He used to stand downtown, outside Michigan National Bank, in his green homburg and bushy mustache and greet the ordinary people of Flint. He would eat his lunch with the workers. He was so visible, so gentle. He mixed with . . . he had empathy for, poor people.

"But in the last twenty to twenty-five years, we have changed, our society has changed. We're heading for the two societies that the War on Poverty was trying to prevent. I fear it will result in terrible violence. Right now it's smoldering. Getting worse. But one day, unless something is done, America will wake up to an explosion of hostility. And they'll be wondering where it came from and what went wrong, just like when we had race riots in the 1960s. But it won't go back to the peaceful demonstrations and marches—those days are long gone.

"There is too much pain being laughed at, too much hostility brewing. One third of our population are being swept under the rug. For them there is no American Dream, just the American Nightmare. But their nightmare will become America's nightmare, unless something is done. Clinton has tried to make one America, but not even the President has been able to fight this attitude. There is, increasingly, no other way to work on the consciousness of this nation other than violence. The new leadership will come from the youth. It won't be long. Maybe ten years."

Dover's is not the only voice in Flint warning of future violence. There are heads more youthful, and hot, than his predicting of the same thing.

Alvin James, the twenty-nine-year-old pastor of the Flint Free Methodist Church and leader of the Olive Branch Mission in Flint, says that he grew up in Brooklyn, New York, and that he has lived in Chicago, but that Flint is the most racially segregated city he has experienced, with the starkest gaps between the haves and have-nots. "When I saw it, it blew my mind," he says. "I don't know how to solve it short of God coming down here and fixing it himself. Our society is heading towards a crisis that may have a violent end. As nasty as it may sound, it may be the only way to cause people to address the problem."

There are some who argue that a meltdown may have occurred already if not for crack cocaine, which took out a generation of young people who would have been the angry young men, the leaders of this uprising. Yet others draw parallels with apartheid South Africa—the physical segregation of the haves and have-nots, of whites and blacks—and the violent unrest that resulted and brought about permanent change there. But it is in this comparison to South Africa that the limitation of the threat of violence becomes most apparent: in South Africa, there was a black majority that posed a severe and credible threat. In the United States, African-Americans are in the minority and their ability to put pressure on the haves is comparatively limited.

Tocqueville nevertheless recognized a danger: "If ever freedom is lost in America, that will be due to the omnipotence of the majority driving the minorities to desperation and forcing them to appeal to physical force,"[11] he says.

Tocqueville believed, however, that the chance of violent confrontation in America was limited. This had less to do with the system of democracy and everything to do with conditions of equality, he thought. "Almost every revolution which has changed the shape of nations has been made to consolidate or destroy inequality," he wrote in his chapter "Why Great Revolutions Will Become Rare."[12] "You will almost always find that equality was at the heart of the matter. Either the poor were bent on snatching the property of the rich, or the rich were trying to hold the poor down. So, then, if you could establish a state of society in which each man had something to keep and little to snatch, you would have done much for the peace of the world."

America, he believed, was such a society. Equality had made it "the most stable of all the peoples in the world," he wrote. "While all the nations of Europe have been ravaged by war or torn by civil strife, the American people alone in the civilized world have remained pacific. Almost the whole of Europe has been convulsed by revolutions; America has not even suffered from riots." Equality had brought about a large middle class in America who—"not exactly rich and not quite poor"—displayed an alert passion for the accumulation of property and "set immense value on their possessions." Since any revolution is a threat to property, he wrote, "the majority of citizens . . . do not see what they could gain by a revolution, but they constantly see a thousand ways in which they could lose by one."[13]

If equality is the key to peace, how might Tocqueville revise his thoughts under conditions where the trend to equality had been reversed? Could he conceive of a situation in which America became fertile ground for revolutionary transformation? "I am far from asserting that democratic nations are safe from revolutions," he wrote. "I only say that the social state of those nations does not lead towards revolution, but rather wards it off . . . If there ever are great revolutions there, they will be caused by the presence of the blacks upon American soil. That is to say, it will not be equality of social conditions but rather their inequality which may give rise thereto."[14] (Within thirty years of Tocqueville writing this, the U.S. was embroiled in the Civil War.)

It is not my intention to overdraw this point about the potential for violent confrontation, but I do want to emphasize that Tocqueville did believe that equality of conditions was the key to the peaceful well-being of society. It is worth noting too that Tocqueville's primary fear for America was not revolutions, but more subtle than that. It was that in blindly following the pursuit of wealth, American citizens who had accumulated property would "dig themselves in."

"If the citizens continue to shut themselves up more and more narrowly in the little circle of petty domestic interests and keep themselves constantly busy therein, there is a danger that they may in the end become practically out of reach of those great and powerful public emotions which do indeed perturb peoples but which also make them grow and refresh them," he wrote. "The prospect really does frighten me that they may finally become so engrossed in a cowardly love of immediate pleasures . . . that they will prefer tamely to follow the course of their destiny rather than make a sudden energetic effort necessary to set things right."[15]

It is just such changes in society that James Dover, Alvin James, and other African-American leaders in the Flint community are responding to. They point out that the rich and middle classes have dug themselves in, becoming "so engrossed" with their private domestic interests and so "practically out of reach" that the have-nots feel backed into a corner.

They have tried to use their democratic powers to improve their situation, electing an African-American mayor, Woodrow Stanley, to champion their position. But although the formerly all-white police and fire departments are now thoroughly integrated, and the mayor is believed to have their best interests at heart, their initial hopes of him being able to help them lift themselves out of poverty have been dashed. He cannot force whites to open businesses in Flint that offer decent-paying jobs. He cannot stem the tide of General Motors factory closures. He cannot entice the well-to-do back to Flint city, whence they ran, taking their taxable income

with them and leaving behind a shrunken, desiccated tax base and
a run-down inner city. In short, the financial resources at his dis-
posal are extremely limited. That's why they call him, I am repeatedly reminded, "the Mayor of Poverty."

It is the job of Jack Litzenberg, director of the Poverty Program at
the Mott Foundation, to spend his working day worrying passion-
ately about poverty in America. Each year he spends $41 million
of the foundation's money to try and improve things. The Mott
Foundation is the number-one money manager in Flint, investing
$405 million in the Flint area since 1964, and also the sixteenth-
largest philanthropic foundation in the U.S., with a net asset value
of $2 billion.[16] Litzenberg has lived forty years in Flint, his previous
job being head of community and economic development for the
city of Flint. He is well placed to suggest solutions.

If this is a society that seems to be splitting irreconcilably into
haves and have-nots, are there any core American values that can
be used as building blocks to bring the two Americas together?

"Core values . . . core values," repeats Litzenberg. "The core
values are not helpful. For example, we don't believe in society
today, we believe in individuality. We're into the Gates era, where
a small number of people are amassing huge fortunes. In their image, we hang on to the myth that rugged individualism is what
counts, that we can make it financially simply and exclusively by
our own actions. It is an entirely false belief. Because for the vast
majority of Americans, the most important determinant of their
success, or lack of it, is the situation they are born into and the
opportunity that affords. Equality is a myth. Social mobility is increasingly a myth. The American Dream is a myth. But we hold
on to these myths and they define who we are."

If the core values are not useful, I persist, then under what conditions will Americans care for one another?

"I think," says Litzenberg, "Americans will care for their own
families and for people they get to know."

"But if they live in gated communities, like in Flint, they never
get to interact socially with poor people," I interject.

"That's it. They see poverty on TV, but it's not real. What TV doesn't allow me to do is *this*"—he reaches over and touches me. "I've got to be able to feel you to care about you."

So absence makes the heart grow harder. What is the solution?

"I wish I had solutions," he says. He pauses. "Education is part of the solution. We already have a pretty good collegiate system in this country. The question is: how do you connect the whole school system to the collegiate system? I think that is the answer; I know of no other. We need to target the schools that are in the poor urban areas. I think it is possible to accomplish. Believe it or not, we have only eight million people of our entire population living in concentrated areas of poverty. We can implement a Marshall Plan on them. Education is still the best path out of poverty. We need to invest in people, not buildings. For example, in Flint the Mott Foundation put money into redeveloping the downtown, into erecting buildings like Autoworld, which failed miserably. We have changed our philosophy. We have realized that what we really need to do is build people. Human capital redevelopment, that is the answer."

In this enterprise, the Mott Foundation can lend its name, credibility, and some millions too, but it does not, spokesmen say, have the financial muscle to implement it on its own. It needs to forge partnerships and it needs help. General Motors and the city of Flint seem obvious candidates. But the former has yet to step up to the plate in a significant way, says the Mott Foundation, and the latter is economically depleted.

What of the haves?

They live in Flint, but not in Flint. Their world is a world apart. The connective tissue frays and tears. In pursuing their lives, they fail to see their connection to the have-nots. To borrow the jargon of the stock market, they are "locking in" their gains for the next generation.

They are digging themselves in, shutting themselves up more and more narrowly.

The outcome that Tocqueville most feared for America is happening in Flint.

3

THE OHIO RIVER VALLEY

Hard Work and the American Dream

To the west, to the west. The train from New York City to Pittsburgh, where the Monongahela and Allegheny rivers collide to form the Ohio River, is called the "Three Rivers Train," evoking images in my mind of the great American outdoors. It exits Manhattan via a tunnel hewn under the Hudson River and then rumbles south down the Eastern Seaboard through the bleak industrial backlots of New Jersey. We pass a mangle of highways, factories, truck depots, junkyards, and derelict property that is surely the most blighted peri-urban landscape in America. After an hour or so, the train trundles into Philadelphia, where it takes on a new engine, and it is only here, I reassure myself, that the journey due west *really* begins. The Ohio is nine hours of rail away, through deepest Amish country, over the Allegheny Mountains, across wide open plains. Green hills and big skies beckon.

Tocqueville's journey to the Ohio and onward to the Mississippi had also begun in Philadelphia. He and Beaumont traveled by stagecoach in November 1831, completing what was then a seven-day trip in double speed of "three times twenty-four hours." The French commissioners were not to know it then, but it was the beginning of the coldest winter on record for fifty years. Their excursion west by stage and steam was to be a brutal one, dogged by dramatic transportation disasters that would test their physical endurance to the limit and very nearly cost them their lives. For now, though, stiff limbs and unseasonably severe weather were the worst of their problems. The dirt roads were "detestable," the carriages "even worse." When they reached the Alleghenies, they were "pounced on by a horrible cold" and forced to complete the rest of the journey in a "tornado of snow."[1]

An hour out of Philadelphia, the Three Rivers Train begins to stretch her legs and I settle back to enjoy the spectacle rolling past my window. To my left, I gaze out over the rear end of a strip of fast-food joints—Pizza Hut, KFC, Taco Bell, Burger King—followed by BIG Mart, Dollar Express, car dealerships; it goes on for miles. To my right, I look out over washing lines, jungle gyms, swings, tricycles, and fences—the accoutrements of suburban backyards. The train, a once potent symbol of freedom, is wedged into a narrow vector between the backside of a commercial strip and an unbroken suburban sprawl that extends halfway across the state of Pennsylvania. It is hours before I see anything resembling a cow.

Rocked by the rhythm of the train and dulled by the unrelenting tameness of the surroundings, I doze off—only to be awakened by what appears to be a mild commotion in the compartment. The ticket collector has been moving through the train checking passengers' destinations on their ticket stubs, which are posted above their seats. It is nighttime now, and he is waking those who need to exit at the next stop; but when he gets to the row directly in front of me, he stops, his brow all puzzlement.

"You moved places, didn't you?" he says to a thin, besuited gentleman seated there.

"No, I didn't," the man responds.

"You moved from that side of the aisle to this," he persists.

"I did not."

"Well, you must have."

"Well, I'm *telling* you I *didn't*."

The bizarreness of this squabble grabs the attention of the passengers seated nearby. Our energy is sucked in as we start trying to figure it out: What exactly is going on? Is the man in the suit telling the truth? Why, when the seats are unreserved anyway, is the ticket collector making such a fuss?

The ticket collector points with rising irritation to the placement of the ticket stub across the aisle from where the man now sits, incontrovertible proof, as far as he is concerned, that this man has changed places. He appears to be demanding simple clarification of this fact.

"I'm asking you one more time: did you move?" he says forcefully.

"Okay, okay . . . well, I suppose that, maybe, I did."

The passenger in the suit sits red-faced, like a schoolboy who has been publicly humiliated. There is an unmistakable tension in the carriage that takes me by surprise. On the one hand, I muse, this petty little incident could be instantly forgotten as an everyday disagreement over nothing at all. But on the other, I cannot help feeling that a veneer has been pierced, and that something about American society has been unexpectedly revealed.

Tocqueville devoted an entire chapter to the subject of American etiquette, arguing that the poor manners of Americans were reflective of their social condition.[2] Unlike class-based societies, he wrote, where everyone knows one's proper place and where, as a result, there is a "dignity" and "regularity" of manners, in democracies people are not quite clear on the precise code of behavior to be followed or their place within it. As a result, messy social situations such as the one I have just witnessed are inevitable. The apparent "rudeness" of Americans, Tocqueville suggests, actually has its roots in a far greater societal good, that of broad-based social mobility and equality.

But the feeling that I am left with is less subtle. It is simply this: when the ticket collector stood his ground and insisted that he would not be lied to, it was the first time that I noticed, *really noticed,* the person in the ticket collector's uniform. You lie to me, you deny my existence, and that is not acceptable, he seemed to be saying.

Ticket collectors are part of the burgeoning service sector of the economy, many of whose employees make up the "working poor." It strikes me that even in a democracy with apparent social equality, the working poor and their like are invisible to most of us.

I take out my notepad and scribble a shortlist of the people I have done business with that day. I try to recall. There is:

- the Red & Tan Line bus driver
- the New York City subway-token salesman
- the Pennsylvania Station ticket clerk
- the Roy Rogers fast-food cashier
- the Roy Rogers cleaning person
- the woman checking tickets at the top of the train platform
- the onboard conductor
- the onboard buffet-cart vendor

Apart from the bus driver who often transports me to and from my American base in Rockland County, New York, I cannot recall what a single one of them looks like. Except, that is, for this on-board ticket collector: a middle-aged African-American man with a loping walk, a genial look in his eye, and a steadfast determination to be treated honestly and taken seriously.

SILENT WITNESS

In the beginning was the river. Its waters flowed at an unrushed but steady clip in a southwesterly direction through a gently sloping fertile valley. The Iroquois called it "Ohio," later translated by the French as "beautiful river," and it came to delineate the natural border that licked at the shores of six states. Starting at the Y-shaped confluence of the Monongahela and the Allegheny rivers in western Pennsylvania, the Ohio pushes west, cutting the line between northern and southern states, between Ohio, Indiana, and Illinois to the north and West Virginia and the blue grass of Kentucky to the south. After 981 miles, at a bend in the river marked by a town called Cairo, Illinois, it intersects with the faster-flowing upper Mississippi, and it is here that the silvery, sedate Ohio ends and the wider, muddier, and more treacherous lower Mississippi—Ol' Man River—begins.

Although the dimensions of the Ohio are much the same now as they were in the beginning—the length, width, depth of the channel, and speed of the current are reassuringly timeless—the river's geographic destiny as the "gateway to the west" has meant that it has borne silent witness to an epic tale: the evolution of the Midwest into the engine room of America and the building of America itself. More than any other region, the Midwest showcases the evolution of the American economy—from agrarian to industrial to postindustrial information age—and illustrates the changing relationship of hard work to the American Dream.

It is a transformation in four acts, each precipitated by a revolutionary invention:

- the steamboat
- the railroad
- the automobile
- the microchip

We are daily witness to the last act; Tocqueville was our eyes and ears for the first. The esteem with which his commentary is held gives us pause to wonder: what did he see about the American character in his journey down the Ohio—from Pittsburgh via Cincinnati to Louisville—that might inform our understanding of the way the American nation operates, thinks, views itself today?

ACT I: TOCQUEVILLE IN THE ERA OF THE STEAMBOAT

The era of steam on the Ohio began with the maiden voyage of Robert Fulton's *New Orleans,* which sailed from Pittsburgh to Louisville in October of 1811. Until that moment, nothing bigger than a raftlike flatboat, which made its way as silently as a fish, had ever been seen on the river. Now, all at once, a floating triple-deck palace, ablaze with light and powered by a giant water-churning paddlewheel, was surging downriver, rendering the pioneers who witnessed this first sailing totally awestruck. "The fearful rapidity with which it made its passage over broad reaches of the river excited a mixture of terror and surprise among the settlers on the banks," a reporter wrote at the time. "The general impression among the good Kentuckians was that a comet had fallen into the Ohio."[3]

By the time Tocqueville arrived in 1831, the steamboat era was in full swing. More than 270 steamships had been launched onto the Ohio and the Mississippi, unleashing a flood of immigrants and products down the river, and the industrial character of the region was already apparent.[4] "The Birmingham of America," is how the French commissioners described Pittsburgh, where "the air is constantly obscured by the multitude of steam engines that run the shops."[5] In addition to the steam-powered textile mills and glassworks, a host of gunsmiths, blacksmiths, tanneries, and merchants had set up stores to supply the pioneers continuing westward, and the town had evolved into a bustling commercial center. Further downriver, Cincinnati's growth was even more prodigious: its population had doubled to 30,000 in five years, making it the fastest-growing city in America. In the 1840s, Cincinnati would briefly become the nation's chief pork-packing center, for which it earned the sobriquet, "Porkopolis." Pigs were herded through the streets hundreds at a time on their way to the slaughterhouses. Pork by-products such as lard were turned into soap and candles and gave rise back in 1837 to a company we still recognize today—Procter & Gamble. "Streets encumbered with debris, houses under construction, no names on the streets, no numbers on the houses, no outward luxury, but the image of industry and labour obvious at every step,"[6] observed Tocqueville.

But the mystery that intrigued Tocqueville was this: what explained the population explosion on the Ohio side of the river while the Kentucky side remained rural, despite the fact that the latter region had been settled twenty years earlier? According to the 1830 census, Ohio had attracted nearly one million immigrants, the whole lot having arrived in the last thirty years, making it the fourth-most-inhabited state in the Union, whereas Kentucky's population lagged behind by a quarter of a million.

Sailing between the two banks, Tocqueville described what he saw and the profound realization he came to:

> On both banks of the Ohio stretched undulating ground with soil offering the cultivator inexhaustible treasures; on both banks the air is equally healthy and the climate temperate; they both

form the frontier of a vast state . . . There is only one difference between the two states: Kentucky allows slaves, but Ohio refuses to have them.

So the traveler who lets the current carry him down the Ohio till it joins the Mississippi sails, so to say, between freedom and slavery; and he has only to glance around him to see instantly which is best for mankind. On the left bank of the river the population is sparse; from time to time one sees a troop of slaves loitering through half-deserted fields; . . . one might say that society had gone to sleep; it is nature that seems active and alive, whereas man is idle. But on the right bank a confused hum proclaims from afar that men are busily at work; fine crops cover the fields; elegant dwellings testify to the state and industry of the workers; on all sides there is evidence of comfort; man appears rich and contented; he works.[7]

It was a stark visual contrast, almost biblical in its imagery, and one that Tocqueville never forgot. He would invoke it years later to argue for the abolition of slavery in the French colonies; and it also critically informed his emerging theory on race relations in America. What Tocqueville saw, and immediately understood, was that slavery perverted the lives of the master as well as the slave, not least in terms of their relationship to work. "On the left bank," he wrote, "work is connected with the idea of slavery, but on the right with well-being and progress; on the one side it is degrading, but on the other honorable." Slavery made work shameful and masters lazy, he thought, not only preventing them from making their fortunes but "even diverting them from wishing to do so."[8]

On a macro scale, slavery limited the economic potential of entire states and regions. It had brought about "a vast difference in the commercial capabilities of southerners and northerners" and would lead, he predicted, the North to economically dominate the South. "The North alone has ships, manufactures, railways, and canals," he noted.[9]

But these were observations made after the fact. Tocqueville wondered: what had motivated Americans in the North of the Union to abolish slavery in the first place?

The notion that whites in the North abolished slavery for moral reasons—out of altruism or unconditional love for their fellow black Americans—is given short shrift by Tocqueville. He does not deny that for some Americans, groups like the Quakers, for example, slavery was a moral issue.[10] But for the majority, the abolition of slavery did not coincide with an outpouring of interracial brotherly love. In fact, he had observed just the opposite: "Race prejudice seems stronger in those states that have abolished slavery than in those where it still exists,"[11] he wrote.

It was a mystery that intrigued him, and of which he had only latterly become aware as his travels progressed. The fact is that prior to reaching Philadelphia, Tocqueville had not encountered a significant black populace, and until he sailed down the Ohio, he had not really thought much about slaves. His prior destinations—Manhattan, upstate New York, the Michigan frontier, and the cities and towns of New England—all had tiny black populations. According to the 1830 census, "Negroes" numbered less than 2 percent of the total population of the states in which slavery had been abolished, just 120,520 in aggregate, compared with 35 percent (2.2 million) of the southern states.[12]

So it was that sailing between slavery and freedom, Tocqueville thought that he divined two things: that "in the United States, people abolish slavery for the sake not of the Negroes but of the white men,"[13] and that freedom for blacks, once given, did not mean equality. In Ohio, for example, although one statute abolished slavery, a raft of other statutes shredded their civil rights: the entry of "free Negroes" into Ohio territory was prohibited; blacks who already lived in Ohio were prevented from owning land there; and blacks were denied entrance into public schools.[14]

Tocqueville's interview with a young lawyer, Timothy Walker, while he was in Cincinnati, illustrates the mindset of the time:

"You have in Ohio some very severe laws against the blacks," prompted Tocqueville.

"Yes," replied Walker, "we are trying to discourage them in every possible way. Not only have we made laws allowing their expulsion at will, but we annoy them in a thousand ways. A Negro has no political rights; he cannot be sworn in, he cannot bear witness against a white. This last law leads sometimes to the most revolting injustices. Lately I was consulted by a Negro who had furnished a very great number of foodstuffs to the master of a steamboat. The white denied the debt. As the creditor was black, and his workmen, who were black also . . . could not appear in court, there wasn't even any way to bring suit."[15]

In other northern states, discovered Tocqueville, where laws did promote equality between the races, it was custom and public opinion that slammed the door. For example, although in some states intermarriage was legal, "public opinion would regard a white man married to a Negro woman as disgraced." Although blacks had electoral rights, "they would come forward to vote at the risk of their lives." And although they could bring an action at law, "they will find only white men among their judges." Segregation was a cradle-to-grave phenomenon, dividing birth units, hospitals, schools, theaters, prison cells, and graveyards along racial lines. "Oppression has deprived the descendants of the Africans of almost all the privileges of humanity," he wrote. "The black man's inequality stops only just short of boundaries of the other world."[16] The white man in the northern states, he declared, was "without the courage to be either completely wicked or entirely just."[17]

Tocqueville's description of the maltreatment of blacks (and Indians) at the hands of whites in America is extraordinarily detailed, compassionate, and, at times, poetic. He devotes more than fifty pages to the subject, and it forms the basis of the longest chapter in his book, "Some Considerations Concerning the Present State and Probable Future of the Three Races That Inhabit the Territory of the United States." Peering beyond the horizon, the Frenchman discerned with remarkable prescience three clear trends: toward the eventual abolition of slavery, toward the entrenched separation of the races by custom, and toward increasing inequality of conditions between blacks and whites.

And yet Tocqueville's account of race prejudice and inequality raises a deeply troubling question. If equality screeched to a halt just short of the color line, how could he, in all honesty, begin his book with the now immortal lines: "No novelty in the United States struck me more vividly during my stay there than the equality of conditions"?[18] How could he say in his conclusion: "Therefore, the time must come when there will be in North America one hundred and fifty million people all equal one to the other . . . All else is doubtful but that is sure"?[19]

He did not qualify these statements. He did not say that he was talking only about the white immigrants, that blacks were excluded from this picture. It is not as if sheer numbers rendered them irrelevant. In 1830, the census tells us (and Tocqueville footnotes this too),[20] there were 2,329,766 "Negroes" in the United States, of whom 2,010,327 were slaves and 319,439 were emancipated—all in all, a little over 20 percent of the total population.

What Tocqueville did was to compartmentalize his findings on blacks and Indians and segregate them from the main text of his argument. He put them all into the last chapter of his Volume 1, which he prefaced with the words: "I have now finished the main task that I set myself . . . In the course of this work I have been led to mention the Indians and the Negroes, but I have never had time to stop and describe the position of these two races within the democratic nation I was bent on depicting." He calls this chapter a "tangent" to his subject. He does not explicitly say so, but the rest of his seven hundred-page treatise is really about American democracy and equality for the whites.

It is incredible to realize that though sympathetic to blacks and Indians in his diaries, and alert to the "tyranny" they suffered, he appears to have fallen prey to the dominant ideology of the time, which is that blacks and Indians were inferior and therefore not to be considered on the same page as whites.

Call it a lacuna, a blind spot, but the effect has been dramatic. It has allowed Tocqueville to be read, quoted, and canonized in a way that distorts a most basic truth about the original American character. His unqualified conclusions, which stand as a widely respected and contemporary critique of America, are taught in schools, evoked by politicians and invoked by Presidents as a clarion call to describe the formative character traits of "this great nation."

President Clinton's 1995 State of the Union Address is just one example. "If you go back to the beginning of this country, the great strength of America, as de Tocqueville pointed out when he came here a long time ago, has always been our ability to associate with people who were different from ourselves and to work together to find common ground," said Clinton. "And in this day, everybody has a responsibility to do more of that. We simply cannot wait for a tornado, a fire, or a flood to behave like Americans ought to behave in dealing with one another." (Applause.)[21]

One cannot blame President Clinton for using Tocqueville in this way. By marginalizing his findings on blacks and Indians, Tocqueville trivialized them. By failing to qualify his conclusions, he helped to perpetuate an idealized view of America that he never saw. He played into the hands of latter-day politicians who prefer to fudge the tough questions. He helped the cause of the spin doctors of Madison Avenue who like to say: it's not important what actually happened; what is important is what people *think* happened. And he did a disservice to those who genuinely wish to address the unfinished business of race relations in America; for how much more difficult it is to face up to the truth of the present when the truth of the past has been muddied and obscured.

We can only speculate as to why Tocqueville structured his book in this way. We could surmise that as he was writing primarily for a French audience, overwhelmingly white, he sought to capture the essence of American democracy and equality as it affected the portion of the population his readers would relate to. We could surmise that he did not want to spoil the pitch of his traveling companion, Gustave Beaumont, who was shortly to publish a book, *Marie, or Slavery in the United States,* part novel, part social critique, about the experience of blacks in America.[22] We could surmise that it was because Tocqueville believed, as he did, that the Indians would be destroyed by the advance of white civilization, and the blacks so outnumbered and swamped by the tide of white immigrants from Europe that their plight would eventually pale into statistical insignificance.[23] We could surmise that he came from an aristocratic background and that he was unable to rise above its mindset; that he was a product of his time.

But there is, I believe, a clear clue as to how this distortion came about. It lies buried in the Tocqueville journals, in the cast of characters he interviewed. "I have tried to consult the best-informed people,"[24] he says in his introduction to *Democracy in America,* and his diaries show he was as good as his word. The social positions of the six people he interviewed in Cincinnati, for example, make for interesting reading:

- Bellamy Storer, leading Cincinnati lawyer and subsequent Congressman
- Timothy Walker, Harvard graduate and co-founder of the Cincinnati Law School
- Salmon Portland Chase, lawyer in the antislavery movement
- Daniel Van Matre, Yale graduate and prosecuting attorney
- Dr. Daniel Drake, leading medical practitioner and founder of a medical college in Cincinnati
- John McLean, former postmaster general under Presidents Monroe and Adams and, by appointment of President Andrew Jackson, associate justice of the Supreme Court of the United States[25]

This was about as educated and knowledgeable a group as one could assemble in 1831—what modern pollsters would call the opinion elite. But it was not a balanced group. They were all professionals, all male, and all white. Throughout Tocqueville's nine-month journey, the typical informant he sought out was successful, professional, white, male. It would have been their voices, therefore, that reverberated about his inner ear when, months later, he sat down at his bureau in France with only his notebooks and memories for company.

Apart from a notable exception where Tocqueville requests, and is granted, interviews with prisoners alone in their cell in a Philadelphia penitentiary and asks them about prison conditions,[26] one is hard-pressed to find even one diary entry where Tocqueville interviewed African-Americans, American Indians, women, or the poor. He asked *about* them, sure, thoroughly and at length, but he never got it from them directly. He never went that extra mile. The result is that where Tocqueville attributes inner feelings and attitudes to African-Americans in his text, it sometimes reads like racist stereotypes that have been regurgitated whole.

"The Negro hardly notices his ill fortune," he writes in *Democracy in America*. "He admires his tyrants even more than he hates them and finds his joy and pride in a servile imitation of his oppressors . . . If he becomes free, he often feels independence as a heavier burden than slavery itself, for his life has taught him to submit to everything, except to the dictates of reason; and when reason becomes his only guide, he cannot hear its voice."[27]

Such sentiments (and there are more) sound like they might have spilled directly from the lips of white slave owners, and they strike a rare false note in the Tocqueville canon. To my ear, they are also eerily reminiscent of the rhetoric used by some white South Africans to assume knowledge about the inner world of black domestic and farm workers during the days of apartheid.

It becomes clear that there was an America Tocqueville did not access directly. Yet right in front of his eyes, as he sailed down the Ohio, this other America was immediately at hand. For on board the steam packet *Fourth of July,* as with subsequent steamships he used, Tocqueville would have had his needs met by, and interacted daily with, a group of people we would today call the working poor. There were the chambermaids, cabin boys, berth makers, pantrymen, stewards, and waiters, but the most colorful and unforgettable of all would have been the roustabouts, the black, Irish, and German immigrant deckhands who made up half the steamship crew of the *Fourth of July.* They worked backbreaking twenty- to forty-hour shifts, sang rhythmic songs called "coonjine" as they carried cargo on their shoulders, and downed tots of whiskey given them by the first mate every four hours to keep them going. Sometimes first mates beat them with fists or clubs, and in extreme circumstances threw them overboard. In the early part of the nineteenth century, roustas were paid $20 for an entire voyage (as compared to $10 for berth makers, $15 for chambermaids, $30 for watchmen, $90 for the pilot, and $115 for the captain).[28] Between shifts, they slept on deck between the freight and the machinery, ate leftovers from the main dining room, played cards, and told outrageous tales about the onshore saloons, dances, and cockfights they had frequented. The roustas were hard to miss.

Yet Tocqueville never mentions them once. Nor, apart from

the captain, does he mention any of the other crew members. Not even when, in the middle of the night, their steamboat struck the Burlington Sandbar between Pittsburgh and Wheeling, "smashed itself like a nutshell on a rock in the middle of the Ohio," and sank. Even in his account of the boat going down, even in the face of this dramatic and potentially uniting near-death experience, even as it was the roustas who would have hauled his and Beaumont's luggage to the safety of a passing steamship, the *William Parsons,* the Frenchman's account of the disaster fails to even acknowledge their existence. "The cry of *we sink,* resounded immediately," he wrote. "The vessel, the gear, and the passengers started in company for eternity."[29]

So it was that sailing down the Ohio between freedom and slavery, Tocqueville marveled at the transformative power of hard work and its centrality to the American Dream. But the working poor themselves were as invisible to him as they had been to me, nearly 170 years later, retracing his route as I struck out west, hemmed in between strip malls and suburban sprawls aboard the Three Rivers Train.

ACTS II AND III: THE RAILROAD AND THE AUTOMOBILE

The steamboat era was brief and its effects mild compared to what was to follow. In the mid–nineteenth century, life in the American Midwest began to be transformed by the railroad, heralding the next prolific phase of the Industrial Revolution and sparking the biggest economic boom history had seen.[30] Unlike the steamboat, the train was fast, unaffected by weather, and went everywhere. On October 12, 1852, the first locomotive pulled into Pittsburgh from Philadelphia. It cut a seven-day journey to fifteen hours, set off an insatiable demand for iron and steel, and changed the nature of work in the region.

Pittsburgh began to pump iron. Its factories shifted from small-scale manufacture of commercial goods to large-scale production of iron—first to satisfy demand for the locomotives and railway tracks as they fanned out across America, subsequently for just about everything, from weapons, munitions, and iron-clad boats to supply the Union army in the Civil War to girders for the construction of bridges and skyscrapers around the country. But it was only with the invention of the Bessemer converter by Henry Bessemer in 1865 in Sheffield, England, and its introduction into western Pennsylvania by Andrew Carnegie and others in the 1870s, that the region really leapt forward. Whereas steel had hitherto been time-consuming and expensive to make, done in small crucible furnaces, the Bessemer process converted iron into steel on a grand scale. It also provoked a huge increase in demand for the converter's essential fuel, coke, a derivative of coal. Communities called coal patches sprang up around the coal mines to house coal workers and their families as iron, steel, and coal production flourished in both western Pennsylvania and eastern Ohio. African-Americans in search of work journeyed up from the South to the Midwest, and great waves of European immigrants flooded the region, the latter often recruited by agents representing Carnegie directly in the villages of Eastern Europe. By the 1870s, Pittsburgh was known as the "forge of the Universe," turning out half the iron, half the glass, and much of the oil in the United States.[31]

It was the age of heroic industry. Everything about it—the process, the products, the danger, the fortunes it generated, the environmental blight, the heat, the weight, the sheer physical size—was epic. "Hell with the Lid Taken Off" was how one nineteenth-century journalist described it.[32] It was an age that was to last one hundred years.

For a start, the steelworks were up to seven miles long, rows upon rows of mammoth furnaces that threw flames into the night sky with such spectacular luminosity that later, after the airplane was invented, the pilots of passing aircraft plotted their routes by them. The product—molten steel poured into ingot molds that hardened into giant girders and that rolled off the production line into the bellies of waiting locomotives—was so massive that even a slight error often meant the loss of limbs or death for workers. The human being as worker was totally dwarfed by the scale of the production process, but the human being as entrepreneur found his bank balance immeasurably enlarged—Henry Clay Frick, Andrew

Carnegie (who sold his steel interests to U.S. Steel in 1901 for almost $500 million, then a world record for the sale of a company), and the brothers A. W. and R. B. Mellon, owners of Mellon Bank and Gulf, an early oil combine—all amassed hitherto unimagined wealth. The pollution was similarly dramatic: businessmen had to change their shirts at lunchtime; laundry hung out to dry at noon would be covered in grime by evening. Later, in the 1940s, the region took on a heroic patriotism as it powered the United States war effort, producing 52 million shells and 11 million bombs. Pittsburghers liked to boast that they had done more to defeat Hitler than any other American city.[33]

The Midwest had become the engine room of America: it built the products that built the infrastructure of the country. The Chrysler Building and the Empire State Building in New York, for example, were erected with Pittsburgh steel. In this process of terrific expansion, the cities and towns of the Midwest were settled by a mix of working-class immigrants—English, Irish, Scottish, German, Italian, Polish, Jewish, African-American, Chinese—that reflected the ethnic composition of the emerging nation. Steelworkers formed unions and negotiated favorable wage rates: $17 an hour plus $7 in fringe benefits, not bad for the late 1960s. Like the Michigan autoworkers to the north, steelworkers were able to afford a middle-class lifestyle and send their children to college. In subsequent decades, Pittsburgh even cleaned up its act as civic and business leaders formed a partnership to find a solution to pollution.

In the meantime, the rise of the automobile was well under way. Cars rolled off the production lines to the northwest in Flint and Detroit. Whereas the train had afforded people (and freight) mobility between cities, automobiles gave people mobility within and around cities, allowing them to live miles from their workplace yet commute easily. But it was with the Federal-Aid Highway Act of 1956, signed into law by President Dwight D. Eisenhower— whose ambitious aim was to connect 90 percent of all cities by way of a national system of highways—that the era of the automobile took off.

It is said that the 1956 Highway Act did more to change the landscape of America than any other act of Congress of the twentieth century. The interstates opened up the country like never before, bringing a string of consequences, positive and negative, few could have imagined. Predictably, they were a boon for interstate commerce and long-distance truck haulage. But they also gave birth to the suburbs, the strip mall, the supermarket chain, the megastore, the suburban shopping center, and the covered mall. They spawned suburban sprawl, sucked the life out of the inner cities, and mowed down the great American outdoors. They precipitated a boom in car-related businesses—such as gas stations, drive-through fast-food restaurants, hotels and motels—that made a few highly enterprising Americans enormously wealthy and, in the process, homogenized the nation and vastly expanded the minimum-wage sector of the economy.

It seems hard to believe it now, but prior to the 1950s there was hardly a single franchised hotel or fast-food outlet in America. There were just one-off diners and mom-and-pop stores and motels. Now, all at once, with talk of the interstate in the air and the love affair with the automobile blooming, here was a concept whose time had come. Franchises took root and spread throughout the nation, each with its own instantly recognizable name and color scheme. It began in 1952 when Kemmons Wilson built the first Holiday Inns in Memphis, Tennessee. Then, in 1955, a sixty-five-year-old by the name of Colonel Harland Sanders in his trademark white suit threw all his possessions into his car and traveled cross-country to bet the house on his secret recipe and to franchise outlets of the Kentucky Fried Chicken restaurant he had started in Corbin, Kentucky. In the same year, Ray Kroc opened the first McDonald's franchise in Des Plaines, Illinois, just outside Chicago. Three years later, in 1958, two college students, Frank and Dan Carney, borrowed $600 from their mother and opened the first Pizza Hut in Wichita, Kansas. Around the same time, James McLamore and David Edgerton began franchising their joint venture, Burger King, which they had founded in Miami, Florida. And in 1969, a relatively late arrival, a pudgy-looking fellow by the name of Dave Thomas, opened the first Wendy's in Columbus, Ohio.

The rest, as they say, is history. By the end of the 1960s, the main characters who would father empires, employing millions of people in America and across the world, had arrived. These were ordinary people, most of them without much education, who seized a moment and in their own way became real American heroes. Their workforces, on the other hand, came to be dubbed the working poor: people who worked full-time at or near the minimum wage, but whose meager pay packets never amounted to much more than the poverty level—and if they had large families to support, amounted to much less. For this new nonunionized sector of the economy, the service sector, the future was unraveling with breathtaking elasticity; but for another, the factory workers of America, that band was about to snap.

In the 1970s, in the face of foreign competition by Japanese and European suppliers and shrinking demand for steel as a commodity due to the rising popularity of plastics and aluminum, the bottom fell out of the American steel and coal market. Factories closed, thousands of workers were laid off, unemployment soared, hundreds of thousands of people migrated—the population of Pittsburgh alone fell from a peak of 700,000 to around 350,000. The steel mills comprised an industrial center so massive, they took ten years to dismantle.

We did not know it then, but just like that, *phhttttttt,* the hundred-year heyday of steel was over. The Industrial Age was over. American cities would no longer *make* things, and they would certainly no longer be identified with, or make, such dramatically big things. Motor City (Detroit), Vehicle City (Flint), Steel City (Pittsburgh)—these were about to become rusting relics of the past. As dramatically as it had been erected, the engine room of America was dismantled, to be rehoused in Mexico, Asia, wherever the cheapest labor could produce the most competitive price.

And we did not know it quite then, either, but the postindustrial, computer-driven, globalization age was about to begin.

Pittsburgh and other midwestern cities—like Cleveland, Akron, and Cincinnati in Ohio—made attempts to gradually reinvent themselves. For a variety of reasons, these mid-sized cities proved more adaptable than both the heavyweight metropolis of Detroit and the smaller, one-dimensional Flint to the north. In Pittsburgh, civic and business leaders joined forces to curb pollution, revitalize the downtown, and foster a new economy. With characteristic American optimism, they motivated themselves by grandly dubbing the process "the Pittsburgh Renaissance." And although, as Pittsburghers today are quick to admit, their attempt to find a new identity is still a work in progress, the term "Renaissance" is not entirely a misnomer. In 1985, the city received recognition for the strides it had made when it beat out Boston and Philadelphia to be rated "America's most livable city."[34]

The key to success has been diversification. Today, less than 20 percent of Pittsburgh workers are in manufacturing, down from 40 percent, and less than 5 percent are in steel and other metals. The city, and the region, has had to shift from a predominantly blue-collar, manufacturing economy to a diversified service and a high-technology economy. And when you look at the details of what this has meant, the service and high-tech economies comprise the kind of businesses that are the enduring legacy of the automobile (Act III) and the microchip (Act IV), respectively.

A quarter of a century after the beginning of the postindustrial age, Ohio has so successfully diversified that it is dubbed the Bellwether State: in other words, it most closely mirrors the economic, demographic, religious, and political makeup of the nation. The ethnic mix of the 11.2 million people who live there, and the work they do, offer a snapshot of the country as a whole.[35] Electorally, it is a swing state, voting Democrat in the 1980s, solidly Republican in the 1990s. All this serves to make it, in the minds of the pollsters, the home of "the average American," and hence the "test-market capital of America." Social scientists use it as a "one-stop shop" to decipher what's on the mind of John and Jane Doe and their 2.2 children; research-and-development experts use it to pilot new products, and advertisers to fly new pitches.

You take the temperature of Ohio, you take the temperature of the nation.

ACT IV: THE NEW ECONOMY

Along the north bank of the Ohio River, a solitary, mocking voice rings out: "Can someone change this guy's diaper?"

"Change your diaper! Change your diaper!" A chorus of taunts aimed at the opposing team's outfielder rises up from the bleachers inside the amphitheater along the river as the final home game of the Pittsburgh Pirates' season gets under way against the Houston Astros. I have come to Three Rivers Stadium because it stands at the base of the Ohio River, at the very point where Tocqueville set sail all those years ago, and because, as an American friend suggests to me (only half in jest), I can never claim to understand the American character unless I at least attempt to come to grips with their national sport.

I do not think I shall fast make the grade, but it does occur to me that baseball and the English sport of cricket have much in common. Both of these games involve a duel between bat and ball, both unfold at an excruciatingly slow pace, and both have a streak of perversity about them. Cricket is the only game in the world that is played over five days and yet, more often than not, ends in a draw. Baseball, on the other hand, actually defines "a perfect game" as one where every single batter either *misses* the ball entirely or fails to get on base. For nine innings, the ultimate thrill is watching batter after batter swing the bat and either miss (he's struck out); pop it up in the air to be caught (he flies out); or hit it along the turf to a fielder, whose throw to first base beats him (he grounds out). As a kid, I grew up to appreciate the painstaking perversity of the game of cricket, and I have to admit that I find the guessing game that unfolds between pitcher and batter equally compelling. To watch Bernie Williams, the Yankee with the silken swing, anticipate correctly and crunch a fast ball into the left-field bleachers is not unlike watching South African batsman Graeme Pollock clip an oncoming swerving ball with the subtle flick of his wrist through the covers for four runs. Such effortless ease, such exquisite timing! Both baseball and cricket attract types who revel in the minutiae of statistics, but who appreciate that the real drama in life is in the fine details.

Tonight, though, the game is backdrop to details of a different sort as I trample the ground of Tocqueville's point of departure. I am curious to discover: Whom might I meet? What sounds will I hear? (References to diapers were not on my list of expectations.) What does the place look like, smell like?

The first thing I do is walk down to the river's edge, where a replica steamboat disgorges fans for the game. I find myself intuitively drawn to dip my hands in the water, to feel at source the strength, the movement, and the flow of the current that has for centuries been the life source of this land. As the water falls through my fingers, and as I look across and see the shimmering skyscrapers that comprise the compact Golden Triangle at the epicenter of the Pittsburgh downtown, it strikes me that the feel of the water—neither icy nor warm, but pleasantly cool—is the only sensation that I can realistically hope to share with Tocqueville. Almost everything I see around me will have changed so radically as to be unrecognizable to the Frenchman.

I pause to listen to the clink of little waves of water lapping against the riverbank, now mingling with the plunk of a guitar as a man strums tunefully, his dog stretched alongside his hat, which lies on the ground upturned and open for donations. As I pass, the strummer motions first to his hat, then to a red sign flashing electronically on the mountain above the far bank of the river. The sign reads: NATIONAL DOG WEEK—BE KIND TO CANINES.

"Who gets to decide which animal gets which week?" I ask.

"There is a committee," he says.

"Why not go the whole hog and have National Dog *Month*?"

"A week costs less," he fires back.

The sign makes me recall a rather more daring proclamation I had spied amongst the advertisements in the *Village Voice* in New York. "August Is Anal Sex Month," it had proclaimed to readers. Tocqueville had enjoyed contrasting Midwesterners (who, New Yorkers maintain, are friendly folk who have no edge) with New Yorkers (who, Pittsburghers say, are edgy but not friendly). The thought crosses my mind that he might have found the two proclamations revealing in precisely this way.

Back in the stadium, the aroma of hot dogs rises along with

ululating cries of "Beer sold here! Beer sold here!" . . . "Cotton candeeeeeeeeee!" . . . "Programs—only a dollar, only a dollar!" There I meet Joe, a middle-aged program salesman; Paul, a pimply, candy salesman; and Claudia, a pregnant cashier. Later, I meet Misty, a thirty-four-year-old mother of two children who is a housekeeper at the Cross Country Inn, and who makes my bed, cleans the toilet, wipes down the bathroom, and vacuums the carpet for three dollars a room. And . . .

. . . And this is the trouble when you pay too much attention to detail. One minute, a whole class of people is invisible; the next, you discover the place is thick with them. From the moment I wake up in the morning, I can't go anywhere without bumping into card-carrying members of the working poor. Of course, as a traveler, I am in their domain. They staff wherever I sleep, eat, drink, buy groceries, books, go for coffee, or seek live entertainment.

At the same time, it strikes me that I am also in the domain of the men who created this service economy in the first place. I am referring to the original founders of the fast-food and hospitality franchises, many of whom have headquartered themselves in and around the Midwest. I cannot help thinking how fascinating it would be to meet one of these men, to listen to his rags-to-riches story and to figure out how it has shaped his perspective on the people who staff his empire today.

But first, in the interests of perspective, I have to stop and ask: in a country where the unemployment rate is just 4 percent, where employment is projected to grow healthily by 14 percent between 1994 and 2005,[36] and where just about everyone who wants a job can have one, how significant are these people, the so-called working poor? And how representative are they of the American experience at the turn of the millennium?

For a start, it is necessary to define the category itself: families are regarded as working poor in America if at least one adult works full-time but the household is still unable to earn enough to cover the most basic financial costs of life, which most social scientists estimate as $30,000 a year for a family of four, $25,000 for a family of three, or up to two times the federal poverty line.

Second, it is useful to get a grip on their numbers: according to the U.S. Bureau of the Census, more than 35 million American families fall into this category.[37]

Third, it is important to investigate whether they comprise a growing or a shrinking portion of the population.

It is only when one tackles this last question—disassembling the aggregate or big-picture economy down into its component parts—that one measure, little remarked upon, stands out, and is startling in its implications.

It is this: *46 percent of the jobs with the most projected growth in America to the year 2005 pay poverty-level wages.*[38]

According to social scientists at the research organization National Priorities Project, which interpreted Bureau of Labor Statistics data and published its findings in a 1998 report called "Working Hard, Earning Less: The Story of Job Growth in America," almost half of the twenty fastest-growing occupations in the US are expected to be in the following eight low-wage, service occupations:

- Child-care workers (average annual wages of $9,360)
- Cashiers ($12,324)
- Waiters and waitresses ($14,092)
- Teachers' aides ($14,114)
- Nursing aides ($14,612)
- Retail sales workers ($14,924)
- Janitors, cleaners, and maids ($15,236)
- Home health aides ($15,444)

"The four jobs with the *most* growth in the nation," emphasizes the report, "are cashiers, janitors, retail sales people and waiters and waitresses. These trends exist in all 50 states."[39]

A local study by the University of Cincinnati[40] adds a key missing piece to this picture. It notes that while almost half of the jobs with the most projected growth to 2005 in greater Cincinnati will be in the "low-wage, few-benefits, service jobs" whose median starting wage is $6.63 an hour, the other half of fast-growing jobs will be in the relatively well-paid high-tech-related occupations, such as computer systems analysts and engineers.

In other words, the two fastest-growing groups of occupations are the ones at the bottom of the economic spectrum, which require little education, and the ones at the top of the spectrum, which have high education requirements. The report notes that as much as "74 percent of jobs" in the latter type of occupations require "some post-secondary or college education."

What the Cincinnati report makes abundantly clear is that more and more, the United States is becoming a two-tier economy with access between the tiers mediated primarily by a highly rationed good—namely, postsecondary education. This is new to the United States—a distinctive feature of the postindustrial economy that has emerged in the last twenty-five years—but it is not unique to the United States. However, the unprecedented impact of the role that higher education—*not hard work but higher education*—now plays in affording upward mobility between the two tiers is only beginning to be addressed by American politicians. Though in private life Americans understand absolutely that higher education is critical to their own children's success, they have not yet digested the long-term implications of this structural shift in the economy for society as a whole.

It is sobering to realize that despite enjoying the best peacetime economic expansion in its history, a large slice of the growth in future employment in America will come from jobs that pay poverty-level wages. It is sobering to realize that despite a work ethic that holds it as an article of faith that those willing to work hard will achieve a better life, the number of people who will work hard but stay poor is structurally set to rise, not fall.

Yet this part of the story of the transformation of America that has unfurled along the banks of the Ohio and throughout the hinterland is seldom discussed among middle-class Americans and their representatives in Congress. These facts struggle to make any impact upon the consciousness of the nation or get any significant or sustained airtime on the networks. At times, it seems to me, to dwell on such issues is regarded as "un-American."

A plan takes shape in my mind. If, like Tocqueville, I want to use this leg of the journey to investigate the changing role that *hard work* plays in accessing the American Dream, I will need to explore it from at least two points of view. I will need to explore it from the perspective of the working poor themselves, and from that of the entrepreneurs who created employment for the working poor in the first place. There is a third perspective too, belonging to the politicians who have the power to impact the lives of the working poor through social policy, and which I will want to explore at the state level, and in more detail when I get to Washington, D.C.

I set out to follow the road that follows the river and—starting with some interviews in Pittsburgh—to delve deeper into the unseen working-poor segment of American society.

"THE BITCH" AT THE GIANT EAGLE

"Hey, mom, tell him the story about the customer who wanted to beat you up!" Paul shouts from the living room.

Helaine Clark reddens behind her prescription eyeglasses, like a reluctant soldier egged on to recall life on the front line. "Oh, I had a guy tell me he was gonna shoot me 'cause his change was ninety-two cents and he said I should round it up and give him a dollar.

" 'You cashiers are so fucking brilliant,' he says to me.

" 'Well, we can't all be rocket scientists like you,' I reply.

" 'I should give you some of this,' he says, and he puts his hand out in a motion to shoot me."

"Naaah, Mom, not that one—tell the one about the *woman* who wanted to beat you up," bellows Paul, fourteen, sticking his head around the corner, his hair a peroxide blond, a heavy-duty chain around his neck, and a T-shirt, emblazoned with the name of the rock group Coal Chamber scrunched around his torso.

"Oh, awright," says Clark, cradling a can of iced tea. "I had a woman who said she'd wait for me after work to beat the shit out of me. You know, she was one of these welfare types and she arrived at my cash register with a stack of coupons that she had got from the Salvation Army. This woman bought nothing but garbage with them—pop, cookies, candy—and after I rang up her coupons, she demands change in cash.

" 'You know we can't give no change for coupons,' I say.

" 'This is a bunch of fucking shit,' she says. Then she calls me a white bitch. 'You and your fucking hairdo,' she says.

" 'Look,' I say, 'I don't make the rules. Why don't you go and take some more candy?' Meanwhile a long line of customers has formed behind her and people want to know what's going on. So I tell them: 'She's on welfare. You know, coupons.'

" 'I don't appreciate you telling other people my bidness,' she says. 'I'm gonna wait outside until you finished work, and then I gonna kick your white bitch ass.' "

Clark's eleven-year-old daughter, Heather, runs in from the living room, where she has been lying, full of a head cold, watching *Grease* on video. She throws her arms around her mom and gives her a hug. "My kids know that I'm a tough old broad, that I can handle myself," says Clark. "I've been called an asshole and a fucking bitch more times than I care to count."

Helaine Clark, age forty-four, is a checkout cashier at the Giant Eagle, one of the oldest and largest supermarket chains in the Midwest, their 140 stores employing 25,000 people in western Pennsylvania, eastern Ohio, and northern West Virginia. Clark started at $5.45 an hour. She now gets $7 an hour after eight years in the job.

Demographically, Helaine Clark is as classic working poor as you can get. According to a 1999 joint national survey of the working poor by Rutgers University and the University of Connecticut,[41] "the typical working poor individual is a single white woman between 30–49 who works one full-time job for 40 hours a week that she has held for at least a year, earns less than $25,000 a year, is paid by the hour, has a child under the age of 18, has little or no paid vacation time, has not received cash welfare, but at some time has received some form of public assistance, most likely an Earned Income Tax Credit." The report adds: "Most (71%) of the working poor have been in their jobs more than one year, and 42% have been in their job more than three years." So, contrary to stereotype, the typical working poor persons in America are neither students, nor are they African-American or Hispanic (though minorities are disproportionately represented in the working poor), nor are they changing jobs every few months. They are white, middle-aged mothers who are either divorced or never married, and who stay in their jobs for a substantial period of time.

Clark can't survive on her full-time cashier job, from which she takes home just $600 a month after tax, union dues, and medical aid deductions; so she moonlights as a domestic cleaner on her day off. She charges $15 an hour, and it brings in an additional $240 a month. The cleaning pays better, she says, but it is backbreaking work and she would never contemplate doing it full-time.

The Saturday I visit, it is her morning off. "I'm sorry the house is a mess," she apologizes. "I'm always cleaning other people's houses, never seem to find time to clean my own." She wears slippers, tracksuit pants, and a grayish T-shirt that has long since lost its original color and shape. Clark is half Irish, half Scottish, and her home is in Morningside, a mostly Italian working-class neighborhood on the east-side of Pittsburgh, two blocks from where she grew up, the daughter of a police officer. She shows me round her three-bedroom house, which she owns, apologizing again, this time for the gaping holes in the kitchen wall, for the clothing piled up everywhere, and for the disembodied furniture cabinets with cardboard boxes for drawers. Her place looks like it needs the builders, the plumbers, and the electricians in for a week.

The question on my mind—which I know is impolite, but I ask anyway—is this: for a seemingly intelligent person, how did you end up staying so long in such a low paying, dead-end job?

"Some people had childhoods," she says, unflinching. "I didn't. You see, my dad was a policeman when he was alive; he was also an alcoholic. He would come home at around three in the morning after a Friday night out, drunk, wake me and my sister and my younger brother, and beat the hell out of us with his police belt. The first time I was beat up, I was five years old. He'd hit us, knock us down, then he'd kick us. Oh, God, it was horrible—horrible. He went on behaving like this for years. For some reason, he never laid a hand on my mother or my older brother, just the rest of us. We begged mom to divorce him, but she was a religious fanatic and she thought that if you prayed, everything would be all right. So we grew up in fear, and as soon as we were old enough, we left home. I married the first man I met, age nineteen. My sister became an alcoholic; has been in AA for twenty years. My younger brother is an alcoholic." She pauses. "Me? I don't drink, but I guess it affected my . . ." She trails off.

"Your what?"

"Belief in myself, I guess. I wanted to be a vet, but it was never an option for us to go to college. It was like, 'You've finished school—*get a goddamn job!*' "

But Clark offers her childhood as only part-explanation for her present difficulties. The rest is due to a far more common trap: no education beyond high school combined with the acute demands of single parenthood.

Her first job was on the fish counter for Robert Wholey Company, a food supplier to restaurants. She made good money there, she says, $20,000 a year. She was offered a managerial position but had to decline, she says, because by now she had remarried and was expecting her first child. "It makes me sick to think this, but if I had stayed, I would be making $14.85 an hour like my friend who works there," she says. Instead, she took time off to raise her two children. But eight years ago, after her second marriage hit the rocks, she was forced back into the workplace. Needing a job that would end early so that she could be home for the children's homework after school, she sought work at the Giant Eagle in the nearby Polish neighborhood of Lawrenceville. "There are about seventy-two employees there," she says, "most in their thirties and forties, most of them Polish, and actually, most divorced mothers like myself."

Clark describes her working day: Up at 6.30 A.M., cup of tea, a cigarette, catch the news on television. Wake the kids at 6.50, put out the breakfast cereal; by 7.30 she's outta there, all dressed up in her blue smock uniform. Then from 8 A.M. to 4 P.M., she's on her feet, scanning people's groceries, taking their money, bagging it—nothing a monkey couldn't do, she says, except that she's really quick, and customers like to be in her line. At slow times during the day, the manager gets her to stock shelves or clean the toilets. "Our manager finds things for us to do that are degrading. But what he doesn't realize is that after four hours on the cash register taking people's rudeness, I actually prefer cleaning toilets to serving customers." Especially when those customers are what Clark calls "those ignorant, low-class scrounges who get their money free on welfare." "They get $541.40 a month—I know, because we cash their checks—plus food stamps, plus free medical, plus housing vouchers. And with each kid they have they get more. I work my ass off and those welfare scrounges live for free, treat me like a piece of shit, and get almost as much as I do," she says.

The unfairness of it all to Clark is compounded by the fact that at the end of the day, after supervising homework, making dinner, throwing a load of laundry in the washing machine, just before she falls asleep in her clothes on the sofa, her feet throbbing, her body numb and exhausted, she has to wrestle with the fact that she still barely makes enough money to cover her expenses, even with the help of child support from her ex-husband. She takes home $840 a month from her two jobs combined and receives $800 a month in child support from her ex-husband, which totals $1,640 a month, or just under $20,000 a year. But it costs her $1,540 a month just to cover her basic monthly expenses, which she lists as follows:

Mortgage on $23,000 home loan	358
Interest on home-improvement loan	130
Food	400
Utilities (gas, electricity, water)	220
Telephone	35
Cable TV	40
Video rental (their only entertainment)	44
Home insurance	50
Car insurance	63
Gasoline for the car	40
Braces for her daughter's teeth	160
Total	$1,540

That leaves just $100 a month for repayment of interest on her credit-card debts and a panic when it comes to forking out for vehicle repairs, house repairs, clothing and shoes for the kids. In the early years after her divorce, Clark sunk deep into debt, borrowing on one credit card to pay another, and amassing arrears of $14,000. She's whittled her debt down to $8,500, and has reduced the charge cards she carries from ten to five, which she now lays out for me on the table—Citibank Platinum Select, Discover, JC Penney, Kaufmann's, First Platinum Mastercard. "Every month I cut one up," she says. "That's how I know I'm making progress."

If it wasn't for the federal Earned Income Tax Credit (EITC)—which refunds income tax to working poor families in a lump-sum payment—the family would never have a vacation. This year, they spent half of their $1,000 tax refund on stuff needed to be done round the house (like plumbing—"the kitchen sink was without water for months") and the other half on a four-day summer vacation on Lake Erie, which, she says, was great, and their first *real* vacation in years. "Before, I used it all for emergencies and we'd just go stay for a weekend at a hotel in the area and swim in the hotel pool."

Another thing. Clark hasn't dated a man in seven years. "Between working . . . being there for my kids . . . you gotta be joking," she says.

"They say the economy is booming, that the country is flourishing. Oh, really? That's news to me. Apart from my kids, my life is just miserable. I didn't figure that at forty-four years old, I'd be working so hard for so little money. I have three messages to my children—go to college, go to college, go to college." And she pep-talks herself too: "This job's below my intelligence; I can find another; soon the kids will need me less, I can do better," she says.

But in the absence of a new job, there is one thing that Clark believes would immeasurably improve her life: a raise. Just $2 an hour, to $9, should do it, she says. It would give her the extra $200 take-home a month that makes the difference between a life that feels like a slow death and, well . . . a life.

Ironically, the joint Rutgers and University of Connecticut national survey of the working poor notes that "when asked how much additional income is necessary to take care of their family needs, two-thirds (68%) of respondents indicate that they need less than $200 in additional income per month." So Clark is in good company. The difference between those working poor who had the critical additional $200 a month and those who didn't was like night and day, concludes the report, with the former group more stable, satisfied, and confident about the future; the latter just the opposite. The report notes that a $1-an-hour increase in the minimum wage to $6.15 an hour would almost get them there, filtering upward to workers on the next tier and adding another $170 to full-time workers' pay packets.

Recently Clark had an opportunity to make a dent in her ambition for higher pay when she was chosen to represent her fellow workers at the Giant Eagle wage negotiation. She got dressed in her best blouse and dress suit and, together with a representative from the local Amalgamated Food Workers Union, went in to do battle with the store owner and his two sons (the branch she works for is one of the few franchised Giant Eagles; most are corporate-owned).

"Our plan was to ask for a 50-cent raise in the hope of getting 25 cents an hour," she says. "But before we could begin, the owner started by saying he wanted to *cut* our wages. That was his opening bid. He said a new Shop N Save was opening down the road, that they had to take out a $4 million loan to remodel the store to stay competitive. So we dropped our 50-cent plan and asked for 25 cents. They left the room. They came back. 'The Shop N Save are paying all their cashiers $5.15 an hour, and they have no union,' they told us. After five hours of back-and-forth—of them leaving the room, us leaving the room—finally they said, 'Okay, we'll give you a dime, and no more raises until the year 2001.' A *dime*! And guess what? We settled. It was them or the Shop N Save. It made me sick—I knew we'd get screwed, but not to that extent. At this rate, getting to $9 an hour will take another twenty years!"

Just a few hours after meeting Helaine Clark, I find myself in the living room of Gerald E. Chait, age fifty-three, one of the five owners of the Giant Eagle chain of supermarkets. I am immediately struck by how modestly he presents himself, dressed in out-of-shape tracksuit pants and a simple shirt. If you saw him on the street, he could pass for Clark's older brother. His environment, though, tells you otherwise. He sits in a sumptuously decorated living room in a mansion in Fox Chapel, perhaps the richest neighborhood in Pittsburgh, with deep plush sofas, marble tables, rugs, a fireplace, a grand piano, each item handpicked, much of it from exclusive designer stores in Manhattan. Lingering out of sight there is a cook, a gardener, a full-time nanny for his young children, a personal trainer. His guest bathroom, which I have occasion to visit, has disposable paper napkins with CHAIT embossed in thick silver across the corner.

Chait, who is soft-spoken, recounts the story of how his Jewish grandfather, Benjamin Chait, came to America from Poland in 1917, "a young man, poor, but looking for freedom." Together with another Pole, Joseph Porter, whom he met as a fellow boarder, he started a small convenience store called Eagle Grocery in East Liberty, then a thriving immigrant section of Pittsburgh, much like the Lower East Side in early New York. Over the years, the two men acquired three more partners, like cowboys in a western assembling their gang, and the five men and their families have ridden together ever since. In the 1940s they expanded from a small convenience store selling nonperishable goods and embraced a new trend—a store with multiple food departments called a supermarket. When the postwar automobile and consumer booms hit in the 1950s and people began to migrate to the suburbs, Giant Eagle followed, becoming anchor tenants in the new suburban shopping centers. Later came covered malls, and the spreading fast-food business, which was so cheap that it severely threatened their supermarket business, and to which they responded by adding features like an inside "ready-prepared" pizza shop. For three generations, from 1931, the Chaits, the Porters, the Goldsteins, the Moravitzes, and the Weizenbaums have run the Giant Eagle, and amazingly, says Chait, a combination of luck and good management has meant that they have never had a major fight or a falling-out.

Part of the secret, says Chait, is that the families are philanthropic—they believe in *giving back* to the community, and they have established a foundation that is used to fund vast numbers of good works. Chait's personal reputation in Pittsburgh, from what I have been told, is of a caring, unostentatious, and decent man involved in the community.

"But why does your company pay cashiers minimum wage or thereabouts?" I blurt out. "Why not do the decent thing and give back to the very people who work for you by paying them a *living* wage?"

Chait says nothing. He takes a sip of mineral water. Then he says nothing some more.

"That," he says at length, "that is a very good question."

I cannot be sure whether Chait genuinely feels it is a question worthy of further exploration, or whether, brain whirring, he is just buying himself time to marshal his defenses and construct an elegant escape.

"The problem is," he says, "there is no agreement on what a living wage actually is."

"I have a recent report[42] in my bag that claims to have calculated a living wage for each state," I counter, "and which in the region of your stores would come to eight to nine dollars an hour, and—"

"We couldn't do it on our own," he interrupts. "Because if we raised wages to a living wage, we'd have to pass the cost along to consumers and raise prices. Then everyone would buy from the competition and we'd go out of business. Profit margins in our business are very low, one percent to three percent after tax. We make our money on volume."

"Would you be in favor, then, of the government raising the minimum wage for everyone?" I ask, pursuing the logic of his answer.

"I don't think the minimum wage should be artificially set; the marketplace should decide," he says.

"But you just explained how the market cannot deliver a livable wage on its own," I say.

"Still, it's a difficult question," he says.

There is a short silence while we negotiate the impasse. But then Chait goes on to make an important point. He says that his company has a policy of promoting from within. "Most of our management were employees at store level who worked their way up through the organization to their current positions. Almost one hundred percent of them," he says. "We do this not out of the goodness of our hearts, but because we've learned to spot those employees who have management potential and to bring them on."

If it is true that upward mobility out of working-poor jobs really is an open channel, then two deductions flow naturally from this premise. First, since the worker can easily achieve advancement, the onus of rising out of poverty rests with the worker, and so no intervention by social policy is necessary. Second, raising wages becomes less critical to well-being, because the amount of time people spend in poverty need only be brief. People endure hardship more readily if they know it's for a limited time only.

Tocqueville himself marveled at how in a democracy, there is nothing degrading about the status of low-paying jobs, "because it is freely adopted and temporary and because it is not stigmatized by public opinion and creates no permanent inequality."[43] It is this *temporary* aspect to working in low-paying jobs that is crucial in modifying people's attitudes and relations, insisted the Frenchman. But Tocqueville concluded his critique on upward mobility in America with a warning. A system that goes halfway, that promises upward mobility but delivers immobility for significant numbers of people, "such a condition is revolutionary, not democratic," he said.[44]

The popular perception of America today, both domestically and abroad, is of a culture and economy of rampant upward mobility, more so than any other Western democracy. But checking whether this perception corresponds to reality by attempting to accurately measure social mobility—let alone making scientific comparisons between countries—is a difficult if not impossible task. There is, though, an emerging body of evidence[45] which shows that upward mobility through hard work is profoundly more difficult in today's postindustrial era than it ever was in the industrial era of the 1950s and 1960s. Today, the argument goes, without a solid education behind you—not just to high school but beyond—your chances of a job in the well-paid, knowledge-based information economy is slim indeed. Against this backdrop, then, in which a lack of college education limits upward mobility and probably consigns you to a job in the low-paying service sector, what of Chait's argument that upward mobility is available for uneducated employees who display the right mix of attitude, smarts, and aptitude?

On the one hand, Chait is right—it *is* possible to move up. And not just at the Giant Eagle. In my travels through the Midwest, I meet many people who have started out as lowly minimum-wage crew members in a McJob and who have stuck it out and risen to become managers and even, in some cases, multiple-store franchise owners. Their stories are impressive. There is no doubt that Wendy's, McDonald's, Burger King, for example, all encourage promotion from within (though, as each will tell you, too, by far the faster track to management is from without).

But what Chait doesn't say is this: the structure of his organization, like every other in the service sector, is a pyramid. That means that there are few chiefs and many, many Indians. The limited number of managers in relation to the very large number of cashiers/crew means that when viewed from the bottom, upward mobility is more of a theoretical possibility than a practical one. Twenty cashiers doing their damnedest to be promoted to the one position in management that *might* come up "next year" can translate into a long wait for the other nineteen. Helaine Clark maintains that in her eight years with the Giant Eagle, not one cashier—not one—has advanced to a management position.

The change in the American economy is structural, not cosmetic. This means that for minimum-wage-paying businesses to train and promote from within is a good first step. But alone, it is not enough.

Walking me back to the car, Chait chats about how back in the 1970s, he read Tocqueville as part of his philosophy degree at Cornell University. "Tocqueville was impressively contemporary," he says, momentarily deep in thought. "This country," he starts up again, a wistful look flickering across his brow, "we started with this kinship that we were all in the same boat. We've gotten away from that. I'm not sure when it happened. It's not just a class divide . . . it's a . . ." he gropes for the word—"it's a *feelings* thing." And then he looks me in the eye. "This country . . . we've lost our ability to *feel* for the people in the other boat," he says.

The emotional charge that Chait gives to these words, in contrast to his unflappable and mellow tone throughout the interview, makes me feel that he is talking about more than his country. I may be mistaken, but I get the impression, generous philanthropist though he is, that he is grappling with these issues in himself.

ON THE ROAD THAT FOLLOWS THE RIVER

Unlike the unforgiving camera, which captures everything within its frame, the human eye operates with delicate discernment, automatically screening out sights which—though directly in its line of vision—the viewer has no desire or interest to see. You might call it a built-in buffer against boredom, or a protection against unnecessary pain. So it is that as I journey to seek an interview with one of the founding franchise barons, and as I make my way from Pittsburgh through the northern tip of West Virginia and into the "Bellwether State" of Ohio and beyond, I am tempted to say I see nothing worth reporting at all.

But after a while, I begin to observe that this "nothing" regularly repeats itself, guarding the entrance and exit to every town or city I drive through, and that there is a something to this nothing after all.

I leave Pittsburgh on Highway 70 heading west, the day breaking fall-warm and sublime, the sun beginning its arc across a cloudless sky. I have gas in my tank, a wholesome breakfast in my stomach. For one perfect moment I feel in need of nothing at all—it's just me, the big sky, a purring engine and the open road.

FOOD EXIT, shouts a sign. And then, rushing toward me, flanking both sides of the highway, Wendy's, McDonald's, Eat 'n Park, Grand China Buffet. Whoosh. GAS EXIT, says the next, and I whoosh past that too. The last sights as I leave Pittsburgh are a Hampton Inn and a Holiday Inn Express (ROOMS $49 SUNDAY

THRU THURSDAY). WELCOME TO WEST VIRGINIA, offers a new sign, and my eye picks out, in the distance, a plume of smoke ascending lazily from an unseen factory chimney. MCDONALD'S, SIX MILES, INDOOR PLAYLAND, notes a giant tower billboard, immediately followed by WENDY'S SIX MILES, HOLIDAY INN, and PIZZA HUT. I shoot through Wheeling near the site where Tocqueville's steamship sank in 1831, onto the West Virginia side of the river, through little riverside villages called Paden City, Sistersville, and Friendly, where the trees are turning a stunning fusion of red, yellow, and orange. WELCOME TO OHIO, says a big blue sign as I cross the bridge and turn left onto Highway 7, which runs directly alongside the river. I overtake long flat barges laden with coal and enter the eighteenth-century town of Marietta, the earliest permanent settlement in the Northwest Territory. The sight that greets me is one of banners. Everywhere banners that say, NOW HIRING, APPLY WITHIN, and which adorn the strip populated by Holiday Inn, Comfort Inn, Wal-Mart, Kmart, Bob Evans, Appleby's Grill, Taco Bell, Burger King, Long John Silver, Wendy's. BILLIONS AND BILLIONS SOLD, adds the sign outside McDonald's. At the center of the old town is a wide street with lampposts and beautiful period buildings that date back to another century, like the facade of a town in a John Wayne western, perhaps. But there are few shops or shoppers, and the place appears commercially dead.

I drive on toward Columbus, through the central plains of Ohio that have been rendered flat as a pancake by an ancient glacier that left it dull to the eye but ideal for corn farmers. The usual suspects—Cross Country Inn, Holiday Inn, Wendy's, Burger King, Pizza Hut, McDonald's, KFC—hulk along the highway, offering food and lodging. This is Anywhere, USA, an anonymous place on the way to another place. It hardly seems to have an address.

By now I am hungry, and so I pull up at McDonald's. I order from a cashier wearing headphones, a middle-aged woman having a bad-hair day who is also the manager, and who tells me she started at four A.M. She hands me my order, but as she does so, something in the back of the kitchen catches her trained eye. "Jason," she bellows to a man momentarily reclining against his work station, "if you can lean, you can clean!"

"If you can lean, you can clean." The catchphrase sets bells dinging in my head and transfers me back in time to an experience I had all but forgotten: in 1995, I surreptitiously took a job at a McDonald's in London for one week, my aim to describe the experience of working there to readers of the London *Evening Standard*. My reign as "Lord of the Fries," though mercifully brief, gave me a taste of the fast-food production line:

They kitted me out in their maroon and gray uniform (cap, striped shirt, trousers, apron) and instructed me to pin my "May I help you please" name badge directly in line with the "M" on my apron. Then they started me on bun duty. Now there are two types of bun: the ordinary top-and-bottom bun for "regulars," and the Big Mac bun, which has three parts—crown, club, heel—all of which are toasted in different ways on different trays, at different times, for different lengths of time. The average turnover of 1,000 Big Macs a day translated into 3,000 toasted sesame-seed buns and the pace was unrelenting. I kept getting confused, mixing things up, causing delays for the person dressing the crowns two feet to my right, creating bottlenecks which put pressure on the crew at the counter who were unable to dispense orders within the standard time of 60 seconds and which left customers waiting more than the prescribed two minutes. By the afternoon though, I'd got the hang of it and a rather kind manager installed me in the less hectic universe of quarter-pounders which is a one-person production line and which—snigger if you will but it felt like an achievement—allowed me to make whole hamburgers on my own! And I've been here ever since, responding to orders: "Pull 6 quarters! Pull 8! Pull 12," and measuring out my day in pre-rationed squirts of mustard and ketchup, sprinkles of onion shavings and pickles placed side by side on toasted buns, relentlessly chasing the clock in an all-consuming yet strangely empty way. The dressings make a layered pattern that I find fascinating and, like Andy Warhol, the hamburger becomes for me a work of art. Occasionally, I contemplate rebellion, like making eight burgers in a batch when they've called for only six, but it never goes further than a delicious thought. After each batch I scrape the grill clean, squeegee down the non-stick coating (which at 450 degrees Fahrenheit gives rather nasty oil burns) and begin again. And again. Each grill and dressing cycle lasts just 120 seconds. Cleanliness is no mere buzzword—I scratch an itch on my face and an ever-prowling manager makes me wash my hands in one of the soap, water and hot-air dispensers. They call it "clean as you go" and if ever there is a lull in production there are always trays to wipe, rags to wash, floors to sweep. A culture of non-stop work is inculcated so that crew members hardly ever indulge in conversation beyond the occasional "Y'all right?" As the manager says, reprimanding one of the Spanish workers leaning momentarily on his mop: "We don't pay you good money to stand around and look idle. If you can lean you can clean."[46]

Working for McDonald's was the ultimate existential experience: time and the world contracted and nothing outside my 120-second Quarter Pounder cycle existed. Even at night I dreamt frenetically about making hamburgers, confirmed by other crew members as a common side-effect. And like them, I was so tired when I got home from work that I fell asleep in the bath. But at the end of the day, I was on an assignment, and so I was able to leave that all-consuming world before it consumed me.

Now as I travel through America I feel consumed in a different way. Now I am a buyer, not a worker, for whom there often seems little choice other than standardized, franchised fast food, whether on the road or in the environs of the big cities. As I approach Cincinnati, for example, pushed up against the Interstate 275 beltway, I am confronted by mile after mile of mega-malls, shopping centers, and strips . . .

It is a franchise wasteland. I have seen the same thing encasing Flint and Detroit, in suburban New York, and even on the Three Rivers Train chugging west through Pennsylvania. In each case, the franchises repeat themselves every mile—the same half-dozen places to eat on the tarmac front lots and the same half-dozen places to sleep on the back lots. There is no doubt that this fungus-like spread of the franchise has homogenized America, throttling cities in a series of interlocking suburban strips that suck the life out of the downtown and drain the identity out of entire regions. Things have gotten so out of hand that Republican Senator John McCain muses that "with all the chains like Gap and Chili's, there's only three unique American cities left—San Francisco, New York, and New Orleans."[47] Throughout the Midwest, as city councils attempt to counter this trend, proposing multi-million-dollar schemes to "revitalize the downtown,"[48] I cannot help wondering why something that is so depressingly ugly is cloned and repeated across the country, in rich areas as well as poor.

Traveling through these parts, Tocqueville had encountered a uniformity that was less tiresome to the eye than it was to the limb. "America is still nothing but a forest," he and Beaumont complained, somewhat grumpily, when their transport broke down and they were forced to trudge twenty-five miles through the snow, without food or lodging. "We were all marching, on foot, in the midst of the woods and mountains of Kentucky, where a loaded wagon had never been seen since the beginning of the world," he wrote. "It got through, however, thanks to the good shoulder shoves and the daring spirit of our driver; but we were marching in the snow, and it was up to our knees. This manner of travelling finally became so fatiguing that our companions began to abandon us one after the other." Tocqueville described the region as filled with hills and shallow valleys cut by a multitude of small streams, and almost entirely covered by trees. "Once every so often a line of rails, some burnt trees, a field of corn, a few cattle, a cabin of tree trunks placed one on the other and roughly squared, announced the isolated dwelling of a settler. You see hardly any villages. The habitations of the farmers are scattered in the woods."

Tocqueville went on to note that the houses built by the pioneers all bore a "perfect resemblance to each other, whether they are to be found in the depths of Michigan or at the gate of New-York."[49]

Even then, he had picked up on the American tendency to clone concepts that worked, in this case the settler's dwelling. He put it down to "the inherent practical nature" of Americans, their ten-

dency for turning everything into "an industry," and their "preference for efficiency over aesthetics." I put it down to an
ineffective, at times nonexistent, town planning system. "Unplanned development is the norm in America," a Cincinnati-environs
town planner, William McErlane, tells me. A TIME/CNN poll
throws some light on why this might be: Americans' dislike for
urban sprawl, they say, is outweighed by their distrust of government planning.[50] Whatever the core reasons, it is, at the very least,
a curious paradox that a country that so embraces individualism
should tend toward such bland uniformity.

Driving through, I feel like a guest at the Mad Hatter's tea party.
Except instead of demanding "More tea! More tea!" and passing it
down the table, the reflex refrain has become "More Wendy's!
More Holiday Inns! More McDonald's!" and passing it down the
strip. Catherine Barrett, a Democrat in the Ohio state legislature
who sat on a zoning board for eight years, throws up her hands in
exasperation and tells me: "Any time you sell land to a Burger King,
McDonald's will come, and there is not a damn thing we can do
about it."

Their influence permeates the airwaves too. On television, and
over the radio, advertisements for the various fast-food and hotel
franchises proliferate. When I listen to the news on the car radio,
the bulletin includes the following items: "One hundred Wall
Street analysts have accepted McDonald's invitation to be put to
work on their new system in the midday rush"; "No one has won
the $16 million Ohio Super Lottery, which means that Wednes-
day's Super Lottery is now $20 million"; and finally, "McDonald's
have just opened their two hundredth Ronald McDonald House,
which aid the families of sick children."

When even the news is McDominated, when advertorial and
editorial become indistinct, the word "ubiquitous" comes to mind.

The cumulative effect of it all is mind-numbing. Our eye pro-
tects our soul, screening out the bland franchise wasteland—we see
nothing, taste nothing, feel nothing. Where once the franchise concept delightfully enhanced our free choice and prided itself on quality—who can forget the thrill of the occasional burger at the lone

McDonald's in town?—now in the name of free choice our options have been homogenized. And even worse, the quality is gone. As Cindi Sims, a veteran Ohio manager with twenty years in the fast-food business (McDonald's, Burger King, and now Wendy's), says to me: "The biggest change in the fast-food business is this: in the beginning we took pride in delivering what we thought was a quality product. But nowadays it's just rush, rush, rush—who cares what it looks or tastes like. Just get it out."

Meanwhile, after a slow start, my attempt to glimpse the world from the perspective of a franchise baron is nearing its conclusion.

Dave Thomas, the sixty-seven-year-old founder of Wendy's, the third-largest hamburger chain in the world, is my first choice. But he is not in when I call ahead to their headquarters in Columbus, Ohio, and being in Florida for the season he will not, I am informed, be available for interview. I drive on to Louisville, Kentucky—to the gleaming white brick-and-glass headquarters of Tricon Global Restaurants, owners of KFC, Pizza Hut, and Taco Bell. The building is decked out like a shrine to the late Colonel, who died in 1980.

I meet a tattooed security guard who tells me that he knew the Colonel. "When I was nine years old," he recalls, "I set up a lemonade stand on the pavement out front of a Kentucky Fried Chicken store. Next thing this big white Cadillac pulls up and a man in a white suit and a walking stick gets out. He walks up to me and . . . I was expecting a cuff around the ear, but he puts his hand in his pocket and offers me ten dollars for my whole supply. I will never forget that as long as I live. A lot of men would have said, "Now get, scoot, *goooo*," but the Colonel was just so kind." All over Louisville, I encounter similar tributes to the Colonel, who appears to be much loved by the locals and venerated as a smart but generous pioneer who made time for ordinary people. Tricon, however, seems unwilling to continue the conversation and repeatedly rebuffs my request for an interview.

I am seemingly out of options, when, stroke of luck, I have a breakthrough. Just a few hours drive south of Louisville, another peerless pioneer, by the name of Kemmons Wilson, takes my telephone call and says: "Sure, c'mon down here to my office—you can pick my brains if you like . . ."

THE MAN WITH 300,000 BEDS

You could say that Kemmons Wilson was the daddy of it all, and that the franchise concept began with his vision on the road to the capital in the summer of 1951.

Wilson had bundled his wife, Dorothy, and their five children into their Oldsmobile and had set off from Memphis to Washington, D.C., "to see how the country ran." Then a thirty-eight-year-old builder, Wilson had never before taken a vacation in his life, but as he wended his way cross-country at an easy pace, spending nights at four different motels on the journey down and another four on the way back, he became increasingly disgusted by the erratic third-rate accommodations on offer and by the surcharges he was asked to pay: $2 for each child and $1 for a television. A room that should have cost $6 came to $17!

"You know," he said to Dorothy, "there is a real opportunity to make some money in a chain of hotels that people will trust."

He pulled out a tape measure from his pocket (as a builder, he carried one with him wherever he went) and began measuring and sketching the dimensions of the rooms in which they were staying.

"How many would you build?" asked Dorothy.

"Four hundred," he said.

And Dorothy laughed.

But Kemmons hunkered down and wrote up a shortlist of the ways his hotel chain would differ from the motels he'd stayed in. They would have standard room rates of $6 for a double; they would be air-conditioned; there would be a double bed for Mom and Pop and another for the children, who'd stay free. There would be no charge for TV, a policy of never putting up No Vacancy signs, standard levels of cleanliness, the same decorations throughout, and each hotel would have a restaurant and a swimming pool. He would make luxury both inexpensive and predictable, he decided. He asked his mother, Ruby, whom he adored, to pick out the drapes and hired a local draftsman by the name of Eddie Bluestein.

It so happened that while drawing up the plans, Bluestein watched an old Bing Crosby movie called *Holiday Inn* and scrawled the name on the bottom of his plans. Wilson liked the name and within a year the first 120-room Holiday Inn was erected, six times the size of the typical motel establishment.

Wilson now acted on his plan to take Holiday Inns national, and as it became clear that the country was gearing itself up to build a national interstate-highway system, he become more convinced than ever of the brilliance of his concept. He sent letters to every major home builder in the country which said: "We invite you to come to Memphis, and we will show you how to make a million dollars. Don't ask any questions, just get on the next plane."

So was born the hospitality franchise—indeed, he claims, the first significant franchise operation in America. By the early seventies, he was opening a new Holiday Inn, on average, every three days, and in 1979, when he retired as chairman of the board, his 1,759 hotels in 50 different countries amounted to the largest hotel chain in the world. In the process he had amassed a personal fortune estimated at more than 250 million dollars.

The Kemmons Wilson who ushers me into his office exudes a magnetic zest for life and a boyish sense of humor. He digs his hand into his jacket pocket and pulls out his tape measure: "I still carry this in my pocket," he says, his blue eyes sparkling like a hundred-watt bulb. "I still like to measure everything I like."

The extraordinary thing is, the man is eighty-six years old.

Wilson no longer owns the Holiday Inn group (it was sold to Bass Brewery), but he is still active in the family business, an enterprise that includes more than thirty Holiday Inn franchises and one of the world's largest time-share complexes in Orlando, Florida.

He settles back in his chair and, draining a can of Coke, recounts for me in quick takes the rollicking story of his life. When he was nine months old, his father died of Lou Gehrig's disease and his mother, who never remarried, went to work full-time as a dental assistant. She made twenty-five dollars a month ("Can you imagine paying someone twenty-five dollars a month?!" he says), and they were so poor that dinner meant, at best, a plate of dried butterbeans or black-eyed peas. When his mother lost her job in 1929, at the beginning of the Depression, Kemmons, then sixteen years old, quit high school and took a job cleaning the local movie theater. Spotting a gap in the market, he bought a fifty-dollar popcorn machine—paying a dollar down, a dollar a week—and was soon making more than the theater owner. Before long, he was into every type of business imaginable: pinball machines, ice-cream machines, movie theaters, real estate, all bought on credit at knockdown Depression-era prices, the profit on one parlayed into the down payment on another. "When you ain't got no education, you just got to use your brains," he says, referring to his innate street smarts. One of the first things that Wilson did was to take his pinball profits and, for $2,700, purchase a vacant plot of land and build his mother a house. When he finished, he proudly showed the house to the farmer who had sold him the plot. But the man looked puzzled. Consulting his map, he said: "You have built your house on the wrong lot—I sold you *that* one." And he pointed to the adjacent piece of land! Kemmons laughs. "People did business differently back then. It was kinder, less cutthroat. We just swapped title deeds," he says.

As he regales me with delightful anecdotes, I look around his office. His walls are covered with a lifetime of honors and framed pictures. There is Kemmons meeting the Pope; the 1965 designation by the *Sunday Times Magazine* of London as "one of the 1000 makers of the twentieth century"; the 1972 *Time* magazine cover dubbing him "The Man with 300,000 Beds"; and in and among the tributes, the honorary degrees, and the awards are dozens of portraits of his wife, children, their spouses, and his fourteen grandchildren. "You want to know the true measure of my success?" he asks. "Married fifty-six years to the same woman, all my children married at least twenty-seven years; nobody in our family ever had a divorce!"

Wilson's story embodies what the American Dream at its best

was meant to be about: a man of humble beginnings, without much education but with grit and ingenuity galore, triumphs magnificently over adversity without losing his family or his morals along the way, and rounds it off at the end by creating a foundation to give back to churches, hospitals, and "deserving causes." The uncanny thing is that his story is not unlike that of at least two other franchise barons—Dave Thomas and the enigmatic Colonel Sanders.

All three men knew what it was to be working poor, all three were high-school dropouts, followed through on a single great idea to build empires that made them rich beyond their dreams, and all became generous philanthropists. They had trampled an altogether different path from the educated, middle-class route afforded Gerald Chait, for example. Yet how differently, how empathetically, I wonder, might such a man view the plight of the minimum-waged working poor today?

"As my mother told me, anyone who works hard enough and has ambition can make it in America. This is the land of opportunity," begins Wilson, and he starts to trot through his well-rehearsed "twenty tips for success,"[51] homilies that he believes strike the right attitude to enable us to pull ourselves up by our bootstraps. Like many self-made men, Wilson displays a blend of down-to-earth modesty and massive ego: he both underestimates the ingenuity it took to actualize his ideas, and tends to look at the world and wonder why people can't be more like him: "If I can do it, so can they," is his bottom line.

"The minimum wage is for people who are lazy, lack ambition, or have some personal problem," he continues.

"Is that how you would have described your mother?" I am inclined to ask him. But what I end up saying is this. "Given the experience of your mother as a single-mom wage earner in the early part of the century, do you believe that in America today, more than half a century later, someone working full-time ought to be able to earn enough to support their family? In other words, that they should be paid the equivalent of a *living wage* rather than a minimum wage?"

"I have never looked at it from that point of view," he says. He thinks a minute.

"I will say this. That is not the way businessmen think."

"Even enlightened businessmen?" I ask.

"Your question reminds me of a story," he says. "I will never forget how, when I was twenty-five years old, Franklin D. Roosevelt introduced the minimum wage into America, twenty-five cents an hour, and compared to my mother's eleven cents an hour, I thought it was wonderful. Soon after that, I remember opening the newspaper and Henry Ford had taken out a full-page advertisement offering to pay his employees fifty-five cents an hour— thirty cents above the minimum wage! I thought to myself: Now *that's* wonderful, *that's* the way to run a business.

"In the hotels we own today, we pay employees a starting wage of fifty cents above minimum wage. I cannot even tell you what minimum wage is, but whatever it is, we pay fifty cents more.

"Is it a living wage? I have no idea. But if you ask me, do I have any objection to the politicians raising the minimum wage?, my answer is no, we got to share the wealth. Whatever the minimum wage is, we, like Henry Ford, will pay a little more. And that's about as enlightened as we businessmen can get if we want to stay competitive. But raising it in the first place—that's a politician's business."

THE BURGEONING WORKING POOR AND THEIR SHRINKING SHARE OF THE AMAZING AMERICAN ECONOMY

Two extraordinary facts distinguish the American economic boom at the turn of the millennium. First, the length of the boom. Its longevity has led everyone to speculate where the top of the cycle might be, how much further upward it can go, and even to wonder whether, powered by technology, we have entered a new non-cyclical economy that can keep growing steadily, defying gravity, defying recession, for the foreseeable future. Second, economists tended to believe that it was a law that as unemployment fell, inflation would necessarily rise, that there was an inverse relationship between them. Yet despite unemployment declining to record low levels—4 percent at last count—wage and salary inflation has held remarkably steady at around 3 percent. This is one of the key reasons why the American economic expansion has been able to continue apace, for if inflation were to rise dramatically, the Federal Reserve would immediately have to dampen it by raising interest rates, thereby raising the cost of borrowing and depressing the economy.

The question is this: At whose cost has wage and salary inflation been kept under such tight control?

An examination of the statistics reveals the following. Between the late 1970s and the late 1990s, the after-tax income of the richest 1 percent of the population rose by 115 percent in real terms, after adjusting for inflation. For the richest 20 percent of the population, real income increased by 43 percent. For middle-income households, the rise in income was a modest 8 percent. But for the poorest fifth of the population, real income actually *declined* by 9 percent.[52] So the working poor really are earning less.

Tocqueville would have been astounded by this development. "One can assert that a slow, progressive rise in wages is one of the general laws characteristic of democratic societies," he wrote. If this no longer becomes the case, he added, such a situation is "serious" and demands "the particular attention of legislators."[53]

Tocqueville thought that workers had greater organizing power than their bosses and would be able to use their collective power to constantly improve their wages. Contemporary research shows that trade unions do indeed make a significant difference, and that service jobs that are unionized pay substantially higher wages—an average of 24 percent more than the exact same jobs that are not unionized.[54]

However, some of the largest categories of service jobs have almost no union representation. The fast-food-services industry, for example, has a meager unionization rate of less than 3 percent.[55] William D. Gross, the principal officer of the Teamsters Local 250 union, a miscellaneous local representing service employees in different industries, tells me that organizing fast-food workers is difficult, if not impossible, for a number of reasons. "The staff turnover is very high, the gains you could force out of management very limited, and the rules are such that if you organize one outlet, you have to organize them all, so logistically it's a nightmare," he says.

Another reason for the fall in real wages seems to be that the minimum wage has not kept pace with inflation. If you made minimum wage in 1968, your earnings were 111 percent of the poverty line, whereas in 1999 a minimum-wage worker earned 82 percent of the poverty line—this despite the fact that President Clinton twice raised the federal minimum wage in the 1990s, from $4.25 to $4.75 in 1996, and to $5.15 in 1997. The US Department of Labor admitted that these increases were long overdue, because by 1996 the minimum wage adjusted for inflation was approaching a forty-year low.[56] In the 1980s, the Reagan administration had increased minimum wage by just 45 cents, so that by 1996, the minimum wage had fallen to 60 percent of the 1968 inflation-adjusted minimum wage. Even with the increase in minimum wage to $5.15, it is now only 70 percent of the 1968 level. A Democratic bill, initiated by Senator Edward Kennedy, to further raise the minimum wage to $6.15 an hour in 2000 and to $7.25 an hour by the year 2002, thereby restoring the buying power of the minimum wage, was put down by the congressional Republican majority.

More than a dozen major cities across America have recognized this problem of declining wages and have enacted living wage ordinances to help their working poor. These ordinances require all companies that do business or have contracts with local government to pay a living wage to their workers, usually around $8 to $9 an hour.[57] Such cities include, for instance, Los Angeles and Detroit, but, apart from Dayton, none of the major cities in Ohio.

Catherine Barrett, a Democrat in the Ohio State legislature, had told me when I visited her office that despite the service industry being the fastest-growing industry in Ohio, raising the minimum wage to a living wage is not on the agenda of their Republican-controlled state government. "It's mostly unmarried mothers who get stuck in those low-pay jobs, and its mostly white men who are the politicians, and so there's the disconnect right there," she said. "There is very little empathy from my fellow politicians, and very little acknowledgment that upward movement out of these jobs may be impossible without further education. Most of these white male Republican politicians take the tired old view that these women have brought their situation upon themselves, and that the way to deal with it is to promote marriage and prevent teenage pregnancies.

"They are wrong, of course. But by the time we get them to realize it, we may have a much bigger problem on our hands than we know how to deal with."

It becomes clear that the problem of the burgeoning working poor and the rising income gap is a structural one. With half of the fastest-growing jobs paying poverty-level wages, and the other half requiring postsecondary education, the once direct relationship between hard work and the American Dream has never been more fragile.

Such a situation, as Tocqueville said, is "serious" and demands "the particular attention of legislators." For as he also said, so eloquently, "it is hard when the whole of society is on the move to keep one class stationary, and when the greater number of men are constantly opening up new roads to fortune, to force some to bear in peace their needs and desires."[58]

4

THE MISSISSIPPI DELTA

"Luck Available One Mile"

They say the Mississippi Delta begins in the lobby of the Peabody Hotel in Memphis, Tennessee, where William Faulkner
and other literary types used to hang out, and where, every morning at 11:00 A.M., five mallard ducks ride the elevator from their
duck penthouse—*ding-ding*—down to the marble-columned foyer,
waddle in single file down a red carpet, and, to the acclaim of
assembled hotel guests, hop into an ornate fountain, where they
swim round and round until 5:00 P.M., duck bedtime apparently,
whereupon the grand ritual—*ding-ding*—is reversed.

This celebrated and genteel gateway to the Delta for wealthy
out-of-towners could not be more different from my own, which
begins in the back of a rattling casino shuttle bus with Louis "Fat-
boy" Fender, "Smokin' " Joey Peterson, and Loraine Hawkins.
These newer strangers, locals all three, squeeze up against me and
share their dreams of avarice as we hurtle forty-five minutes
through the night from Memphis, Tennessee, across the state border into Mississippi, and on toward the cornucopia of casinos that,
these days, light up the Delta.

"Did I tell you . . .'bout the time I hit red, white, and blue
sevens on the slots?" starts Louis. "For a car."

"You won a car?" says Joey.

"Only had in one quarter. It was a progressive payout—had to
have put in three quarters to win the car."

"Damn!" says Loraine.

The dream—gamble, get lucky, win a million dollars, change

your life—has a familiar, delicious cadence. It might be frayed from overuse and underachievement, but upfront, on the drive to the casino, it's the only one that packs a punch. The luck of the gambler, the freewheeling, recalcitrant stepsister of the American Dream, is with us on this bus, and it makes for a heady travel mate. I am along for the ride, my mission to explore the role that luck plays in the modern construction of the American Dream.

The conversation on the bus shifts restlessly. Louis and Joey fall into intense debate about the finer art of blackjack; about whether playing the end box raises your chances of winning. Loraine lights up a Kool Mild cigarette and waves her frequent-player card in the air. "It's my birthday tonight," she announces. "The Grand have comped me a room, and I'm in the mood for partying."

Two white pensioners, Edna and Ida, occupy the front seats and huddle like a couple of armadillos behind heavy-duty handbags.

"How long are you going for?" I ask them.

"Until tomorrow evening, perhaps the next," says Edna.

"Where will you sleep?" I ask, noticing that she has no luggage.

The bus driver, overhearing my question, guffaws. "Tell him! Tell him!"

"We don't," says Edna, grinning all over herself. "We aint gonna sleep. Nnnn-hmm. We gamble right through the night."

"They gonna get the money," the driver says, slapping the steering wheel in delight and revealing a mouthful of missing and gold-capped teeth. "Tell him! Tell him what you do."

"We's widows. We go with a $100 limit, and we gamble until we can't push that button on the slots anymore, or until we've lost everything, whichever comes first. It might take two hours, or two days, or two—"

Edna shrieks as a child's stroller, improperly stowed on the overhead rack, plummets down and clatters to the floor, narrowly missing her leg. Somewhere in the bus a baby starts to howl. You can almost feel everybody thinking, seething: Make your kid shuddup! What kinda place is this to bring an infant? Gradually the baby's cries are drowned by the reassuring roar of the engine.

The driver smiles and puts his foot on the gas. His name is Stan Robinson, age forty-nine, and he too dreams of changing his life.

He earns eight dollars an hour, he tells me, and lives with his wife, Violet, a cosmetician, and her five-year-old daughter, in a shotgun house in "a poverty area" of Memphis. (The style of house is so named because if you shoot a shotgun through the front door, the bullet will travel the length of the two-room house and go straight out through the back.)

Robinson won big once, and he likes to share with his passengers the memory of the day he went to Tunica with $100 in his pocket. "For some reason," he begins, "I was angry that day, so I decided to take out my aggression on the slots, and before I knew it I had $600 and pretty soon $2,600, so I took a rest, tried another machine, lost, came back to the same machine where I had won the first $600, hit mixed sevens twice, won me $900. And then I got on a $5 machine, which is way out of my league, I never play those machines—I mean, they're for high rollers and I'm a nickel-and-dime guy—but I started playing the $5 slots and then the $10 slots, and two double double diamonds with a single bar came up on the pay line and the machine went crazy, and my pockets were bulging with coins and hundred-dollar bills, I mean my pants were actually sagging under the weight, and when I emptied my pockets and started counting, I had $7,200! Did you get that? Seven thousand dollars! I was wild, I'd never held that amount of money in my life. Some lady said to me, 'You're so lucky tonight, why not try the $25 machines?' I looked at my watch, it was four-thirty in the afternoon. I had been gambling for fifteen hours and suddenly I felt wiped. I said: 'Sweetheart, this is a year's earnings to me, this can change my life—I'm getting my black ass on the next bus out of here.' "

But it wasn't quite enough to change Robinson's life. That, he now estimates, will take $150,000—the amount of capital he thinks he would need to activate his dream and start his own casino-shuttle-bus company. "I love my job, but I work 365 days a year and I'm still in poverty. I have this thing that one day I will hit the megabucks jackpot and break out," he says.

And so in the twenty minutes free time between dropping passengers off at the casino and picking up the ones returning to Memphis, Robinson either watches the guys playing the $100 machines or feeds the slots himself. He is convinced that the next lucky spell, the indescribable elation of winning big, is just a coin away.

"How much have you put back?" I ask him.

"At least $5,000." He pauses. "Probably more." And then, quietly, so that only I can hear, he adds, "All of it."

"All of it?"

"I'm afraid to calculate the total amount I've lost in the last few years—maybe $10,000, maybe close to $15,000." He laughs. "Nobody's up in the long run. The casinos are there to take your money, not to make you rich."

He drops his voice again. "The people who ride this bus, ninety percent of them are poor and cannot afford to be here. They don't understand that the casinos are not there to make *them* rich."

"Why do you think it will make *you* rich?" I press him.

"Ask my wife. She says I've developed a gambling problem. Maybe she's right. But with me being black an' all, it's hard to think that investors would fund me and that I could achieve my dream the normal way. So gambling is like my only shot at it. I have one rule, though—I always make sure my family has enough to eat. I'll go hungry sometimes. I have my player's card that gives me free meals at the casinos according to how much I gamble, so I eat that way.

"Hell, I don't want to depress nobody," he laughs. "I usually save this part of the story for the way home."

It is half past midnight on this, the last bus of the night from Kirby Terminal to the casinos, and we thrum through the southern outskirts of Memphis and turn onto Highway 61. At this hour, you expect little traffic out in the Midwest, but one side of the road blinks red with an endless stream of taillights heading for the casinos and the other blinks white with a constant stream of headlights returning.

Alongside the highway, the flashing neon of shops with names like America Pawn and Doc Holliday's Pawn offer the passing motorist easy money at a prohibitive price. CHECKS CASHED, they advertise in florid pinks and greens. CASH LOANS ON CAR TITLES! You can also (as I later discover when I visit these shops) hand over your electric guitar, lawn mower, power tools, handguns, rifles, CD collection, videos, watch, jewelry, even your child's Beanie Baby collection, and in return they will furnish you with a cash loan at a fraction of their value. The catch is that you have to repay the loan at the prohibitive compound annual interest rate of 300 percent, and that if you default on the repayments, they are free to pawn your goods at whatever price they decide. Since the casinos opened, pawn superstores have proliferated along this stretch of the highway, like vultures, say the locals, preying on the fallen gambler.

In truth, though, with your instincts tuned to winning, you hardly notice the pawnshops on the drive there. Instead, as Highway 61 crosses the state border from Tennessee into De Soto County, Mississippi, your eyes are drawn to the twenty-story-high billboards and their seductive messages of riches that light up the night. FIRE YOUR BOSS, says one. MEET RELATIVES YOU NEVER KNEW YOU HAD, says another. CONSIDER THIS YOUR FIRST SIGN OF GOOD LUCK . . . REEL LOVE . . . LOOSEST SLOTS . . . Spaced every five hundred yards or so, like a column of giant foot soldiers marching to the horizon, the billboards pull you inexorably onward, toward Tunica County, Mississippi, where the casinos are.

Memphis was just twelve years old when my French companion pulled into town by stagecoach, his plan to sail by steamboat down the Mississippi to New Orleans. The town had been laid out by Andrew Jackson, in 1819, on a five-thousand-acre parcel of land which he and two others had bought from the Chickasaw Indians and promoted for settlement. Now Jackson was President of the United States, and Memphis had become a modest town with a few hundred immigrant settlers, mostly of German and Irish origin.

Tocqueville's journey to Memphis had been hampered by arctic weather that had left the Ohio River frozen over and caused unplanned overland diversions. Full of cold and flu and frustration, Tocqueville commented only on how disappointing Memphis was. "Memphis!! . . . What a fall! Nothing to see, neither men nor things."[1]

Yet the potential he saw in the fertile Mississippi Delta was to move him greatly. He was to describe it as "the most magnificent habitation ever prepared by God for man . . . yet . . . still only a vast wilderness"[2]

From Cairo, Illinois, in the North to the Gulf of Mexico in the South, the Mississippi River winds more than one thousand miles. Together with its feeder rivers, the Ohio, the Missouri, and the Arkansas among them, it drains an incredible 41 percent of the contiguous United States, making it the third-largest drainage basin in the world after the Amazon and Congo Rivers.[3] The Delta floodplain—a portion of the river 200 miles long and 65 miles wide, from Memphis to Vicksburg—is perhaps the most famous stretch of the Mississippi, its very name conjuring images of white-baubled cotton fields, slavery, and the Delta blues.

At the time of Tocqueville's visit, the river served a dual and practical function. It was, like the Ohio River, the equivalent of the highway, the easiest means of transport of both humans and produce. But it also demarcated the frontier—beyond it lived mostly Indians, the region's first inhabitants who had given the river its name, Mississippi, meaning "Father of Waters."

In the early years of white settlement, and for many decades thereafter, cotton was not only king of the Delta, it was the only show in town. But, as Tocqueville predicted, the South was held back by its dependence on cotton and slavery and never developed the industrial infrastructure of the North. The mechanization of farming in the mid–twentieth century exposed the South's over-reliance on farming, and the workers that were laid off struggled to find alternative work. Unemployment soared. Many southerners moved north and sought work in the steel mills around Pittsburgh, in bustling cities like Chicago, and in the auto plants of Flint and Detroit. Later, the arrival of synthetic materials threatened the supremacy of cotton itself, and further layoffs ensued.

By the 1980s, Mississippi was described by the census as the poorest state in America. Tunica, dubbed "America's Ethiopia," and infamous for its wretched open sewers like Sugar Ditch, was its poorest county.

Then in 1990 an unexpected event occurred that was to change this Bible Belt state forever. A long-serving Democratic senator in the Mississippi State Senate by the name of Tommy Gollott introduced legislation that contained an outrageous idea. His plan was that Mississippi should follow the lead of two states upriver, Iowa and Illinois, and legalize riverboat casinos. He also wanted to legalize floating casinos on the Mississippi Gulf Coast to the south—in other words, casinos that floated on the sea as well as on the river, including in his home constituency of Biloxi.

Gollott had little reason to be hopeful. For years he had tried to introduce horse racing, dog tracks, and the lottery, and each time he had been defeated. Indeed, gambling was so frowned upon in Mississippi that until the late 1980s, even church and school raffles were outlawed. But Gollott sensed that with their backs against the wall economically, his fellow senators might finally be ready to take a risk. His own constituency, Biloxi, was on the verge of bankruptcy. He argued that a well-regulated casino industry could form the nucleus of a tourist industry, providing jobs and raising state revenues without them having to raise taxes. In the days before the final vote, Gollott realized that many senators who would normally flatly oppose such an idea were wavering, and that the final tally would go down to the wire. He managed to convince eight senators who would have felt compelled to vote against the legislation to take sick leave.

The legislation squeezed through by a single, solitary vote. "I will admit that some of them were asked not to be there so it would have a chance to pass, and they agreed," Gollott tells me, granting me, he claims, the first detailed interview he has ever given on the subject since that day. "By the time your book comes out," he explains, "I will have retired from the State Senate. And since I am proud of this legacy, I want people to know the truth about it. And the truth is, as I have said . . . I probably asked a few of them not to be there. I think the reason they agreed was that they wanted it to pass for the good of the state, but they might have lost their seats if they had been seen to vote for it."

Gollott's legislation went further than the states upriver. Whereas those states had imposed strict limits on the number of casinos they would allow and where they could place them, Mississippi adopted an unfettered free-market approach. Each county situated on the river or the Gulf Coast could vote on whether they wanted the casinos, but if they decided to let the casinos in, no artificial limitation could then be placed on the number of casinos that set up shop. In addition, the drafters of the new legislation cleverly added a provision that was to make Mississippi the gambling destination of choice in mid-America. They allowed their casinos to be built on giant barges permanently moored in moats set back from the river, and this facilitated the construction of much larger and more impressive casinos than the cramped, poky riverboat-casinos that had hitherto operated upriver. The sheer scale of the operation was of another magnitude altogether, and with greater potential volumes of gamblers for each location, it attracted the Vegas Big Boys and led directly to the construction of huge land-based hotels right alongside. The casinos were limited to the waterfront—that was the method of zoning, of town planning—but beyond that it was a free-for-all.

The gambling boom that resulted exceeded everyone's most florid expectations. Suddenly the state had economic lift-off from a source that, given its Bible Belt credentials, had to be the most unexpected imaginable.

In the space of a few years, straightlaced Mississippi has lost its virginity. It has become the nation's third largest casino gambling jurisdiction after Las Vegas, Nevada, and Atlantic City, New Jersey. Today twenty-nine casinos operate in Mississippi, either on the river between Tunica and Natchez or on the Gulf Coast between Gulfport and Biloxi.

These are not casinos as we know them in London, Paris, or Monte Carlo, with private memberships, entrance fees, ornate buildings, exotic locations, and mainly targeting the rich. The Mississippi casinos make no pretense at exclusivity. They offer free entrance, bargain-basement $8.99 buffets, $29-a-night hotel rooms, and massive barnlike gaming halls—they are Kmart casinos for the wage-earning ordinary people.

But what has happened in Mississippi is not unique—it is part of a nationwide trend. Two decades ago there was not a single casino outside of Nevada. Today there are more than five hundred casinos in twenty-one states. Only thirteen states had lotteries then;

thirty-seven have them now. Some states, like Massachusetts, boast eight separate lotteries a week and can't add new "Pick Six" or "Powerball" games fast enough.

Gambling is no longer perched on the illegal margins of society, but has become an accepted part of mainstream American culture. Within the space of a generation, legalized gambling in the form of lotteries, casinos, and horse racing has become the nation's most popular form of entertainment. In the late 1990s, Americans spend $50 billion a year on gambling, including $24 billion on casinos and $16 billion on lotteries, more than on movies, spectator sports, theme parks, cruise ships, and recorded music combined.[4]

To put this in context, the amount Americans spend on gambling is more than the entire gross domestic product of two-thirds of the countries of the world. It is approaching the gross domestic product of Ireland ($59 billion), exceeds the GDP of Kuwait ($46 billion) and Kenya ($45 billion), and way exceeds, for example, the GDP's of countries like Ghana ($36 billion), Croatia ($23 billion), Paraguay ($22 billion), and Jamaica ($9 billion).[5] If you had to pick one statistic to capture how wealthy America has become, how much spare income its citizens seem to have at their disposal, this might be the one.

Except that it is more complicated than that, because according to the research (of which more later), the Americans who gamble the most are those who can least afford it.[6] It appears that for them, for the poor, gambling is not simply light entertainment, as benign as going to the movies, but rather a serious attempt to get rich.

Something new and significant is happening to alter the role that chance—dumb luck—is playing in the pursuit of the American Dream.

How might such a shift be explained?

The conservative religious lobby insists that supply creates its own demand. Their belief is that gambling is an exogenous evil, a corrupting influence not unlike alcohol, visited upon an innocent nation. (The Protestant churches tend to regard gambling as immoral, whereas the Catholic Church takes a neutral line on its morality, on the grounds, they say, that there is no scriptural prohibition against gambling.)

The counterperspective is that a propensity for gambling was always latent in the American character, a robust force just below the surface that had long been repressed. Eugene Martin Christiansen, an author and well-known social commentator on gambling, writes that "a propensity to gamble was . . . effectively repressed by temperance reform prohibitions but not eradicated from the American character, a subsurface, powerful force, waiting to be tapped."[7]

Tocqueville observed something similar. He said that the American character was particularly susceptible to the lure of chance, especially when the game of chance involved the potential for financial gain. This applied "to everyone in a democracy, rich or poor," for Americans "love the emotions it provides," he wrote.[8] When Tocqueville sailed down the Delta, gambling was illegal, and although professional gamblers worked the salons on the riverboats and were tolerated by crews, if a passenger complained, the gambler was tossed overboard and forced to swim ashore.[9] Such a threat was not to be taken lightly, given the hazardous currents of the river, and gamblers could easily be swept to their death.

The suppression of gambling in Tocqueville's time was proof of the powerful grip that religion had over the morality of Americans. It was also testimony to the self-evident fact that then, hard work was universally regarded as both the moral and the fastest route to the good life.

Could the explosive rise in gambling in the last decade also have something to do, then, with the perception that for growing numbers of Americans—for people like Stan Robinson in Memphis, Helaine Clark in Pittsburgh, Anthony Harris in Flint, and Carlos Reyes in New York—"hard work" may no longer cut it as the means to access the American Dream?

LUCK AVAILABLE ONE MILE, says a road sign.

My fellow travelers on the bus fall silent. Talking is now in bad taste, disrespectful of the private bubble that gamblers withdraw into just before they pounce on the casino. They seem to be concentrating their talismanic energies, going over in their heads their carefully constructed game plans one last time before exploding out of the traps.

Suddenly the casino-hotels are upon us, a thousand points of mesmerizing light shimmying out of the Delta flatlands. First stop, the Grand: "the largest gaming resort between Vegas and Atlantic City," it calls itself. Birthday girl Loraine swings her bag over her shoulder. "You only live once," she says lightly, and disappears down the throat of the hotel foyer.

"Good luck tonight—you have a good one!" Robinson shouts after her.

Down the road is a choice of eight more casinos built in two half-moon crescents. It's junior-league Vegas, but instead of a strip bisecting a desert, it's a cul-de-sac in a cotton field. Each casino is built on a moored barge and boasts near-identical layouts, distinguished only on the outside by their varied attempts at a theme. The Sheraton is all towers and turrets and is lit up like Merlin the Magician's castle; Sam's Town has a western saloon theme; Fitzgerald's is green and Irish, with all its luck-of-the-Irish, Blarney Stone connotations; Gold Strike towers thirty-one floors above the rest in reflective gold-tinted glass like a luminescent gold chip; Horseshoe simply has two horseshoes above its entrance; and Bally's is just red and round.

Yet the millions spent by the casinos on themes and billboards to entice customers into their particular establishments are as nothing in the face of direct financial inducements. To a person, every one of Robinson's remaining passengers disembarks at the Sheraton. Why? Because the Sheraton offers a five-dollar refund on the ten-dollar bus ticket. And so, like the Peabody mallards, we head straight for the refund counter, where—quite pathetically on reflection, but in a totally focused way at the time—we wait in line to collect.

"Good luck tonight—you have a good one!" Robinson shouts after us.

I take in the scene: a windowless zone with no natural light, operating around the clock, day running undetected into night. Thousands of slot machines sound off at once, creating a relentless sonic bombardment, a cacophony that rapidly becomes white noise. Cocktail waitresses in black tights, miniskirts, and low-cut tops with push-up bras offer playing patrons free alcohol—White Russians (vodka, Kahlua, and milk on ice), screwdrivers, or beers, all they want. People on the slots tend to commandeer two machines. Not content to push one button, they sit in front of one and slouch over another, feeding both. There is a totally focused shape to their mouths, a glazed look in their eyes. Win or lose, they show no emotion. At the blackjack, roulette, and dice tables, the air is acrid with cigarette smoke as heavy smokers rule. Hard paper currency is sent down a chute and replaced with plastic chips that go clickety-click in your hands. It is an environment brilliantly designed to help you lose track of your time, your senses, and—of course—your grip on your wallet.

What new truth, I ask myself, can I hope to discover about the role of luck in the American Dream from inside a place as obvious as a casino? That the luck of the gambler holds no regard for race or class? That a casino is one of few places in society where the haves and the have-nots rub shoulders, sit at the same table, and face the same odds, the same (un)even playing field?

But who wins and who loses on the velveteen tables is just the most superficial manifestation of luck on offer. I do not expect to discover that "dumb luck" has a history reaching back—and this is the eerie part—precisely to the year Tocqueville journeyed through these parts.

THE HISTORY OF LUCK

It takes barely two minutes to drive from the clutch of casino-hotels to Shea Leatherman's farmhouse in the Mississippi River Valley. I idle down Lucky Lane, which is newly built, and then turn onto a larger, busier road that was recently renamed Casino Strip Boulevard. The Leatherman house is set back off the latter. The house is an antebellum white clapboard with green window shutters, and according to the sign posted outside, the Leathermans have been there SINCE 1832. I think it an amazing coincidence that their

arrival date should coincide with the year of my French companion's visit, but then I push it from my mind and think nothing
further of it.

I have come to visit Shea Leatherman because according to the
local gossip, he is one of the luckiest men in Mississippi. I'd first
heard it mentioned in Judge Joe Brown's chambers in Memphis
late one Friday afternoon when a few policemen with heavy medals
adorning their chests had gathered after court to shoot the breeze.
My tape recorder had chosen that day to jam, and while a deputy
sheriff was kindly trying to fix it so that I could interview the fast-
talking judge (who was even more fast-talking than usual that day
because he had just flown in from Los Angeles, where he had been
shooting his syndicated court TV show and hadn't slept in forty-
eight hours), the policemen began bantering about how bankrupt-
cies in Memphis had soared to a record high since the arrival of
the casinos in 1992.

"You see more homes being lost," elaborated one.

"Yup, more cars being repossessed," agreed a colleague.

"So there's more burglary, more robbery, more—"

"More work for us."

Judge Brown, dozing on the edge of his desk in his black leather
jacket, had been watching this drawn-out interchange through one
half-shut eye when he decided the time was ripe for a summing
up: "Gamblin' bad for Memphis but good for Tunica. Gamblers
come from Memphis—they lose. Tunica hands that once picked
cotton now countin' money—they win. But the big, big winners,
that would be those Tunica plantation owners."

"You mean," says one policeman, "the Leathermans and—"

"Yeah, that'd be the ones."

Shea Leatherman, forty-seven, sits in a room hung with ordinance wall maps of the region, sun rays diffusing softly through his
windows. He is dressed casually in loafers and tan trousers and exudes Old World charm, his swept-back, silver-gray hair giving him
a distinguished look. This farmhouse has been in his family for five
generations, he tells me. For more than 150 years, it looked out
over flat, low-rent fields of cotton and soybeans. Now it looks out
over a surreal landscape—neon-lit casinos—and has become,

virtually overnight, about the most commercially desirable land in the whole of Mississippi.

Leatherman's story reaches back almost the life span of America itself. "In 1832 my great-great-grandfather Richard Abbay came from Nashville and settled here in what was called the Mississippi Bottom Wilderness," he begins. "He came with his twin brother, who returned to Nashville after a year, but Richard Abbay, who had been apprenticed as a house builder and had helped build the Kentucky residence of the late senator Henry Clay, famously known as Ashland, decided to stay and start a cotton plantation." Leatherman pulls out a yellowing obituary of his great-great-grandfather, dated 1884, from under the glass top of his desk. "Death of a Well Known Cotton Planter," it says. It ascribes the cause of death to "sheer exhaustion" and the "wearing out" of the old man's vital system—he was eighty-seven when he died—and goes on to say: "He became wealthy and owned many slaves."

"Before Richard Abbay died," continues Shea, "he had a daughter, Mary-Susan, who married a doctor called George Washington Leatherman. After the War of Northern Aggression, or 'the recent unpleasantness,' as it was also called [the Civil War], George and Susan had three children. Two of the children died, but one son survived. His name was Samuel Richard Leatherman, and he was my grandfather."

Shea's grandfather expanded the plantation from 1,600 to 10,000 acres and became a cotton factor as well as a cotton grower, buying and selling cotton from his office at the Cotton Exchange in Memphis. He had two sons and three daughters, including Shea's father, William Leatherman, who was born in this house. In 1947, the farm was divided up among four of the five children, who from Shea's vantage point in the family tree were his father, his uncle, and two of his aunts. The fifth heir—Shea's third aunt—got a parcel of land on the Arkansas side of the river, "where the casinos aren't." The Leatherman plantation, I later discover, is also where legendary Delta blues musician Robert L. Johnson grew up in the 1920s with his mother, sisters and stepfather, plunking his scratchy guitar at local juke joints, and is also in the close vicinity of the former home of another blues master, Howlin' Wolf.

Skip ahead to 1990. Shea, his brother, and sister have inherited their father's plantation, and his cousin, Bobby Leatherman, has inherited the uncle's. But farming is having, as Shea puts it, "a difficult time of it," and his sister and brother moved elsewhere, leaving Shea to manage the affairs of the plantation on his own. Then, out of the blue, the news breaks that the Mississippi legislature has voted in Tommy Gollott's plan to legalize riverboat gambling. Each county along the river will have the right to vote for or against the casinos.

The casino bosses from Vegas swarm over the place. It becomes apparent that the biggest plum is to tap the buying power of Memphis, eighteenth-largest city in the United States, with a metropolitan population of 1.1 million and located just over the border in Tennessee, and where, crucially, gambling is banned. Everyone assumes that the northernmost Mississippi county on the river, De Soto County, which borders Tennessee, will get the casinos. But the religious community prevails and De Soto votes "no thanks" on moral grounds. Tunica is the next county down the river. It votes to legalize casinos, and the first one—called Splash—opens in October 1992.

But not on Leatherman's land: they overshoot him by about eight miles. As do the next three casinos—Lady Luck, Bally's, and President's—all of which are built on the river at a place called Mhoon Landing. The land at Mhoon Landing is owned and leased to the casinos by two farmers, Dick Flowers and Dutch Parker. Right place, right time. Their lucky break.

And that could have been that. But the next thing that happens is that all four Mhoon Landing casinos go belly-up. They are too small, with inferior facilities, and unable to compete with the swanky casinos opening closer to Memphis, and so they either close, go bankrupt, or move, leaving behind a derelict site and two farmers who wonder what hit them. Wrong place, it turns out—too far down the river. Now the place to be is as far north toward Memphis as possible, tight up against the Tunica/De Soto county line and right on the Mississippi River in a part of Tunica called Robinsonville.

This is where Leatherman's land is, all 6,400 acres of it, all ten square miles.

Soon representatives of the Boyd family, an old Vegas casino-owning family, are beating a path to Leatherman's door to explore the possibility of building a casino-hotel on his plantation. The remaining land along the river running north to the county borderline is owned by four other local cotton-farming families, and they too are besieged by Vegas magnates. Within three years, each family has at least one casino-hotel on its plantation. According to Shea, they are split up as follows: Bobby Leatherman, his cousin, has Harrah's and Hollywood; Burt Robinson has the Sheraton, the Horseshoe, and Gold Strike; the Adams family has Bally's and the Grand; two women by the names of Jean Michaels and Betty Carlos have Fitzgeralds; and he has Sam's Town. Suddenly rural dirt roads are replaced by four-lane highways, gas stations and hotels go up, and the place starts to feel like Boomtown USA. Hotel accommodation in Tunica County goes from one moldy motel offering 20 rooms in 1992 to eighteen state-of-the-art hotels offering 6,093 rooms in 1999.[10] The story is told how the water and sewerage system was so poor at first that if someone took a shower in Sam's Town Hotel at the same time as someone flushed the toilet in Hollywood, the water pressure was reduced to a trickle. Shea had had his initial reservations. "My preconception was that the gambling industry was Mafia-controlled and not an industry our family should be involved with," he says. "It took a leap of faith to get beyond that." But the amount of money on offer by the casino moguls was no small incentive. He declines to divulge the financial details of the deal he did on Sam's Town, saying only that "it has been a wonderful boon" and that "the future of the Leathermans is secured for generations to come."

"Are there any black landowners in the region?" I ask him.

"Yes, on the east side of Tunica County, there are some that own small pieces of land."

"None along the river?"

"No. Those are owned by the whites."

These days Leatherman prefers to see himself as more of a land developer than a plantation owner, the latter having "negative historic connotations associated with slave ownership and sharecropping." Daily he pores over builders' plans for shopping centers, apartment buildings, and more casinos, whose arrival is "just a matter of time." He uses the house mainly as his office, commuting every day to East Memphis, where he lives with his wife and his two teenage daughters who go to a private girls' school. "This area is destined to become a great tourist and gambling mecca because of its central location within the United States. Of that I have no doubt," he says. Three states in close vicinity—Tennessee to the north, Arkansas to the west, and Alabama to the east—have no casino or lottery gambling.

"To what do you feel you owe your recent prosperity?" I ask him.

"It's sheer dumb luck. Fluke. Like striking oil," he says. "There is no precedent. No one could have foreseen it. Nobody. It's simply pure luck that we owned the land."

But is it? It is only when I pick up Tocqueville's diaries that I realize that this apparent dumb luck to which Leatherman refers has a history, a history that goes back to 1832 and is tied to one of the most unsavory events in American history.

It was in the 1830s that President Andrew Jackson passed the infamous Indian Removal Act. This act, together with a series of treaties, provided for the forced removal of what were known as "the Five Civilized Tribes," including the Choctaws and the Chickasaws, from their ancestral lands east of the Mississippi to uninhabited territories west of the river. The act was passed so that white immigrants could settle. In the eight-hundred-mile "forced march," or "Trail of Tears," as the Indians later called it, ten thousand Indians died.[11] Historians described how many white speculators came down and grabbed the land even before the Indians had departed. "I expect there never have been such frauds imposed on any people as the Chickasaws," one commentator wrote at the time. The map of Mississippi circa 1820 shows that the Tunica region (named after an Indian tribe) was Choctaw territory, and that east and south of that was Chickasaw territory.[12] Traces of the

Indians are etched on the face of the present landscape. Rising above the Delta floodplain, which Tocqueville described as "flat as rolled lawn," are manmade mounds which served as Indian burial sites. Bobby Leatherman's house is, so I am told, built on such a mound.

Tocqueville witnessed the forced march while waiting for the steamboat *Louisville* to take him from Memphis. He describes what he saw:

> As we were debating there on the bank, we heard an infernal music echoing in the forest; it was the noise of a drum, the whinnying of horses, the barking of dogs. There finally appeared a large troup of Indians, old men, women, children, belongings, all led by a European.
>
> Here began a scene which, in truth, had something lamentable about it. The Indians advanced mournfully toward the bank. First they had their horses go abroad; several took fright and plunged into the Mississippi, from which they could be pulled out only with difficulty. Then came the men who, according to ordinary habits, carried only their arms; then the women carrying their children attached to their backs or wrapped in the blankets they wore; they were, besides, burdened down with loads containing their whole wealth. Finally the old people were led on. Among them was a woman 110 years old. I have never seen a more appalling shape. She was naked save for a covering which left visible, at a thousand places, the most emaciated figure imaginable. To leave one's country at that age to seek one's fortune in a foreign land, what misery! Among the old people there was a young girl who had broken her arm a week before; for want of care the arm had been frozen below the fracture. Yet she had to follow the common journey . . . In the whole scene there was an air of ruin and destruction, something which betrayed a final and irrevocable adieu; one couldn't watch without feeling one's heart wrung.[13]

Tocqueville follows up his description with cutting social comment:

The Americans of the United States, who are reasonable and unprejudiced, and great philanthropists to boot, have taken it into their heads, as did the Spaniards, that God had given them the new world and its inhabitants in full ownership. They have discovered, furthermore, that, it being proved (listen well to this) that a square mile could nourish ten times as many civilized men as savages, reason indicated that wherever civilized men could establish themselves, the savages would have to move away. What a beautiful thing logic is. Consequently, whenever the Indians begin to find themselves a little too close to their white brothers, the President of the United States sends them a messenger, who represents to them that in their own best interests it would be well for them to retreat ever so little toward the West . . . [to] magnificent lands, where the game has never been disturbed by the sound of the pioneer's axe, where the Europeans will never come. Add to this presents of inestimable price, waiting to reward their complaisance: hogsheads of brandy, necklaces of glass, earrings and mirrors: the whole backed up by the insinuation that if they refuse, it may perhaps be necessary to use force. What to do? The poor Indians take their old parents in their arms, the women load their children on their backs, the nation finally sets out, carrying with it its most precious possessions. It abandons for ever the soil on which, for a thousand years perhaps, its fathers have lived to go establish itself in a wilderness where the whites will not leave them ten years in peace.

The Spaniards, like real brutes, throw their dogs on the Indians as if on ferocious beasts. They kill, burn, massacre, pillage the new world like a town taken by assault, without pity as without discernment. But one can't destroy everything; fury has its end. The remainder of the population ends by mingling with the conquerors, taking their customs, their religion; in several provinces they are to-day reigning over their former conquerors. The Americans of the United States, more humane, more moderate, more respectful of right and legality, never bloody, are more profoundly destructive; and it is impossible to doubt that before a hundred years [have passed] there will no longer be in

North America . . . a single man belonging to the most remarkable of the Indian races.

The combination of Tocqueville's poignant description and the sign SINCE 1832 innocently posted at the entrance to the Leatherman house is a reminder that when you scrape away the veneer of apparent pure chance, dumb luck is not as random as one thinks. Even luck has a history. Even luck has a deeper structure that waits to be revealed.

And yet, speaking of luck, is it not an uncanny twist of fate that casino gambling should have become the economic elixir of many an Indian tribe today? In 1988, Congress passed the Indian Gaming Regulatory Act, allowing land-based casino gambling on Indian reservations, with the proviso that the money be used to promote the welfare of the tribe. Although more than two-thirds of Indian tribes do not have any gambling at all, for 124 tribes casino gambling has become a key source of revenue and employment, and has grown into a billion-dollar industry. The 8,300-strong Mississippi band of Choctaw Indians have one casino on a reservation east of Jackson, the impressive $37 million Silver Star Hotel & Casino, which they own jointly with the Boyd Gaming Corporation of Las Vegas (the owners of Sam's Town on Leatherman's land). Out of the proceeds, the Indians have built a brand-new hospital, new housing, and a house of worship: its name—the New Blackjack Baptist Church—appears to pay literal homage to its source of funding. Average annual household income on the reservation has leapt tenfold to $24,000 in the last twenty years, an increase not exclusively due to gambling. (The Choctaws have enterprisingly developed other business interests as well, notably manufacture of car parts for American automakers and plastic utensils for McDonald's.) It does seem ironic, though, that no social policy should have done more to improve the economic living standards of Indians—the worst of any ethnic group in the nation—than that which sanctioned casino gambling on their soil.[14]

But all that is by way of digression from Tocqueville's route down the Delta.

In viewing the luck of the Leathermans today, Tunica's locals take it at face value. "Those farmers," says Bobby Williams, the part-time mayor of the town of Tunica in Tunica County, "were simply in the right place at the right time."

THE COLOR OF LUCK

Edward Kirby was of the belief that in America, you made your own luck. In his fifty-seven years as an African-American living in the South, nothing ever fell into his lap, he says. But when the casinos began to open in Tunica, he saw an opportunity to realize his dream and he went for it. He resigned from his $30,000-a-year job as a Greyhound bus driver and invested his life savings in a Memphis-based casino-shuttle-bus company. He called it Kirby Charters and Tours.

I first meet Mr. Kirby because he is the owner of the bus company on which I initially journey with Stan Robinson to the casinos. He invites me into his office, which has a run-down feel to it: linoleum floor, cheap wood-paneled walls, pink awnings over the windows. It is tucked away in the corner of his airy terminal building where a dozen passengers—mainly African-American—lounge on hard wooden chairs and wait for the next shuttle. The terminal has a Coke machine, a candy machine, an ATM, a ticket booth, a desk where someone sells cellular phones, and a couple of raised-high televisions to entertain the customers. Kirby is dressed, like his drivers, in Kirby livery—white cap, white shirt, blue jacket—and sits behind a desk scattered with unpaid bills.

Kirby grew up dirt poor, the son of a sharecropper, six miles south of here across the state border in De Soto County, Mississippi. "We lived on the plantation of a white man who gave us a house to live in and some land to farm," he recalls. "It's still there, five miles west of Walls, called T. P. Howard's plantation." Kirby describes the cycle of debt white farmers imposed on the sharecroppers. "In the winter months, when there was nothing to farm, we had no money, so we bought our food on credit from the white farmer's general store. In the summer months we planted cotton, and in the fall we cultivated. It was a bale for us, a bale for Mr.

Howard. I helped my dad and granddad pick the cotton by hand and put it in sacks. It was backbreaking work. Come December, Mr. Howard would sell all our cotton (we never knew the price), deducted what we owed him for the food bought on credit in the winter, and paid us the difference. That's called your settlement. But a lot of years, we came out in the hole. In other words, the farmer said our debts exceeded what he had received for our cotton and we got nothing. Never really could get out of the hole."

Mr. Howard was a preacher, Kirby recalls, and compared with some of the other plantation owners, "who might slap you for no reason and beat you for talking back," he was good to them. Kirby remembers what happened to one of his mates, a kid by the name of Edward Ellis, who made the mistake of being caught looking through the bathroom window of a white man's house. "He was arrested and they gave him twenty years. He was thirteen years old when they sent him to juvenile jail. He served every year," he says.

"We were so afraid of whites. The law wasn't the law back then—the law was the white man, whatever he wanted. If you hit a white man, even if he was in the wrong, you went to jail—or you were killed. We were completely at the white man's mercy," he says.

Kirby used to watch the Greyhound buses barrel through their three-store town. "I didn't really have any dreams as a youngster 'cept one. I used to dream about driving a Greyhound bus, being in cities I'd never been in, getting a ticket out of there." He applied for a job as a driver in 1968, the year Martin Luther King Jr. was assassinated at the Lorraine Motel in Memphis. Greyhound turned him down six years in a row because, he says, at that time they weren't partial to hiring blacks. Eventually, in 1974, things started opening up and he was taken on. For seventeen years, until 1991, he drove for Greyhound, achieving his dream of driving all over America.

But then he began to dream a new dream—of owning his own bus company. "I would be driving in the middle of the night and find myself planning the color of my buses," he recalls. When a Greyhound workers' strike in 1991 coincided with the surge of casino activity south of the state border, Kirby saw it as a lucky break. He resigned and started his own operation, beginning small by carrying just five passengers at a time in his two-door Cadillac and charging ten dollars a person. From there he bought a van, then a bus, and then a fleet of eleven buses which ran return trips to the casinos almost around the clock, seven days a week, 365 days a year: "a bus to a casino of your choice every sixty minutes!"

As the casino business took off, so did Kirby's bus business. Initially, the road to the casinos was a treacherous, potholed two-lane highway, and locals from Memphis preferred not to drive but rather to go by bus. For one thing, if you went by car, you had to line up at the gate, sometimes waiting hours to get into the casinos, whereas passengers on shuttle buses went straight in. Also, passengers could drink alcohol and not worry about the drive home.

"I was one of the first bus companies in there," says Kirby. "The casinos offered my passengers incentives—refunds on their bus tickets plus a $7.95 free meal. I couldn't believe my luck. Business boomed. My company became very profitable. I, the son of a sharecropper, was worth more than $1.5 million in net assets."

It was then, says Kirby, that his luck hit some snags—strongly linked, in his mind at least, to the color of his skin. "Despite my profit record, the banks wouldn't lend me the money I needed in order to upgrade my fleet and stay competitive with the other coach companies that had begun to move into the market," he says. "Why? Because the owners of the banks are white, and I'm black, and they couldn't imagine someone of my color being a good risk and a successful businessman." Then a new four-lane freeway—Highway 61—was built, and with it more casino-hotels were erected, with parking lots as big as small airports, and locals who had cars began to use them. Kirby's clientele became more poor and more black, and as it did so, he says, the perception of his shuttle company changed among the casino managers and owners. "I pitched for a slice of the expanding tourist charter business, but the casino and tour operators wouldn't use me. I say it's because I'm black and I'm perceived as carrying poor blacks from the poor parts of Memphis. If I was a white company, the casinos would have played ball. I tried several times. But they wouldn't give me a contract, not one casino. Then, to make matters worse, the casinos stopped offering my passengers refunds and free meal incentives. One by one they withdrew. Only the Sheraton kept the deal going. That was a killer. I lost thirty-three percent of my business when the incentives stopped."

Kirby is $600,000 in debt and sinking deeper, he says. He has already cut his fleet from eleven to six buses, laid off drivers, and cut his own pay to $100 a week to slash costs. (Any less than six buses and he can't offer a regular schedule.) He continues to lose passengers, money, and sleep. His wife, to whom he has been married for thirty-eight years (they have six daughters), earns $35,000 a year as a bus driver for the city of Memphis, and they are living off her salary until he gets back on his feet, he says. To do that, to break even, he has to double his ridership from two hundred to four hundred passengers a day.

By becoming an entrepreneur, Kirby believed that, unlike his father and grandfather, he would no longer be "at the white man's mercy." Don't believe the hype about the role of pure luck in the American Dream, he wants to tell me. You take financial risks to make your luck. The sad part is that along the way you discover that your luck is tainted by the color of your skin. Of course, this is Kirby's perception. It might also be that his buses do not run on time or are simply no match for the quality of the competition. Kirby concedes that that may be part of the story. But he still feels defeated by "the color of my luck," he says.

Recently, as something of a last-ditch attempt to get back in the fray, Kirby pitched for the casino-employee shuttle contract. He thought he had a great chance, since a high proportion of the casino staff are African-American. He thought that for once his color, and the convenient location of his terminal in South Memphis, where many casino employees live, would be an advantage. "I got dressed up in my best suit and went to present my case to the casino bosses."

He shakes his head. "They didn't go for it."

Kirby stares numbly out the door as a late-night shuttle pulls up. Seating capacity is forty-seven. He counts as the returning gamblers exit the bus. "One, two, three . . . seven, eight." Just eight—all of them African-American, all looking disheveled and ragged. Like a tired team of athletes on a long losing streak and who have just lost an away game, again.

"If I can't find a way to turn things around soon, I face bankruptcy," he says.

FROM THE PERSONAL TO THE POLITICAL

This is the question I grapple with as I gun my rental Buick down the Delta, Howlin' Wolf belting out "Back Door Man" on my cassette deck. Just who is benefiting from the rise of gambling?

The Mississippi Gaming Commission reports that in 1998 alone, the Mississippi casinos took $2 billion from the gambling public.[15] Although for many gamblers, the amount lost is affordable and simply entertainment, the research shows that not all the people who play can afford to pay. A 1996 study by the Stennis Institute of Government at Mississippi State University found that the poor not only spend, on average, a much larger proportion of their income on casino gambling than middle-income people, but they may even spend, quite astoundingly, more dollars per capita in absolute terms.

They found that gamblers with annual family incomes under $10,000 spend, on average, 10.3 percent (up to $1,030) of that income at casinos, whereas gamblers with family incomes of $20,000 to $30,000 spend 3.3 percent (up to $990) and gamblers with family incomes over $50,000 spend only 1.3 percent (as little as $650).[16]

Jed Weintraub, a spokesman for the Memphis Bankruptcy Court, tells me that bankruptcy filings have spiraled by almost 50 percent since the casinos opened, despite the fact that the local economy is booming. "There is no question that gambling plays a role in the equation, but to what degree we don't know, because no research has been done," he says. The president of a local debt-collection agency goes further, telling a reporter at the *Memphis Commercial Appeal*: "When you look down a list of cash advances on a credit card and see Robinsonville, Robinsonville, Robinsonville,"—the location of the Tunica casinos—"you can bet those advances aren't for the dinner buffet."[17]

Yet the majority view I encounter is that the arrival of the casinos is overwhelmingly positive for Mississippi and its 2.7 million residents—36 percent black, 63 percent white. This is why:

Prior to the arrival of the casinos in 1990, Mississippi's per-capita income (average personal income) was $12,719, the lowest in the nation. Unemployment vacillated between 10 and 17 percent, and in counties like Tunica it rose to 26 percent in the winter, when the farmer's fields lie fallow. But by 1996, just four years into the great casino experiment, per-capita income had risen 39 percent to $17,561 and unemployment had dropped to below 5 percent, a level where almost everyone who wants a job can have one. In Tunica, the effect was even more dramatic: per-capita income doubled to $19,139, and the county that was dead last of Mississippi's eighty-two counties leapfrogged into the top third.[18]

The reason for this improvement is that the Mississippi casinos have created 32,000 jobs paying an average of $21,000 per job, plus health insurance benefits, which translates into an average compensation package worth a very decent $35,000 per year. The story told to me by Leslie Haynes is a commonplace one: she is a single mother with a one-year-old child who gave up her job as a "struggling jewelry saleswoman" working on commission to became a Tunica blackjack dealer. She now earns $40,000 a year and she couldn't be more delighted. "I have just bought myself a new house and a new car," she says.

The state has used the casinos to leverage itself as a tourist destination, creating another 50,000 indirect jobs on top of the 32,000 direct jobs. So successful have they been that welfare recipients have declined by two-thirds since the start of the 1990s.

ONWARD DOWN THE DELTA

A few miles south of the town of Tunica, the new four-laner ends abruptly and Highway 61 reverts to a crumbling single-gauge road. I pass falling-down shacks, rusting cars on bricks, roadside stores with ink cardboard signs advertising COLDEST BEER IN TOWN, and dilapidated cotton-processing plants, images of poverty with which Mississippi has long been associated.

But the presence of the casinos is never far away. When I stop to put gas in my tank, a monitor built into the petrol pump entertains me with a casino promotional video. A short while later, I am encouraged by a road sign pointing to Helena Bridge: TURN HERE FOR THE LADY LUCK, it says.

Two pulsating 112-foot, neon-lit guitars dominate the Mississippi River at Helena Bridge. Stuck like carbuncles onto the Lady Luck Rhythm and Blues Casino-Hotel, they bring to mind—in a gaudy, ironic way, of course—Paul Simon's memorable lyrics to "Graceland": "the Mississippi Delta was shining like a national guitar."

That night I play blackjack. I watch the woman in the seat next to me, a gas-station cashier from nearby Clarksdale, amass a small fortune. "I came here with $200 and I'm fuckin' 'em up," she says. She has a beer in one hand, a cigarette in the other, and a skyscraper of black chips (each worth $100) in front of her. She plays $500 a hand. "Give me black, babee, I'm after your black." She screams with raucous laughter every time she wins, and the dealer, Charles, from Arkansas, jokes along with her. When Charles runs out of black and has to ask his pit boss for another box of $100 chips to pay her, it delights the table no end. "Gimme my damn moneee!" she crows.

From Helena Bridge, Highway 61 follows the delta to Greenville and on to Vicksburg. The casinos become progressively more tawdry as you head south, and the roadside billboards—GO FOR THE GREEN!—begin to encounter competition. WHAT COULD YOUR KIDS POSSIBLY DESERVE MORE THAN SUNDAY SCHOOL?, entreats one.

In 1832, when Tocqueville passed through Vicksburg on his way down the Delta, Vicksburg was a Wild West town, its riverfront primped by fine whorehouses the likes of which apparently rivaled any to be found in New Orleans, including the infamous House of the Rising Sun.

It was also a town in the grip of professional hustlers and gamblers. In 1835, a local insurrection occurred when a notorious gambler, Burt Cabler, overstepped the limits and gatecrashed the town's Fourth of July picnic. The Vicksburg citizens tarred and feathered him, and cast him downriver on a skiff. Buoyed by their unexpected success, the locals met at the courthouse and issued an ultimatum for all gamblers to leave town within forty-eight hours. The residents of one gambling house, the Kangaroo, refused and barricaded themselves in. When the leader of the newly formed citizen's committee, a doctor, Hugh Bodley, knocked on the door to demand that they leave, the gamblers' response was swift and severe—they shot and killed him. Enraged, the citizens broke down the door, dragged the gamblers into the street, and gave them an instant "kangaroo" trial. The sentence—death by hanging—was carried out immediately on half a dozen gamblers. Then they burned down the Kangaroo and erected a monument (which still stands today) in honor of Dr. Bodley, "who died protecting the morals of Vicksburg."[19]

Now, after more than 150 years in which Vicksburg, population 30,000, had basked in its reputation as a historic, but sleepy, Civil War city, the gamblers and the gambling houses are back on the riverfront. Within a year of August 1993, four casinos—Harrah's, Ameristar, Rainbow, and Isle of Capri—had opened for business, and Vicksburg had become the third-largest gambling jurisdiction in Mississippi after Tunica and the Gulf Coast. Gamblers journey in from Jackson, the state capital, just forty minutes away, from across the river in Louisiana, and from as far afield as Texas and Oklahoma.

So unexpected was their popularity that when the casinos opened, the city had budgeted zero dollars in gaming-tax revenues for their first year of operation. Instead they got $5 million. Today the city budget has more than doubled to $30 million, mostly as a result of taxes on casino revenues.

I want to know: How has the money been spent? And how has the arrival of the casinos impacted social attitudes in the region?

Charles D. Mitchell, the editor of the *Vicksburg Post,* has watched his city "sell its soul" to gambling. But he's glad. Turns out, it wasn't such a pristine soul after all. As to my two questions, he's cynical about the former, buoyant about the latter. "The money has gone primarily into amenities and egos," he says. "Our police force used to be hard-pressed to put new tires on their vehicles; now they just buy new cars. Of course, there have been new roads, a new swimming complex, baseball fields, but huge amounts have been wasted simply on hiking up the city payroll, which is now $15 million, as compared to the whole city budget, which used to be $12 million. Our police and firemen are currently the best-paid in the Southeast. You gotta ask yourself . . ."

In Tunica County, too, I learned, town and county officials have watched their budgets double and triple. The county has used the revenue to rebuild the infrastructure of the state—its roads, water, and sewerage—to bring a backward part of Mississippi into the twentieth century. The Tunica town mayor, Bobby Williams, his office adorned with a life-size John Wayne cardboard cutout, signed photographs of Newt Gingrich, Trent Lott, and Dan Quayle, and a personal collection of 135 antique miniature cars, had told me that his budget went from $750,000 to $3 million. He doubled his police force, built a new post office and a new city hall.

But the jury is still out on the promise by advocates of gambling that revenues would be used to dramatically enhance the funding of public education—and not just in Mississippi. In Ohio, the use of lottery moneys to fund public education has not resulted in an overall increase of funding for public education. In Tunica, the building of a spanking-new, $8 million state-of-the-art elementary school in a part of Robinsonville where new housing is going up, and where only the middle class can afford to live, is criticized as doing nothing for the county's blacks, almost none of whom will reside in the new school's attendance zone.[20]

Interestingly, Tocqueville describes how in the 1800s, the lawmakers used the prohibition against gambling to redistribute wealth. Tucked away in the appendix of *Democracy in America* is an excerpt from an 1829 American antigambling statute. It says: "Whosoever wins or loses the sum of twenty-five dollars within the space of twenty-four hours by gambling or betting shall be guilty of a misdemeanor, and on proof of the fact will be condemned to a fine equal to at least five times the value of the sum lost or won; the said fine *shall be handed over to the overseer of the poor* for that township. Whoever loses twenty-five dollars or more can bring an action to recover it. If he fails to do so, the overseer of the poor can bring an action against the winner and make him pay the sum won, and threefold as much again, *for the benefit of the poor.*"[21] (Italics my emphasis.)

It is not the law in itself that is so arresting, but rather the unexpected twist in the plot in which the poor are written in as beneficiaries of gambling.

The biggest advantage to the present casino boom, as far as Charles Mitchell is concerned, is that the casinos have altered the balance of power in the region between the haves and the have-nots. "Before the casinos came, there was a culture among employers of treating employees badly," he says. "Unemployment was high, and with long lines of people for every job, employers got away with treating staff as completely disposable: they paid minimum wage, with no medical benefits, no training, and if staff were late for work, they were simply fired. There was also a racist edge to employment policy.

"Now those employers cannot find people to work for them. When the casino-hotels arrived, creating more than four thousand new jobs, they offered health insurance, employee savings schemes, training programs, and affirmative-action policies designed to ensure that their workforce reflected the ethnic diversity of the local population (half black, half white) at every level of the organization, from entry-level jobs through to management. The casinos behaved like responsible employers. Watching employers who had been mean and cruel to employees having to re-examine how they treat them and having to offer benefits, training, and opportunities for promotion has been more fun . . . and it's changed the employee-employer relationship in a profoundly positive way.

"The arrival of the casinos has brought about an empowerment among people that were losing hope, people who had been mired in poverty for generations. And there's no going back."

They say Ol' Man River is a man with a past. Gamblers were part of that past, but marginalized as scoundrels. That Ol' Man River is today a man with a future is in no small measure due to a passion for gambling that, despite decades of suppression, was never eradicated from the American character.

Mississippi has put its faith in the seemingly insatiable demand of the American public for games of chance. So far it seems to be working as gambling helps to move the region forward. But is it a wise course to steer for the long term?

The American government was so concerned at the wildfire spread of gambling throughout the nation that in 1997 it established the National Gambling Impact Study Commission to report on the social and economic impact of the gambling boom. "With little end in sight to the proliferation of gambling, our country stands at a crossroads. Do we allow gambling to expand, or do we halt its growth until we fully understand its effects on individuals, communities, and the nation?" the commission asked. Two years later, in June 1999, it reported back to the President and Congress. It had found that there were "both significant benefits and significant costs" and suggested that states impose a moratorium on gambling expansion to allow states time to digest the possible impact. A pause.

In the meantime, the commission made seventy-six recommended changes for regulating gambling, urging states and the casino industry to face up to the burgeoning number of "problem" or "compulsive" gamblers—people who cannot control their urge to gamble, who, it estimates, account for between 2 and 7 percent of gambling adults, depending on the measure used. These are small percentages but huge numbers of people in absolute terms. The commission estimates that between 1.7 million and 3.2 million adults gamble in ways that damage themselves, their families, and their communities. "Commissioners found themselves at a loss when it came to quantifying the emotional damage suffered by millions of pathological gamblers and their families. How does one quantify the tragic actions of the sixteen-year-old boy in Atlantic City who slit his wrists after losing $6,000 on lottery tickets? How does one categorize the deaths of the middle-aged couple from

Joliet, Illinois, who committed suicide after the wife accumulated $200,000 in casino debt? How can one calculate the 'cost' of the two children who died while locked in cars as their parents or caregivers gambled in nearby casinos?" And then there is the still-unknown impact that such easily accessible gambling will have on the nation's youth. "Especially troubling, 1.1 million adolescents are also estimated to be pathological gamblers . . . and . . . how will children's access to Internet gambling be monitored?" the commission worried.[22]

I arrive in New Orleans and tune into the evening television news on ABC.

A story is breaking of a casino-shuttle-bus crash. The pictures show a bus lying splayed on its side. Shocked-looking passengers are saying how "lucky" they feel to be alive.

I recall a story recounted to me in Memphis by Pastor Don Abernathy, whose Longcrest Baptist Church is within spitting distance of Highway 61 and the route to the Tunica casinos. One day he heard a huge bang and ran out to find that a casino-bound shuttle bus had hit a car. The bus had turned over, killing the driver of the car and injuring thirty passengers. He told me how he watched incredulous as the eight passengers who had escaped injury hailed the next shuttle bus for the casino, even as ambulances took away the dead and the critically injured. It seemed to him a callous act, devoid of compassion for their fellow Americans. "They said," he told me, speaking slowly, and trembling a little, obviously shaken by an attitude he was still trying to comprehend. "They said *they* had survived, so it meant that their luck must be running good."

5

ON THROUGH THE
DEEP SOUTH

The Battle for the Soul of America

I t is only on a Greyhound, and perhaps only in the South, that
a conversation like the one I have with Rhoda can take place.

I board the 3:15 P.M. bus in sun-bleached New Orleans, bound
for Mobile, Alabama, the first stop on my journey onward through
the South, and just over three hours away. As the bus shoots the
city limits and begins to hit its stride on Interstate 10, I look up
from my book and notice a middle-aged woman sitting directly
across the aisle. At that instant she looks up from her book too,
and momentarily our eyes meet. There seems something a little
hardened about her, faintly crusty around the edges, like oatmeal
left too long in the pot, something that makes me want *not* to
engage her. We greet each other politely, as strangers do, and she
proceeds to tell me—in an accent so deeply southern it sounds to
me almost like a foreign language—that she has been on the road
for something like fifteen hours. She is traveling from her home in
Texas to see her parents in Charlotte, North Carolina, to celebrate
her birthday.

"And to tell them some news," she adds.

"What are you turning?" I ask.

"Forty-nine on Monday," she says.

"Happy birthday," I reply, inclining toward my book again.

"I'm going there to tell them that I have just been diagnosed
with cancer," she says flatly.

Cancer? Did she say "cancer"?

"It's vaginal cancer," she adds. And she coughs—a dry, racking, eye-popping cough.

My throat constricts. I feel a little dizzy. *There is no air on this goddamn bus!* As if from far away (though really he is quite close), I hear the driver talking to an African-American woman in the seat in front of me. "Ain't that something," she is saying gently and easily. "Ain't that something." I want to be light and easy too, but my head is a mess, torn between empathy and self-preservation. *How horrible for her. Is she in pain? That cough! Is she contagious? Why is she telling me this? What does she want from me?* Part of me wants to yell to the driver, "Stop! Lemme off!" and bolt from the bus, another part wants to give the poor woman a hug. Well, perhaps not a hug—I have only known her five minutes, and I don't even know her name and who knows what exotic germs are at this very moment lunging toward me in that cough—but maybe I could offer a sympathetic word, a squeeze of her hand.

"I'm going there to tell them that I am going to live." She speaks softly but defiantly. "God will help me. With God's help." And I notice that it is the New Testament that she has been reading.

In short order she introduces herself—as Rhoda B[1]—taking pains to explain the biblical origin of her name as "the damsel who answered the door to Peter in Acts, chapter 12, verse 13." She recounts the basic outline of her life: an adopted child, grew up on a farm in North Carolina, daughter of a part-time Methodist pastor; worked as a nurse's aide; got married in her early twenties; moved to Texas; had three children, all adults now and living in Michigan, West Virginia, and California, respectively; goes to church three times a week, reads the Bible three times a day, is an adherent of the Church of Christ (a conservative Protestant denomination with two million members in the United States); is currently studying by correspondence to be a pastor herself; left her husband four years ago. "You see . . ." she says.

And then, pulling a photograph from her purse, she hands me another dreadful surprise.

I peer into a swollen, barely recognizable face with bruises the size of avocados—one eye painfully closed, the other a mere slit, lips a puffy bluish, greenish black.

"This is what I looked like when he beat me up," she says.

"Who?" I ask, shocked.

"My husband. He used to hit me with a two-by-four."

"What," I ask ignorantly, "is a two-by-four?"

"You know, a plank of wood measuring four inches wide by . . ."
She trails off. "I'm a manic depressive. I take lithium to keep my
chemical imbalance in line. And mostly I'm fine, but with his beating up on me . . . I had nine nervous breakdowns in ten years, each
one following his abuse. Once I was hospitalized for three months."
She talks fast now, needing to vent, her sentences increasingly stac-
cato, recalling how there were times he beat her every day, several
times a day, and spitting out the many dates she was hospitalized.

"But why did you stick with him for so long?" I butt in.

"I had three young kids, no job, no money, and nowhere to
go. My parents lived far away. There was the church. But really I
was alone. As soon as the kids were grown up, I divorced him.
And I haven't had a breakdown since. Not one in four years. And
also because I've stuck close to the Lord . . ."

"Okay, y'all," announces the bus driver perkily over his handheld
intercom, pulling the bus smoothly off the interstate and coming
to a gravel-crunching halt at a gas station on the turnpike to Bay
St. Louis, on the Mississippi Gulf Coast. "Just a coupla minutes to
buy some food, smoke, 'n' stretch . . ."

We pile off the bus and into the convenience store, where several of the rowdier passengers, who have been seated at the back
of the bus, attempt to purchase some alcohol. The cashier declines
them, explaining that alcohol can neither be consumed on the
premises nor taken onto the bus. "Greyhound rules—I don't make
'em an' I don't break 'em," he says. Not to be denied, the passengers approach a motorist in the shop who has stopped for gas and
candy and press him to buy their cheap wine for them, offering to
pay for his chocolate if he'll oblige. But the cashier is wise to their
ruse and thwarts them once again. By the half-fried tincture of these
passengers, already two sheets to the wind, it seems that cashiers at
previous pit stops might not have been quite as vigilant.

The incident gives me pause to observe my fellow travelers for the first time. It had been put to me that if I wanted to meet a cross-section of *real* Americans, the best way was to go by Greyhound. It is apparent that this is an outdated and rather romanticized idea, as few middle-class or well-heeled Americans take a Greyhound these days. They opt instead for planes, trains, and automobiles. Greyhound, still the cheapest way to travel within the U.S., has become a mode of transport where you meet a cross-section of real, low-income Americans. My fellow travelers, Bible scholars and boozers alike, and everything else in between, comprise a diverse ethnic mix—African-Americans, Hispanics, Native Americans, and whites, with ages ranging from college students to mothers with young infants to the elderly.

The bus reloads and, kicking up a cloud of dust, roars back onto the interstate. We pound past the turnoffs to Gulfport and Biloxi, the road rolling to the horizon through the flat terrain ahead, and bisecting on either side the armies of billboards (or should that be "bull boards?") to which I have grown accustomed. They advertise the bevy of Gulf Coast casinos just a few miles away, such as the spanking new Beau Rivage and the Grand—ASK FOR THE MOON, WE'LL GIVE YOU THE STARS—KENNY ROGERS COMING FEBRUARY 4. And of course, standing like giant flamingoes between them, each one competing to be higher and more colorful than the rest, the twenty-story one-legged towers screaming WENDY'S, SHONEY'S, MCDONALD'S, RAMADA, and so forth and so on. They serve as constant reminders of the ubiquitous working-poor segment of society and the burgeoning market for gambling. But rising between them, adding a new ingredient to the mix, is a billboard with a different message. It is a message I had observed in southern Mississippi but never in the north of the country, and it says: JESUS OFFERS ETERNAL LIFE. ARE YOU INTERESTED? CALL 271-3363.

This is the Bible Belt, I remind myself, the most religious region of perhaps the most religious nation in the world. According to a Gallup poll, 99 percent of southerners—99 percent!—profess to believe in God.[2] (Two thoughts: surely these polls are overstated;

and how fascinating it would be to meet that one in a hundred person who has the strength to resist.) In the nation as a whole, the belief factor is said to be only a smidgen lower, with 94 percent of the population claiming that they believe in God, compared, for example, with 70 percent in Britain. According to these polls, 84 percent of Americans believe that Jesus Christ is God, or the son of God, whereas the divinity of Jesus is accepted by less than half the people of Britain. And 40 percent attend church weekly (47 percent in the South), as opposed to just 14 percent in the UK.[3] Remarkably, these statistics have hardly changed in half a century of polling.

Back in 1831, Tocqueville, too, was struck by the apparent fervency of the Americans. "The religious atmosphere of the country was the first thing that struck me on my arrival in the United States," he noted.[4] Tocqueville sketched a picture of a deeply observant nation:

> In the United States, when the seventh day comes, trade and industry seem suspended throughout the nation. All noise stops. A deep repose, or rather solemn contemplation, takes its place . . . On this day places of businesses are deserted; every citizen, accompanied by his children, goes to a church; there he listens to strange language apparently hardly suited to his ear. He is told of countless evils brought on by pride and covetousness. He is reminded of the need to check his desires and told of the finer delights which go with virtue alone, and the true happiness they bring. When he gets home, he does not hurry to his business ledgers. He opens the book of Holy Scripture and there finds sublime and touching accounts of the greatness and goodness of the Creator, of the infinite magnificence of the works of God, of the high destiny reserved for men, of their duties and of their claims to immortality. Thus it is that the American in some degree from time to time escapes from himself, and for a moment free from the petty passions that trouble his life and the passing interests that fill it, he suddenly breaks into an ideal world where all is great, pure, and eternal.[5]

But impressed as he was by this outward show of religiosity, Tocqueville went deeper, challenging the depth of this commitment. "They seem a religious people," he had to admit. But, he wondered, "to what point does their *life* conform to their *doctrine*? What is the true power of the religious principle on their *soul*?" (my emphasis).[6] In other words: does this love of God translate into a love of their fellow man? Does it make them feel more connected to each other? Does it make them more compassionate citizens?

There is something about Rhoda's life story that burns, burns, burns at these questions. "There was the church. But really I was alone," she had volunteered in an unguarded moment. What did she mean?

"Rhoda," I say, turning to her after a long period of scudding along in silence. "Did you tell your pastor what your husband was doing to you? Did you turn to your church for help?"

She shoots me a defensive look. Her church knew that her husband beat her, she tells me, and they knew that her financial position was too precarious for her to just get up and leave. And so her pastor and fellow congregants prayed for her, she says.

"They *prayed* for you?" I try not to sound incredulous. "That's it? And then they went home to their house, and you and your husband went home to yours, and he beat you with . . . ?"

"Prayer and faith—that is what church is about," she says.

"But how did it help you?"

"The church brings me closer to God," she replies. "It gives me a better understanding of the word of the Lord, and it helps me to pass it on to others, to preach."

Rhoda's reply stupefies me. For what is the point of the church if it does not connect with real as well as spiritual life? It is apparent that religion has given her faith and strength—profound and inestimable gifts—but surely church offers something beyond prayer and evangelism. Even the Ten Commandments, the template from which all Western religion proceeds, is only half concerned with man's relationship to God, the other half with man's relationship to man. Of course, I have to consider the possibility that Rhoda's reply might say more about Rhoda than it does about her particular church, and I wonder what her pastor might say were he traveling with us on this bus. But taking her story at face value, I find it incredible that she should have believed, as an involved member of her congregation, that she had to endure, for more than ten years, such an abusive, nightmarish existence—alone.

It stirs in me the questions that stirred Tocqueville: about the relevance of organized religion to real life; about the interest of the church in social issues; and, ultimately, about the nature of American compassion. It leads to a broader question: about the role the church plays in helping the vulnerable, the socially excluded, and the have-nots in society. Under what conditions is compassion given; under what conditions is it withheld? And what does the answer to this question reveal about the American character?

The subject of compassion is also on the lips of the politicians who, as I travel, are fighting for the year 2000 presidential nomination. At times the reference is oblique, as in Democrat Bill Bradley's assertion that "the nation is ready once again to assert its better self." And sometimes it is head-on, as in Republican George W. Bush's decision to run for president under the slogan "compassionate conservative." He could have chosen any word to describe himself, but he picked "compassionate," and that must say something about how he sees himself relative to his fellow Republicans, and, in this age of hyper-polling, how important he believes this quality is to ordinary Americans.

Now, as I travel through the religious South in the last month of the twentieth century, in the weeks between Thanksgiving and Christmas, the time seems ripe to dig a little deeper into the American psyche.

But first I must insert a note of humility. Because the place to begin digging, the place to dissect the meaning of compassion itself, is surely right here on the bus, with a painful observation—about myself. Why have I found it so difficult to show compassion to Rhoda? Why do I keep her at arm's length, resisting her, never actually asking if she is in pain, never saying how sorry I feel for her predicament? Okay, she has needed to talk, and I have listened—so I have not been completely insensitive—but even then

I have engaged her more as a journalist than as a human being. Here is a fellow traveler, an imperfect stranger, vulnerable and in pain, who simply wants to talk and be heard with sympathy. She wants nothing from me save a little of my time. So why does part of me recoil as I listen, unnerved by her intimacy, afraid that I might catch some of what she has?

According to the *Compact Edition of the Oxford English Dictionary,* the word "compassion" is a combination of the Latin words *com* ("together with") and *pati* ("to suffer"), whence it derives its meaning "to suffer together with another." It defines compassion as "the feeling or emotion when a person is moved by the suffering or distress of another, and by the desire to relieve it."

But in order to "suffer together with another," you have to be able to put yourself in his or her shoes. To empathize. That is easy to do when the person you are empathizing with is a lot like you, or is the kind of person you usually relate to. I struggle to relate to Rhoda. Her nasal, syncopated accent (though who knows what she thought of my British–South African hybrid!), her "born again," God-fearing way of talking, the subtle clues to her manic-depressiveness that were evident the first time I saw her—all make her seem "other" to me. It is this "otherness" that makes it harder to activate my empathy, my compassion. It puts an invisible barrier between us that I have to work hard to break down.

The reflective words of Gerald Chait—the midwestern supermarket mogul whom I had met in Pittsburgh—come rushing back at me. "This country," he had said, "we started with this kinship that we were all in the same boat. We've gotten away from that . . . We've lost our ability to *feel* for the people in the other boat." I suddenly appreciate the honesty of his sentiments.

It is good to get to bottom lines. It's real. It's bedrock. It lays bare the magnitude of the challenge that lies ahead.

Because the harsh reality, as I have come to appreciate on my travels, is that the haves confront the have-nots as strangers across a multitude of barriers. In most of the American cities I have visited —the haves and the have-nots tend to live in different neighborhoods, socialize in different circles, send their kids to different schools, play in different parks. Gated neighborhoods are increasingly common.

Most of the haves live geographically separate lives whose only inter-action with the have-nots may be limited to the employees who clean their house, baby-sit their children, make their coffee at Star-bucks, or ring up their bill at the local supermarket.

In the face of these geographical barriers, the connecting role of religion and the church seems especially profound. For it is ulti-mately our spirituality that allows us to pierce physical barriers and to connect to the humanity in strangers, whatever their health, wealth, race, or ethnic group.

The bus crosses the state border into Alabama, the sun setting behind us, illuminating the sky in a plumage of peaceful orange. It is that time of day—silent, calm, beautiful—when anything seems possi-ble. For a moment, enveloped by the orange sky, the road dark and unseen beneath us, it feels as if the bus is flying magically through the atmosphere. I look beside me and I see that Rhoda has fallen asleep, breathing softly, a pen in her hand, the letter that she was writing unfinished and flapping gently with the motion of the bus. I look at her afresh: a large woman, plain in her looks, plain in her dress, with unkempt curly gray hair, glasses balanced on the end of her nose, and a face that has aged beyond her years, a face that shows the breaks of her life. Yet as the diffused light falls aglow about her shoulders, softening the striated lines around her eyes, I see something that I had not seen before: a woman in a Vermeer painting, plain to be sure, but full of poise and strength and great, great dignity. Welling up inside me, I feel an over-whelming sadness. From this new angle—and quite literally in this new light—Rhoda seems, suddenly, almost familiar.

THE POWER OF THE CHURCH—THEN AND NOW

Tocqueville loved to discuss religion. The church, he realized, was one of the great causative influences in the making of America. This was only partially because of how things began, with the Pu-ritans fleeing England to gain religious freedom. "I think I can see the whole destiny of America contained in the first Puritan who landed on those shores, as that of the whole human race in the first man,"[7] he wrote, referring to their pioneering, freedom-loving spirit tethered to a religious zeal. But it was more complicated than that, especially since the first act of the Puritans was to attempt to deny religious freedom to others. So wherever Tocqueville went, he would never miss an opportunity to steer the conversation in the direction of religion. "To what do you attribute the religious tolerance which reigns in the United States?" "What is your opinion of the influence of religion on politics?" From the Great Lakes to Baltimore to the backroads of the South, he peppered his hosts and fellow travelers with questions.

"Never have I been so conscious of the influence of religion on the *morals* and the *social* and *political* state of a people since my arrival in America," he wrote.[8] It is "a subject toward which my imagination draws me continuously and which would end by making me mad if I plumbed it often," he admitted in a letter home. But he couldn't help himself, because, as he said, "the religious state of this people is perhaps the most curious thing to examine here."[9]

That religion should be so powerful in America—in the land of the enlightened and the free—was an irony that Tocqueville marveled at. For in Europe religious zeal had been gradually weakening, and the reason for this, maintained the philosophers of his day, was precisely the spread of enlightenment and freedom. So why did the spirits of religion and freedom march in harmony in America, he asked himself, whereas in Europe they pulled in opposite directions?

"The main reason for the quiet sway of religion over their country was," opined Tocqueville, "the complete separation of church and state."[10] This was not just Tocqueville's view—it was, he said, the unanimous view of all the Christian creeds in America. The clergy held no political appointments, and in return, all religious beliefs were constitutionally on the same footing, the government neither supporting nor suppressing any one. Tocqueville saw a paradox of power here that intrigued him. How could it be "that by diminishing the apparent power of religion one increased its real strength"?[11] The answer was that the clergy in America had traded direct political power for a more enduring influence. They had sacrificed the present for the future, concluded Tocqueville. "Religion cannot share the material strength of the rulers without being burdened with some of the animosity roused against them," he wrote. When religion is directly linked to governments, "it follows their fortunes and often falls together with the passions of a day sustaining them. Hence any alliance with any political power is bound to be burdensome for religion. It does not need their support in order to live, and in serving them it may die." This danger existed in all societies, but was heightened in a democracy, he thought, because of the speed with which power passed "from hand to hand." Whereas American clergy saw that they would have to give up direct political power if they wanted to acquire religious influence, "European Christianity had allowed itself to be intimately united with the powers of this world."[12]

But if religion derived its enduring strength from the complete separation of church and state, how then, could the influence of religion over politics and society be characterized?

Tocqueville put this question to, among others, Dr. Richard Spring Stewart, a distinguished Maryland physician, whose reply makes fascinating reading:

In the United States, the great majority, even among the enlightened classes, but especially among the people, is truly believing, and firmly sustains the opinion that a man who is not Christian offers no social guarantee. This gives the clergy a great *indirect* influence [my emphasis]. Thus, if a minister, known for his piety, should declare that in his opinion a certain man was an unbeliever, the man's career would almost certainly be broken. Another example: a doctor is skilful, but has no faith in the Christian religion. However, thanks to his abilities, he obtains a fine practice. No sooner is he introduced into the house than a zealous Christian, a minister or someone else, comes to see the father of the house and says: "Look out for this man. He will perhaps cure your children, but he will seduce your daughters or your wife, he is an unbeliever. There, on the other hand, is Mr. So-and-So. As good a doctor as this man, he is at the same time religious. Believe me, trust the health of your family to him." Such counsel is almost always followed.[13]

That unbelievers should be untrustworthy was an idea also observed by Tocqueville himself. "While I was in America," he wrote, "a witness called at Chester (state of New York) declared that he did not believe in the existence of God and the immortality of the soul. The judge refused to allow him to be sworn in, on the ground that the witness had destroyed beforehand all possible confidence in his testimony." Newspapers reported the fact without comment, he noted.[14]

The influence of religion on society was tremendously powerful, thought Tocqueville, even though it was indirect.

We see religion exerting an influential role on modern sensibilities too. Observe, for example, the clamor by Republican and Democratic politicians who run for president to publicly trumpet their religious faith. In the 1992 presidential election campaign, Bill Clinton, Al Gore, George Bush, and Dan Quayle all attested that they were born-again Christians.[15] In the 2000 presidential primary campaign, Al Gore publicly reasserted his credentials as a born-again Christian, while George W. Bush claimed that Jesus Christ was his favorite philosopher, "because he changed my heart," he said. John McCain regaled how as a former prisoner of war in Vietnam, he composed a Christmas sermon to rally his fellow POWs. Only former senator Bill Bradley refused to discuss religion, maintaining that it was a private matter.[16]

Why do they go to such lengths to protest their faith? Just like in the story Tocqueville recounts, the men who would be President of America must believe that a simple declaration of their belief in God is vital to their success. Such is the sway of religion over society that their status as religious Christians underwrites the credibility of their testimony and the integrity of their character.

Tocqueville's essential insight—that the majority of Americans regard faith almost as a litmus test of morality—still appears to apply today.

The first time that I personally had witnessed the power of organized religion in America was when, as a journalist, I covered the 1997 Promise Keepers rally in Washington, D.C., for the *Independent* in Britain.[17] Hundreds of thousands of men had gathered on the baking-hot sand of the Washington Mall. What, I wondered, had motivated half a million men to leave their families for the weekend and travel fourteen hours overnight cramped in a minivan? They had not come for the beer, the hot dogs, or the women—none of those traditional male selling points were on offer. So what was the mobilizing force behind their presence? Throughout the mile-long gathering, small groups of men leaned on each other's shoulders in impromptu prayer circles. When I began to probe individuals, I realized that each prayer circle—and there were thousands of them—comprised a separate church group. These men had not traveled there on their own, or with a couple of friends, as you expect to find at public gatherings like rock concerts, but had instead come with their local church groups. Individual motivations might have been opaque that day, but if the gathering revealed one truth that was crystal clear, it was the stunning reach and organizing power of the church.

These mass, open-air gatherings of Christians have, in fact, been a part of American society for two centuries. In Tocqueville's day, they called them camp meetings. These were annual gatherings on the frontier where pioneers would bring their families and camp out for a few days in order to hear the word of God as delivered to them by a circuit preacher. Tocqueville records how one of his hosts described the occasion:

> Almost every summer, some Methodist preachers come to make a tour of the new settlements. The noise of their arrival spreads with unbelievable rapidity from cabin to cabin: it's the great news of the day. At the date set, the emigrant, his wife and children set out by scarcely cleared forest trails toward the indicated meeting-place. They come from fifty miles around. It's not in a church that the faithful gather, but in the open air, under the forest foliage. A pulpit of badly squared logs, great trees felled for seats, such are the ornaments of this rustic temple. The pioneers and their families camp in the surrounding woods. It's there that, during three days and three nights, the crowd

gives itself over to almost uninterrupted religious exercises. You must see with what ardour these men surrender themselves to prayer, with what attention they listen to the solemn voice of the preacher. It's in the wilderness that people show themselves almost starved for religion.[18]

The camp meetings took place at a time in religious history known as the Second Great Awakening. Baptists and Methodists spearheaded the evangelizing efforts which led to the churching of the frontier and to the pre-eminence of these two forms of Protestantism in America over all others, a position they never subsequently relinquished.

Yet, despite all that Tocqueville wrote about the power of religion in America, the extraordinary facts are that by the end of the nineteenth century, only 35 percent of Americans were churched. It is only in the last hundred years, due to a further wave of proselytizing by evangelical Christians, that church membership has doubled to 70 percent.[19]

So, if the reach of the church has endured, as Tocqueville predicted it would, the key question we circle back to is this: What did he think was its influence on the moral sensibility of the people?

"The main business of religion is to purify, control, and restrain that excessive and exclusive taste for well-being which men acquire in times of equality," he wrote. Religion's role was a balancing and restraining one, to keep the pursuit of wealth honest. But it was only a supporting actor, and if religion was to survive and prosper, it had to make sure it channeled, but did not oppose, the materialistic instincts of Americans. "It may be that, should any religion attempt to destroy this mother of all desires, it would itself be destroyed thereby," he wrote. "They will never succeed in preventing men from loving wealth, but they may be able to induce them to use only honest means to enrich themselves."[20]

Tocqueville thought that the Catholic Church, which was growing rapidly with the influx of Irish immigrants, showed greater interest than Protestants in promoting equality and helping the poor—partly because, as he wrote, "most of the Catholics are poor."[21] Protestantism, on the other hand, orientated men "much less toward equality than towards independence." Of the black church—which was already well established and would later lead the civil rights movement—he said not a word.

He mentions the church's relationship to the poor only briefly and in passing. For, interestingly, Tocqueville did not make much of a link between the purported religiousness of Americans and their compassion. It was unparalleled "equality of conditions" which made Americans "extremely open to compassion." Helping others in difficulty was not done out of virtue, but rather out of empathy and out of a "self-interest properly understood." (Once again, without specifically saying so, he was talking about relations between *white* Americans.)

Nevertheless, Tocqueville did describe the role of the church as restraining and softening the worst excesses of materialism. Inequality and the burgeoning gap between the haves and the have-nots has become just such an excess. But is the church interested in bridging the divide between the haves and the have-nots? Or does it simply mirror, and even prop up, this divide?

THE POWER OF PLACE

The first thing you discover when you start to pound the pavements of Mobile, Alabama, is that there is, literally, a church on every corner. Occasionally you tramp three blocks without passing under the long shadow of a steeple, but then, hey, presto, on the next corner, as if to make up for this temporary dearth, you run into three or four churches in a row, all of different denominations. The second thing you learn is that southerners are constantly referring to Jesus Christ as if he is a real live person right there in the room, whom they know intimately. "Thank you, Jesus!" they say when a waitress serves them a hamburger. "Now what would Jesus do?" they ask aloud of themselves and of each other when they're in a quandary.

All in all, nearly five hundred churches,[22] close on half of them Southern Baptist, serve the 200,000-strong population of Mobile, an extraordinary average of one house of prayer for every 400 residents. The state of Alabama has a similar hit rate, with eight thousand churches to serve its population of 4.3 million, an average of one church for every 550 people. Some of these churches, particularly the African-American ones, are tiny, the equivalent of the miniature, whitewashed, one-room schoolhouse, and they serve as few as a dozen people. On the other extreme, there are churches the size of football stadiums, with their own cable TV channels and upward of 4,000 members. "Fort God," they call them, and "corporate Church." "When visitors ask me what's the biggest industry in Mobile, I say, 'Beer joints and Baptist churches,' " quips a taxi driver who had earlier ferried me from my hotel. (Beer joints, it turns out, are gentleman's clubs with nude lap dancers.) "And far as I can tell," he adds irreverently, "they have the same clientele."

Situated on the west bank of the Mobile River estuary on the Gulf of Mexico, and surrounded by bayous and creeks, Mobile was initially a center for the import and sale of human cargo. The French explorer Jean-Baptiste Le Moyne, sieur de Bienville, who was an emissary for King Louis XIV, founded Mobile on its present site in 1711. He founded New Orleans seven years later, and in 1720 he sanctioned the import of Negroes from Guinea off the west coast of Africa for use as slaves on the plantations upriver. Advertisements in the city directory promoted the sale of "Real Estate, Negroes, Horses, Carriages, Furniture and all other kinds of stable and fancy goods."[23] In Mobile itself, few residents owned slaves, and there was a substantial population of free blacks who, while segregated from the white community, were recognized as full citizens. (Unlike slaves, free blacks could own property, earn wages, engage in trades, marry, have children, enjoy a somewhat normal family life.) Initially Mobile was more important than New Orleans, and was actually the first American town to celebrate Mardi Gras. But New Orleans quickly became the focus of French expansion into Louisiana (named after King Louis), and Mobile was relegated to little-sister status. The connections between the two cities persisted, however, and the French-Catholic influence remained even after 1763, when Mobile fell under British rule, and after the American Revolution, when it became part of the United

States. Indeed, up until the Second World War, when large numbers of Americans descended on the region seeking work in the burgeoning shipbuilding industry, Mobile was a Catholic-dominated city, a rare thing in the Protestant-dominated South. When Tocqueville passed through Mobile in January 1832, it was a slave-trading and cotton-exporting town with three thousand residents. Tocqueville, however, did not linger, neither taking in the local French architecture with its delicate wrought-iron-lace balconies nor the still-thriving slave markets on Dauphin Street and the west side of Royal Street. The reason for his haste was a potential audience with President Andrew Jackson, which awaited him in Washington, D.C., if only he could get there in time before his fast-approaching return date to France. On his traverse through the Old South by stagecoach from New Orleans, the Frenchman journeyed northeast, making tracks through Mobile and Montgomery in Alabama; Augusta, Georgia; Columbia, South Carolina; Fayetteville, North Carolina; and Norfolk, Virginia. From there he caught a boat up the Chesapeake to the nation's capital.

My travel plan, by contrast, is to linger, to focus my main investigation in just two of the southern cities Tocqueville visited—Mobile and Montgomery. On rational grounds, Alabama seems a good, average southern state to choose, less conservative than Mississippi and South Carolina (who, until recently, flew the Confederate flag above their state capitol), and less moderate than, say, Georgia and North Carolina. Alabama also has a history that straddles both sides of the political divide. It is where the Confederacy was born, but it is also where the national civil rights movement began with the Montgomery bus boycott in 1955, and where Martin Luther King Jr., then a local preacher, led the famous march from Selma to Montgomery in 1965.

But partly I choose to linger in Alabama for no good reason other than that I have always imagined it to be the epicenter of the South. Perhaps it's simply the allure of the name—Alabama—the way it rolls off your tongue. The structure of the word itself is so unusual—begins with an *a,* ends with an *a,* every second letter an *a*—and there is something freewheelin' about it, light and loose, evoking long, slow cotton-pickin' days and the easygoing,

hospitable lifestyle of a region. And yet tucked inside the word—
bam—is a hardness. The South is the place where racism was at its
most virulent, where human beings were treated as commodities
to be bought and sold, where segregation was institutionalized;
where lynchings were savored.

The South, and with it Alabama, has borne witness to the worst
human rights abuses on American soil. It is the perfect place to
explore the conscience of the nation.

The question arises: Is the church in America part of the problem,
or is it part of the solution? I specify "the church" only because
America is overwhelmingly (85 percent) a Christian nation, with
only 3 percent Jewish, 2 percent Muslim, 1 percent Hindu, and 7
percent with no religious affiliation, though the question may be
asked of all these religions.[24]

Perhaps the place to begin is by acknowledging that there is no
single monolithic church in America, and by briefly delineating the
religious pie chart of the nation.

America is majority Protestant (58 percent), comprising more
than 900 denominations, the largest and most significant of which
are the Baptists (19 percent), Methodists (11 percent), Lutherans (7
percent), Presbyterians (5 percent), Episcopalians (2 percent), Pen-
tecostalists (3 percent), and Church of Christ (2 percent). These
denominations, in turn, are split, often due to historically divisive
issues such as slavery and segregation, or simply along racial or
ideological lines. The largest single Christian body, however, is the
Roman Catholic Church, which accounts for more than a quarter
(28 percent) of Americans. As a region, the South tends to be more
Protestant (71 percent) and less Catholic (15 percent) than the
country, and of the Protestants, the Southern Baptist, Methodist,
and Church of Christ denominations account for more than half of
affiliated Protestants between them. The African-American population is mainly Protestant and pray mostly in separate churches.

Tocqueville prefaced his commentary on religion with a declaration: "I questioned the faithful of all communions; I particularly

sought the society of clergymen, who are the depositories of the various creeds and have a personal interest in their survival."[25]

Taking a leaf out of Tocqueville's book, I too set about meeting pastors and leaders from different denominations. On the basis of what they preach (their words), and what they do (their actions), I seek to understand their deeper philosophy about the causes of, and solutions to, poverty and inequality in America.

Two or three sharply different approaches to the social contract, or social gospel, become apparent. And emerging from them are wildly at-odds interpretations of the very meaning of the word "compassion." First there is the black church in America, whose mission has historically been a dual one, combining a deep well of spirituality with an enormously resourceful social activism. Second, there is the conservative white, Protestant approach; and third, the Roman Catholic and progressive white Protestant approach. What is offered below is not meant to be comprehensive, but rather a fragment, a taste if you like, of how these "broad churches" underpin life, attitudes, and politics in America.

THE MEN FROM THE MINISTRY

Wherever I go in Mobile, the name Clinton Johnson is mentioned, and the opinion offered is seldom neutral.

"Johnson! The man is power-crazy," says Rabbi Steven Silberman, leader of the conservative Jewish synagogue in Mobile. "Johnson claims that blacks have been kept out of power for too long. Many of us agree with his sentiments, but his manner is too hostile. He doesn't endear himself to the white middle classes."

"Johnson is doing a fine job," insists Sister Judith Vander Grinten, director of Mobile's Catholic Social Services. "Mobile used to be run by an elitist old-boy's club—Old Mobile, we called it—and was known for its corrupt white leaders, who had usually been in jail at one time or another. Johnson and his colleagues on the city council are changing that."

Clinton Johnson is a pastor and a politician. He occupies an office on the ninth floor of the Government Plaza Building in downtown Mobile, with sketches of Martin Luther King Jr. on the wall and a sweeping view of the Mobile shipyard. As president of the Mobile City Council, he holds the highest elected office in the city after the mayor. He is also pastor at the Shiloh Missionary Baptist Church, one of the largest African-American churches in the region. His church, which has 850 members, is affiliated with the National Baptist Convention USA, which has 8.2 million members (almost entirely African-American), making it the fourth-largest Christian grouping in America, after the Roman Catholic Church, the Southern Baptist Convention (almost entirely white), and the United Methodist Church.

On the day I meet him, Clinton Johnson, age fifty-two, is dressed in a tailored navy-blue suit, a gold watch adorning his wrist, his fingers festooned with signet rings inlaid with diamonds. His opening gambit is to lean back in his chair and lay his shiny leather shoes up on his desk directly in front of my face. *Clunk. Clunk.*

"See the soles of these shoes," he implores me.

I look a little nonplussed.

"You look at me and you see a man who appears well off, even rich," he says. "But what you can't see is this. I still remember what it feels like to wear shoes where the sole is completely worn through and you have to stuff the bottoms with cardboard. I used to joke that mine were *patent* leathers because the soles of my feet were *pattin'* the ground as I walked. Patent . . . pattin' . . . get it?"

I laugh, thinking this a novel way to kick off an interview, very "feet first" and quite arresting, particularly considering his elevated position in the clergy. As a pastor and a politician (though these days more of a politician), Johnson is perfectly placed to comment on the political and social role that the church has played in Mobile, so I ask him to elaborate. I settle back expecting a punchy, sharp social analysis, but the story he recounts is surprisingly personal. The influence of the black church is so central to who he has become and the role that he plays in the world that he cannot tell me the story of the church without also telling me the story of his life. The black church was *in* his mother and *in* his pastor—

the two most formative influences in his life—and now it is *in* him too.

Johnson was born in Mobile in 1947, the youngest of seven children, at a time when blacks sat at the back of the bus and drank from separate water fountains. His mother was a domestic worker in a white household, his father a longshoreman with a penchant for indulging in drink a little stronger than Kool-Aid and whose job it was to unload the ships on the Mobile docks. Neither had more than a sixth-grade education. They lived, nine of them, in a two-bedroom dwelling that was more an alley than a house. "There were many days we did not eat, many days we did not have ten cents to ride the bus to school, or a quarter for lunch," he recalls.

The one thing they did have was their faith. Their mother would wake them every morning at five to pray as a family, and every Sunday they went to church. Among the first things he experienced as a young black boy, aside from material deprivation, were the psychological limitations imposed on him because of his skin color. "My mother realized how destructive this could be to a child's sense of self-worth, and she used faith to counter it. She taught us that our true value in life is not determined by what others think of us, but what we think of ourselves," he says.

Yet Johnson's mother, Clara, was also a strict disciplinarian. "If there had been a consciousness of child abuse when I was growing up," he says, "Mother would have got ninety-nine years plus two life sentences. Yes! She beat me up! Yes! She had me held down by my two older brothers, who stripped me naked while she whipped me across my back, my bottom, my legs. As she spanked me, she would say: 'I love you, but I'm doing this for your betterment, to keep you out of jail.' I will tell you this, though; I never got whipped for the same thing twice. I remember getting spanked once because I had not said good morning to our elderly neighbor, Mrs. Davis, when she greeted me as I left for school one morning. It made no difference that I had not heard Mrs. Davis greet me. Mother spanked me black and blue. 'Respect your elders,' she scolded. Well, from that day on, whenever I left the house, I would shout at the top of my lungs: 'Good morning, Mrs. Davis! Good morning, Mrs. Davis, wherever you are!' "

Nevertheless, Johnson says that theirs was a happy home. "At the end of the day, my mother had a big, compassionate heart and she taught us to help others. She used to tell us: 'Big G plus little *s* equals big S—God plus little self equals big success. It's the faith that I learned from my mother, and in church, that empowered me to make a difference in society today."

"In what way did your church empower you to make a difference?" I ask.

"The black church has played a unique role in this country," he continues, leaning in like the preacher he is, with barely a pause for breath. "It is the only institution we blacks had control over. It was our community, our entertainment, our social club, our educational forum, our place to gain respect and dignity for our worth as a person. And the pastor . . . he was our counselor, our career advisor, our preacher, our everything. We had a great euphoric view of what a pastor could do. There was no more respected person. He and the church, they gave us our hope and our platform for everything we have achieved . . ."

Johnson is in mid-flow when he catches sight of a colleague sweeping past his open door. "Hey, Fred!" he calls, interrupting himself. "Hey, Fred, come in here a minute. We're talking about your favorite subject!"

Fredrick Douglas Richardson Jr., age sixty, bearded, burly and with the gait of an aging grizzly bear, flops down into the chair beside me. Like Johnson, he is a city councilman, an African-American, and a church man—deacon of the Stone Street Baptist Church, a church that he claims is the oldest surviving Baptist church in Alabama and one of the five oldest African-American Baptist churches in the nation.

"I *luvvvved* church!" he says expansively. "My grandmother would read me the Scriptures every night before bed, and that stirred in me an intense interest in spirituality." But church also served a social function, he recalls. "It was where my community gathered, where my friends were."

Richardson, it turns out, is also a black-church historian. He has written a play, which was performed in Birmingham, Alabama, about the birth of the Stone Street Baptist Church in 1806.[26] And he has authored a book about the rise of the civil rights movement in Mobile, viewed from within.[27] Wrapped up in these social histories, as he tells it, is the fascinating story of his own life, descendant of a slave.

During slavery, he begins, most blacks attended the white church, where they were relegated to the rear or to the balconies. Some free people of color had started their own churches, however, and slave blacks began to attend, but they could only join the black church if they had permission in writing from their white masters. The black church decided to institute what they called "Wednesday-night prayer meetings," which was partially a cover— a nonthreatening way of organizing, and of discussing their pressing social problems, without attracting white censure. After the abolition of slavery, the black church was deluged with new members, and the church was used as a place to map out strategies. Here was a moment in history that was pregnant with possibilities. There was a debate as to how aggressively blacks should pursue their newly won liberty, whether to take the high road and go for broke, or the low road and proceed cautiously. The problem was, they had neither money nor property to sustain themselves, and no weapons to defend themselves. "They were free, but vulnerable in a thousand different ways, so they took the low road," he says. "Many of them returned to work for the same plantation owner they had worked for as a slave. They went from slaves to sharecroppers. They took the low road so that their offspring could take the high road."

But a number of freed slaves, including his own ancestors, opted for a bolder path, he says. In the brief window of time between the abolition of slavery and the subsequent assassination of Abraham Lincoln, blacks were allowed to claim forty acres of farmland as their own, as long as they cleared it. Richardson's great-great-grandparents labored day and night to clear their forty acres and claim it as their own. Their actions meant that Richardson would grow up in a remote farm village, called Nymph, approximately one hundred miles to the northeast of Mobile, halfway between Mobile and Montgomery. By the time Richardson was born, the fifth of twelve children, the farm had been passed down to his grandmother and was down to ten acres, the other thirty having been sold off. Nymph had become a close-knit community of about seventy-five people, with its own little school, church, and brewery, the latter run by his father. The only time that the young Fred Richardson came into contact with whites was when they came to buy the moonshine that his father made. Nymph was a poor but self-sufficient community that was entirely African-American.

He describes the life he led and why the church occupies a special place in his affections. "Our day began with school in a building that had two rooms, and a curtain that served as a partition to make a third room. In those three tiny classrooms, they taught first to ninth grade. Each of those three teachers," he laughs, "taught three grades all at the same time. At three P.M., every kid would pile out of school and that's when our day's work would really begin. Mine started with a half-mile walk to the spring to fetch pails of water for my mother to cook with. After that I had to gather wood for the fire, cut the wood into pieces small enough to fit inside the stove, and then I had to 'feed up'—give the hogs, cows, mules, and chickens their daily meal. After that, I milked the cows and churned the milk until it made butter. By that time, it was good and dark, and I still had homework to finish. During the cotton-pickin' season, we'd go into the fields evenin' time as well. For six days of the week, it was hard labor. But Sundays . . . Sundays we had church. Sundays, we were free. In my mind, Sunday was the best day of the week. Going to church was a reprieve, a respite from work."

Yet Richardson also grew up to love the religious side, and as he matured, he began to realize that his church was preparing him to step into the outside world with confidence. "It gave us opportunities to perform acts of oratory in public, and it developed our minds by making us memorize the Scriptures," he recalls. "It taught me to overcome my fear of speaking before an audience. I learned it at church—I learned to stand up and say what was on my mind."

But the outside world that Fred Richardson and Clinton Johnson emerged into when they began to make their way in society was not ready to hear what was on the mind of a young black man. It was a society that still had separate water fountains, still had blacks confined to unskilled, low-ranking jobs, still had blacks stuck at the back of the bus. Richardson followed his sister to the port city of Mobile where he took a job as a mail carrier with the Mobile Post Office by day and tried to further his education by night. But despite the civil rights movement being well under way, there wasn't a single local college that would admit blacks. Johnson had to leave Mobile to pursue his education, journeying to Huntsville, Alabama, where he got the first of his three degrees (this one in sociology). Richardson would have to wait until 1974 before taking his bachelor's degree in political science at the University of South Alabama.

Richardson responded to the state of the world around him by becoming a political activist, a role that was rooted in his religious values, he says. "The civil rights movement had pretty much bypassed Mobile," he recalls. "Even after the assassination of Martin Luther King Jr. in 1968, the Mobilians wouldn't budge—the schools were still segregated, as were the restrooms." Richardson and four others began a group called Neighborhood Organized Workers (NOW), which met every Wednesday evening at the local black Catholic church, where they organized mass protest meetings. They marched, picketed, demonstrated, got arrested. "The black churches were at the forefront of this struggle, but the white churches, aside from Catholics and a few Jews who were our attorneys, were totally silent," he says. From 1968 to 1974, Mobile wouldn't shift. Then they hit on the idea of a boycott of white-owned shops. Operation Ghost Town, they called it, and as whites felt the pain, they started to take black demands more seriously.

Yet even then, civil rights came slowly to Mobile. So slowly, in fact, that by the mid-1980s there were still no African-Americans in the city government, despite blacks comprising 35 percent of the city's population. The turning point came in 1985, when a successful judicial challenge to the voting system—*Bolden* vs. *City of Mobile*—resulted in city hall being forced to change the way it held elections from an "at large" system to a district system. In the former system, the whole city was treated as a single voting district, so that the candidates with the greatest "at large" support won. The whites, who formed the majority, would never vote for a black candidate, so it was an extremely effective way of shutting out the black minority. "One of Tocqueville's fears for America was that the majority would not take into consideration the wishes of the minority," says Richardson, who also quotes Tocqueville in his book. "The tyranny of the majority, he called it, and he saw it as a grave danger for America. For a long time, it proved true in Mobile—we blacks, we the minority, were completely shut out of power." It was only when the city was divided into districts, each district electing its own city councilmen, that those districts with majority black populations could elect their own African-American city councilmen.

"The turnaround for African-Americans in Mobile since 1985 is phenomenal," says Johnson. "For the first time, we have had blacks entering medium- and high-ranking jobs in the civil service, and joining the middle class. We have begun to catch up with the rest of the country. We now have, for example, two black members of the Mobile County School Board, a black president of the Mobile County Commission, a black deputy chief of police, four black state legislators (out of twelve from Mobile) in the Alabama House of Representatives, one black state senator from Mobile (out of three) in the Alabama Senate, and three black city councilmen (out of seven)—including myself and Fred Richardson—on the Mobile City Council."

The impact on the people, says Johnson, was that the African-Americans who were elected to office brought a firsthand knowledge of the needs of the poorer communities to government. "We put the needs of the have-nots on the agenda. For example, in 1985, the downtown area, which is a black district, was full of empty, derelict buildings. The previous white-controlled city hall had done nothing about it, but in the last ten years, we have spent $400 million rebuilding and revitalizing the downtown through a mixture of public and private funds. We brought essential services to communities that didn't have it before, and we took the lead in building a homeless shelter. We have practiced the politics of inclusion, of reaching out to the have-nots." Both Johnson and Richardson emphasize the dramatic empowerment of Mobile's black population, most of it, they say, in the last fifteen years.

Johnson uses the progress of his own family over three generations to put it in perspective. "My mother left school, age eleven, and spent her life cleaning white people's floors. That's the first generation. She had seven children, most of whom finished school, only two of whom went to college. That's the second generation. My wife and I, on the other hand, have two daughters, both of whom have college degrees, and we have a sixteen-year-old son, who is a straight-A student at a magnet high school. And you know what he wants to be?" Johnson throws back his head and guffaws. "A U.S. senator. A *Uuuu-Esss* sen-a-tor. Yup, says he's gonna be the first black President of the United States!" Johnson is hitting his knee in delight. "And when you consider our economic position: our combined income [his wife is a teacher with a master's degree and runs a travel agency] is $175,000 a year, and we have a 6,200-square-foot, five-bedroom home set on one acre. We've gone from bottom of the pile to upper-middle-class. In the eyes of my parents, I would be considered a millionaire."

Yet, while Johnson and Richardson both acknowledge how far they have come, neither wants to underplay the challenge that lies ahead. They estimate that 20 percent of the city's population—approximately 40,000 people—still live below the poverty line. In Mobile County, the poverty rate is even higher—one in four, almost 100,000 people—and the child poverty rate is a stubborn 26 percent.[28] "That's too much suffering in a country as wealthy as ours," says Johnson.

"What role has the black church played in addressing this suffering?" I ask.

Richardson sighs. "The black church has changed," he says. "In the civil rights era, the black church played a primary role in the protest politics of the day, and as an agent of social reform. Back then, we were all equally poor. But now we have black haves and have-nots just like we have white haves and have-nots. The gap between them is growing, and you know what? The black middle class behaves just like the white middle class. And as that has played out, as we have come out of the shack and into the suburbs, our churches shrink from the community outreach role they once played. Make no mistake, the church is still tremendously powerful. I only got elected to the council because I was known in every church in the district. But by and large, the black church today sees itself as a place to teach morality and to increase their members by evangelizing. It's a place to meet, greet, and eat and raise money so that they can continue to meet, greet, and eat. It's a self-perpetuating cycle.

"And yet"—he brightens—"it might be that the church doesn't know how it can help now that the terms of engagement have changed, now that we are *in* the government, now that bald protest politics is no longer appropriate. I believe that the church's new role should be as advocates of the have-nots. It's not their job to replace government, but they can identify the needs of their constituents and hold the government responsible."

As it happens, Johnson is that very evening running a seminar at a nearby church teaching the local people how to petition city government. "In my judgment," he says, flying out the door, "the contemporary black church has withdrawn from its social role. A few individual pastors still try, but they are a minority, and collectively they've not taken a stand. It's ironic, but as we progress economically, the same church that gave us our compassion for our fellow humanity, our faith, and our platform for everything we have achieved, that same church moves further and yet further away from its commitment to the people and from—" he pauses— "from God."

Is the analysis of Johnson and Richardson unique to contemporary Mobile? Or does it speak to a broader trend of detachment in the black church?

Andrew Billingsley, a professor of African-American studies at the University of South Carolina, surveyed a thousand Protestant black churches across the country in the late 1990s, trying to assess this very question. His book *Mighty Like a River: The Black Church and Social Reform* (1999) tells the extraordinary story of how black churches have helped shape American society and delineates the current state of their commitment. From its earliest beginnings in the 1770s, the black church has had a dual mission, both a religious and a social one, he writes. "Throughout the history of the African

American people, there has been no stronger resource for over-coming adversity than the black church. From its role in . . . help-ing ex-slaves after the Civil War, and from playing major roles in the Civil Rights Movement to offering community outreach pro-grams in American cities today, black churches have been the focal point of social change in their communities."[29]

Billingsley tells me, when I speak to him over the telephone, that according to his survey, there has been a decline in the social role of black churches since the 1960s, but that the decline may not be as widespread as generally feared. Billingsley notes first that the nature of activism has changed. "During slavery, activism could be characterized as subversive. During the civil rights era, it was about protest and confrontation with forces *external* to the black community. Today, it is more subtle, addressing problems *internal* to the black community. It is less about open protest and more about community development, social service programs, and eco-nomic empowerment."

With this shift in mind, the survey shows, he says, that one-third of black churches are still socially activist (creating community outreach programs, such as homeless and health services, reaching out to society beyond their own congregation). Another third offer a traditional charity model (limited to food and clothing collections for the poor at Thanksgiving and Christmas). And a final third are entirely spiritually focused and operate no community outreach programs at all. He divides them into three categories: activist, moderately active, and conservative. The churches that are most likely to be "activist" are those with a mix of working- and middle-class members, and where the minister believes there is an extreme and sustained crisis in the community.

The question is this: Does this rump of activist churches con-stitute enough of a presence to make a difference in society?

That is difficult to assess, says Billingsley, because even in the civil rights era, it was only a minority of black churches that got involved. "Reverend Andrew Young once told me a story about how when Martin Luther King visited Birmingham, it was not just the white ministers and rabbis who shunned him, but the black ministers as well. Only two black ministers met him at the airport.

Eventually the black churches joined the movement, but even at its height, there would not have been a majority involved. And yet, that minority made the difference. I can say categorically that if there had been no organized black church, there would have been no civil rights movement."

And of course, the question as to whether the diminishing yet still sizable activism of the black church in society at large amounts to a critical mass cannot be considered in a vacuum. White churches, with their greater numbers and financial muscle, are an essential part of the picture.

"So what about the white church?" I ask Billingsley.

"Aah," he says. "That is a whole other story."

OF SHEEP AND GOATS

What Jesus Said About Responsibility to the Poor
When the Son of Man comes in his glory, and all the angels with him, he will sit upon his glorious throne, and all the nations will be assembled before him. And he will separate them one from another, as a shepherd separates the sheep from the goats. He will place the sheep on his right and the goats on his left.

Then the king will say to those on his right, "Come, you who are blessed by my Father. Inherit the kingdom prepared for you from the foundation of the world. For I was hungry and you gave me food, I was thirsty and you gave me drink, a stranger and you welcomed me, naked and you clothed me, ill and you cared for me, in prison and you visited me." Then the righteous will answer him and say, "Lord, when did we see you hungry and feed you, or thirsty and give you drink? When did we see you a stranger and welcome you, or naked and clothe you? When did we see you ill or in prison, and visit you?" And the king will say to them in reply, *"Amen, I say to you, whatever you did for one of these least brothers of mine, you did for me"* [my emphasis].

Then he will say to those on his left, "Depart from me, you accursed, into the eternal fire prepared for the devil and his angels. For I was hungry and you gave me no food, I was thirsty and you gave me no drink, a stranger and you gave me no welcome, naked and you gave me no clothing, ill and in prison, and you did not care for me." Then they will answer and say, "Lord, when did we see you hungry or thirsty or a stranger or naked or ill or in prison, and not minister to your needs?" He will answer them, *"Amen, I say to you, what you did not do for one of these least ones, you did not do for me"* [my emphasis again]. And these will go off to eternal punishment, but the righteous to eternal life.

Matthew, 25

Message on the Help Line of Frazier Memorial United Methodist Church, a White Mega-church in Alabama

Our phone lines for financial assistance are now closed for this week. In order to be considered, if you call next Monday, you must show proof that you have a full-time job, your income from that job must be enough to pay your normal monthly bills, you must have proof that you have been on unpaid leave from your job because of illness or a family crisis and that you have not received financial assistance from this ministry before.

In other words, the unemployed, the homeless, the destitute, and the regular working poor need not apply.

COMPASSIONATE CONSERVATISM

It is sometimes said that the ethos of the Baptist Church encapsulates the original, freedom-loving, pioneer mentality of America. This is because each individual Baptist congregation answers only to itself. They appoint their own pastor, who may or may not be formally trained, and they hold it as an article of faith that each congregant retains the right to interpret the Scriptures for himself. The local parish church is the sovereign ecclesiastical unit, and there is no overarching hierarchy or central headquarters that has oversight.[30] In smaller Baptist churches, the pastor is quite likely to be an insurance salesman or businessman during the week and a minister on the weekend. This is the extreme opposite of the Roman Catholic Church, which is centrally controlled by the Vatican and by the American National Conference of Catholic Bishops (NCCB), and where ordained priests determine policy and interpret the Scriptures on the individual's behalf.

The Baptist Church, which grew out of the Puritan and Separatist movements, is probably the most decentralized, democratic, quintessentially American organization in the world. Yet this freedom-loving pioneer, beholden only to himself, has a flip side: he can easily become isolated, withdrawn from society, and interested in helping only himself.

Joe Bob Mizzell is the director of Christian Ethics for the Alabama Baptist State Convention and is therefore perfectly placed to help me sort, as Jesus put it, the sheep from the goats. Based in Montgomery, he represents, he says, more than one million members, which, quite incredibly, is one-quarter of the entire population of the state of Alabama. All in all, 3,180 churches are affiliated, 98 percent of them white, he says, and they in turn are affiliated to the Southern Baptist Convention, the largest Protestant denominational group in the nation, representing more than 15 million Americans.[31]

Mizzell has a cheerful, easygoing demeanor, but he is also rather busy, so I promise to be brief and to the point.

"What is the approach of your Alabama Baptist Convention to helping poor people in America?" I ask.

"We have wonderful Sunday school and evangelizing programs," he replies.

"Do you have any social programs for the poor?"

"We have not taken an official position on that," he says.

"You mean it is not on your agenda?"

"We believe that the way to help people in poverty is to convert them to Christianity. That's number one. When people become born again and choose to live a Christian life, that will help them more than anything."

"But most poor people in this country are *already* active Christians," I say.

"We believe," continues Mizzell, "that Christianity gives people morality and from that comes wealth. We're not the Salvation Army. Our number-one priority is evangelism—to reach people who are without Christ. Our other goal is to teach them the Bible."

Mizzell articulates a philosophy that I encounter among many born-again, conservative Christians, which is that poverty is a sign of personal sin and wealth a sign of God's favor. Accordingly, the way to help a person who is poor is to convert him, or if he is already converted, to bring God more centrally into his life. If you remain poor, it is most likely because you are lazy or immoral, they say.

I should not be surprised that Mizzell holds these views, but I am taken aback by how openly he expresses them. In the UK, when sentiments such as these are articulated by people in public life, they are likely to lead to a national uproar. For example, when born-again English football (soccer) coach Glen Hoddle allegedly made comments about disabled people being as they were because they had, in this or a previous life, been somehow immoral, he was roundly vilified and promptly fired. Besides, the act of offering someone a Bible when they are desperately in need of food, clothing, shelter, or other corporeal assistance (like Rhoda, for example) strikes me as a ludicrous and cruel denial of reality: a modern variation of Marie Antoinette's "Let them eat cake."

"Take me," Mizzell is saying. "Christianity took me out of poverty and into wealth. My father was a lowly high-school janitor, but I accepted Christ and I became a pastor. Right now I earn a salary in the region of $60,000."

"Are you what they call the religious right?" I butt in.

"We are not affiliated with the Christian Coalition, if that's what you mean. Our members' sensibilities range from moderate to fundamentalist, so not all of them would support the more extreme position of the coalition."

"You mean that there is a position on this that is more extreme than your own?"

"I cannot speak for them," he says. "The man you want is the president of the Christian Coalition of Alabama, a character by the name of John Giles."

I have a few hours to kill before my interview with John Giles, so I return to my hotel room for a midday tour of the Electronic Church. I had been told about the televangelism rampant throughout the South, made famous by preachers such as Billy Graham and opportunists like husband-and-wife team Jim and Tammy Faye Bakker, but no amount of forewarning prepares me for the footage that I witness. Cable Christianity, from what I can make out, comes in one of three double-barreled flavors: evangelical fund-raising; faith-healing fund-raising; and undiluted fund-raising fund-raising.

On Channel 10, a middle-aged dyed-blond woman with glossy lipstick, heavy mascara, and the kind of taut facial muscles that scream "Facelift!" sits alongside an older male preacher, and together they read from a pile of letters that they claim have been mailed in by viewers. Paul and Jann are their names, and as they read, tears roll down Jann's cheeks smudging her thick base. " 'Dear Paul and Jann,' " she begins. " 'My name is Mercedes. I'm sending you two dollars because that's all I have. I wish I could send more, but that's all I have.' " She's only nine years old, Jann tells us, her voice quivering. The letter also says, she continues (and here comes the evangelism part), " 'Please pray for my grandparents, for they are Hindu, and believe in false gods.' " Then she gives over another letter from someone who claims to be "eighty-seven years young" and who is "Jewish like Jesus." The camera zeroes in for a close-up. Jann is sniffing now, her voice barely audible above her sobs. "This woman says . . . this woman says . . . we are saving the world for Jesus!"

The fun is only just beginning. On Channel 32, there is the curious sight of a large, double-chinned nun, dressed in full habit, selling religious items. This, it appears, is the pious version of that soporific medium known as the shopping channel. "This Florentine mosaic cross," she says, wheezing, "is imported from Italy . . . just twenty-four dollars." Her presentation skills are unconventional to say the least. She speaks like a stern schoolteacher, spends most of her time looking at her feet instead of the viewer, trails off in mid-sentence; and then, just as you think she might have dropped off to sleep, she rises from her reverie and pulls out the next piece of merchandise. "Now I want to tell you about a fabulous book . . ."

Her name, I discover, is Mother Angelica, of the Catholic order of Poor Clares, and she has her own cable TV station, called Eternal Word Television Network (EWTN), which she runs out of Birmingham, Alabama. "She disturbs and irritates a lot of us," one Alabama Catholic pastor later tells me. "The money she raises goes straight to her TV network. Many of us ask: what is this woman who is vowed to poverty doing selling religious goods for profit on TV? She has, I believe, upset her Catholic diocese of Birmingham, and basically she now answers to no one. But she operates in a gray area, and the bishops face a real quandary as to how to keep her in line."

What Mother Angelica offers, though, is a bargain compared to the deal on Channel 18. There a preacher in a suit tells us about "the law of reciprocity." "Giving money to the church is giving money to God," he says. The church he has in mind is, of course, his own, but this time you get no Italian-imported Florentine mosaic cross for your dollars in return.

But the most bizarre of all are the so-called faith healers. A middle-aged man accompanied by a younger, dyed-blond woman (again the male-female double act) extends his hands and, voice building to a crescendo, booms out repeatedly: "In the name of Jeeeezuzz, heeeeeeaaal them now! In the name of Jeeeezuzz, heeeeeeaaal them now!" All the while, a telephone number is displayed for viewers to call in their donations.

At some point during my journey through the South, I watch a fascinating investigative documentary about how faith healers cheat. *Unmasked: Exposing the Secrets of Deception,*[32] it is called, and the narrator begins by saying: "If you've ever wondered how these religious con men are able to talk directly with God, you'll want to pay close attention to the deception of Reverend Peter Popoff. For years, Popoff drew thousands of followers to his televised crusades with one simple promise: by speaking to God, he could identify their afflictions and heal them with the power of his touch."

We see Popoff working a packed auditorium, organ music rising in intensity, his voice building to fever pitch. "Is that—pause—"John?" he asks a man who has stood up, apparently anonymously, from out of the audience.

The man nods in amazement. Popoff appears to have divined his name.

Popoff now places his hand flat on his own forehead and appears to enter into a mini–spiritual trance. "Is it 3784 Wood Row?" he shouts.

The man nods in amazement. Popoff has divined his address too!

"God is burning those blood clots out of his veins, out of his arteries, right now," he yells at the audience. "You want God to open up your ears too. Get those hearing aids out!"

John stands awestruck. Popoff has even divined his medical ailments.

"Oh glory, here it comes in the name of . . . Get! There it is! When the Lord speaks to me, and the true word of knowledge comes forth, I'll put my life and my reputation on the line, because I know God's voice. Halle-luyah! In the name of Jeeesuz, whoooaa, in the name of Jeeesuz, whoooa, hal-le-lu-yah . . . there it is!"

How does he do it?

Popoff's "voice of God," the footage shows, turns out to be none other than the voice of his wife, who, through the use of a radio transmitter and a wireless receiver that fits snugly inside his ear, is feeding him the key details about his unsuspecting followers from backstage. Her information is based on prayer cards the audience filled out while waiting to get in. According to the documentary, despite his being exposed, viewers continue to tune in and he is "still fleecing the masses in the name of the Lord."

There are times when, as I travel through the South, I feel as if I am on another planet. The sheer gullibility, the desire of some people to believe anything in order to connect to something deeper in their lives—it makes you wonder how those good old-fashioned East Coast qualities of cynicism and irony got so deeply lost in the migration. And yet, one has to acknowledge that the potential for profiteering prophets was there from the start. Instead of religion acting as a restraint, a gentle brake on materialism, as Tocqueville observed, there was always the danger that some might use their religion to reap dishonest dollars, perverting rather than balancing the dominant materialistic drive of American culture.

John Giles of the Christian Coalition has an office located in the overlapping shadows of church and state in downtown Montgomery. Around the corner is Martin Luther King Jr.'s historic pulpit at the Dexter Avenue King Memorial Baptist Church. And up the road are the steps of the gleaming, white-domed State Capitol. It was on those very steps where, after the famous march from Selma, on March 25, 1965, King delivered his memorable speech to America:

> Our feet are tired, but our souls rested . . . We are on the move now . . . Let us march on segregated housing. Let us march on segregated schools. Let us march on poverty. Let us march on ballot boxes . . . How long will it take? Not long . . . Because the arm of the moral universe is long but it bends towards justice. How long? Not long. Because mine eyes have seen the glory of the coming of the Lord.

And it was on the portico of the same State Capitol that Jefferson Davis was inaugurated as the president of the Confederacy in February 1861, and where for the first four months of the Civil War, the renegade government was based.

With all the shops having long since departed to the strip malls on the eastern bypass, Montgomery's city center is as deserted as a museum on a Monday. Yet Tocqueville would have been impressed. Both battles to which these two buildings hold testimony— the Civil War and the civil rights movement—ended in victory for forces that rolled forward the frontier of social justice in America. Tocqueville would have thought his theory that "the gradual progress of equality is something fated" was on track well into the 1960s.

Giles is on the telephone. "Just doin' a little fund-raisin', be out in a min," he winks. I take in the framed copy of the Ten Commandments on his wall, and a picture of Fob James, the former Republican governor of Alabama, whom Giles once worked for.

"Shalom! Shalom! How you doing, guy?" he says to me, warmly pumping my hand. Giles has just returned from a trip to Israel, where he learned, he says, about the "priestly significance" of the name Cohen within the Old Testament, especially "the key role assigned to the Cohens when the Messiah comes . . . You'll look out for me, then, won't you?" he says jokingly, his humor gently couched in a tone of respect.

"Now," he says, "who was that French fellow you are following?"

Giles, forty-five, has blond hair, blue eyes, and forearms shaped like chicken polkas. He sits me down and, in short takes, tells me the story of his life so far, and how he moved from voting for Jimmy Carter in 1976 to heading up the Christian Coalition in Alabama seventeen years later.

Giles grew up in Montgomery in the kind of family, he says, where they went to church every Sunday, prayed before every meal, and were taught to be people of integrity. In high school he rebelled, "got into drinking and sampling the pleasures of the world," though when he married, at eighteen, he was still a virgin, so his dalliances went only so far. Giles intended to go to college, but his father's business, Giles Enterprises, was growing so rapidly that he joined him instead. His father supplied fast-food outlets with food-serving equipment, such as fried-chicken cookers. Giles stayed until he was thirty-three, at which point he had a falling out with his brother and left.

He got into politics in 1976 when a program on TV alerted him to the fact that abortions were going on "right here in Montgomery." "There was a man running for president that year with a fresh smile who said he was born-again, so I voted for him," Giles recalls sheepishly. "I was so naive. I didn't realize that Jimmy Carter was not a conservative."

In 1979, Giles's neighbor, the county chairman for the Republicans, poked his head over the fence and asked Giles to help get Ronald Reagan elected. Reagan's "pro-life" position appealed to

Giles, and so he went door to door and "helped carry the county for Reagan." Six years later, after Giles had moved house, he got a call from the former neighbor, who was now working to elect Guy Hunt, a Republican and a Baptist minister, to governor. "He thinks like we do," the former neighbor told Giles. Giles helped get Hunt elected, then accepted a job in his cabinet. Four years later, in 1993, Hunt was convicted of a felony, says Giles, and kicked out of office. First Carter, then Hunt—his judgment still needed a little fine-tuning.

By now, the Christian Coalition had been launched. Rev. Pat Robertson had run for president in 1988 and, after losing in the Republican primaries to George Bush, had formed the Christian Coalition, building a nationwide TV network and claiming a membership of two million. In 1997, Giles got the call to head up the Christian Coalition in Alabama. His job was to establish coalition chapters and to print up voting guides—hundreds of thousands of them—for distribution to churches throughout Alabama.

Giles was not to know, but he joined the coalition at precisely the time its fortunes went into decline.

In the early 1990s, the Christian Coalition had led the charge of the religious right in national politics, seeking to combine a fundamentalist vision of religion with a conservative social agenda. Their influence peaked in 1994, when they played a significant role in the elections that saddled President Clinton with a hostile Republican Congress for the remainder of his term, and which heralded the rise of Newt Gingrich and his "Contract for America." Five years later, however, the coalition was in disarray. Some of its most experienced leaders had defected and it was $2.5 million in debt. The disaffected leaders admitted, moreover, that the coalition had distorted the size of its support base by "keeping thousands of names of dead people . . . on its list of supporters." The *New York Times* reported that in tours of coalition headquarters conducted for journalists, "a roving group of employees leapfrogged ahead of reporters to fill empty offices and telephones."[33]

The short-lived rise of the coalition would appear to prove Tocqueville right—that the secret to the enduring power of religion is to keep church and state separate. The coalition flouted this canon—and so their fortunes "fall together with the passions of a day."

Nevertheless, the Christian Coalition still wields tremendous influence through its voter guides, particularly since the number of born-again or evangelical Christians shows little sign of declining. According to a 1998 Gallup poll, 44 percent of Americans describe themselves as born again/evangelical, up from 36 percent in 1992. And in the South, where their presence climbs to 56 percent, they really do comprise a "moral majority."[34]

Giles claims that despite their woes (which he acknowledges, especially as he is yet to draw a full salary), the coalition is ranked as the seventh-most-powerful lobby group in the nation, and the fourth in Alabama, after the farmers, the National Rifle Association, and the teachers.

Giles, who is now loudly sucking a sweet, shows me the questionnaire that they send to political candidates, whose answers form the basis of the voter guides. The questions are all about the candidate's response to a litany of moral issues, such as abortion, gun control, school prayer, school vouchers, taxes, homosexual rights, affirmative action programs, capital punishment, and legalized gambling. There are fifty-three questions in all. Not one of them addresses issues germane to the poor or the working poor—such as raising the minimum wage, or expanding the Earned Income Tax Credit.

"Why are the poor not worth a question on your list?" I ask.

"Well, you can't list everything," he says.

"You mean it's not one of your top fifty-three priorities."

"I suppose you could say that. But biblically speaking, it really is the responsibility of the church to take care of the poor, not the government. As the Old Testament makes clear—people should tithe and one of the beneficiaries are to be the poor."

Giles is getting into his stride. "If every church in America adopted one poor family, we could close up our Health and Human Services Department tomorrow. It's a fact."

"You sure about that, John?"

"Absolutely," he says with a flourish.

"Why don't we do the math?"

"It might be two or three families per church—I may be a little off." He backtracks slightly.

"Let's try it for Alabama," I say, reaching for his calculator. "Okay, Alabama has a population of 4.3 million and a poverty rate of 15.1 percent . . ." I punch in the numbers. "That's 650,000 people living in poverty. Okay, now say we assume an average family size of four. That works out to 162,500 poverty households to be taken on by . . . let's see . . . 8,000 churches in Alabama . . . That's roughly 20 families per church, John."

"Aw," he says, looking glum. He removes his glasses, rubs his eyes. "I was sure that someone had done the research on that. You know, this is not just my idea, it's George W. Bush's idea too, and lots and lots of people who think it's a step in the right direction."

I point at the calculator.

"So the math . . . the math ain't right, huh," he says.

Nevertheless, Giles's "idea" is worth pondering for two reasons. It is, as he claims, the new, new thing. And, nobody has dared to expose, for fear perhaps of alienating large swaths of Christians, its essential hypocrisy.

Giles's proposal that the church, rather than the government, should assume more responsibility for helping the poor has been vigorously promoted by George W. Bush, who regards it as a cornerstone of his "Compassionate Conservatism," and, in a different way by Al Gore. Whereas Gore called for a collaboration between government and faith-based groups in helping the poor, without giving much detail on how his plan would work, Bush has gone much further, threatening to substantially redefine the role of the church and the government in the process. In Indianapolis on July 22, 1999, in the first major policy speech of his presidential campaign, Bush said: "In every instance where my administration sees a responsibility to help people, we will look first to faith-based organizations . . . We will make a determined attack on need, by promoting the compassionate acts of others. We will rally the armies of compassion to fight a very different war against poverty . . .

This will not be the failed compassion of towering, distant bureaucracies . . . We will take this path because private and religious groups are effective, because they have clear advantages over government."[35] Bush says he wants the federal government to provide tax incentives and funds to churches to help the needy, and for the government to then be able to step back from its present role of helping poor people directly.

Bush's idea comes straight out of the religious right and was made popular by Marvin Olasky, whose best-selling 1992 book, *The Tragedy of American Compassion,* comes "recommended by Newt Gingrich." Olasky is a professor at the University of Texas at Austin and is the editor of *World,* a weekly Christian newsmagazine. His argument, in a nutshell, is that prior to Roosevelt's New Deal, the church and charities were the prime organizations that helped the poor, and that they did so effectively, with compassion and without creating dependence. He even quotes Tocqueville, noting the French observer's amazement at the strength of "compassion [among Americans] for the sufferings of one another."[36] The tragedy of American compassion, he says, is that governmental handouts hurt the very people they are trying to help, because they created dependency. Furthermore, the government is an impersonal bureaucracy unsuited to helping the poor, he says. But just because government cannot do the job, it does not mean that nobody should. We should revert to the faith-based charitable models of 1900, he suggests, which means the dismantling of the modern welfare state and the use of churches to provide "moral uplift" and a hand up rather than a handout.

The social commentators and clergymen to whom I speak— while challenging Olasky's version of history (even when the church was helping the poor, it was not the major benefactor, they say)— tend to view Bush's ideas with trepidation. They fear that a higher profile for the church will lead to the government abdicating its responsibility to the poor. They worry that if the church becomes an agent for government, the separation between church and state will be compromised. And they are concerned that money given to churches to help the poor will be spent on evangelism instead. On the other hand, they are aware of the deep grass-roots connection of faith-based organizations to communities, and think that, if managed responsibly, the idea could promote the common good.

There is, however, one fatal flaw to the compassionate-conservative plan: the very churches that conservatives like John Giles insist are best placed to help the poor are, in actual fact, not at all interested in helping the poor. Baldly, they tell you so. And I'm not just talking about Joe Bob Mizzell and his fellow Southern Baptists, either.

Later, for instance, I visit a charismatic Pentecostal Assembly of God church in Montgomery and interview their pastor, Michael Rippy. When I ask him about the Gospel According to Matthew, and what Jesus said about helping the poor, he says to me: "Jesus said lots of things. You have taken one parable; I will give you another." And he proceeds to quote me Matthew, chapter 28, "the last words" that Jesus is alleged to have spoken. "Go ye therefore, and teach all nations, baptizing them in the name of the Father, and of the Son, and of the Holy Ghost. Teaching them to observe all things whatsoever I have commanded you." The final words of a man tend to have most impact, Pastor Rippy says. "As far as I'm concerned, it's a matter of priorities. Baptize the poor first; teach them what Jesus said second."

Another line from the Scriptures that conservative pastors quote back to me is "The poor will always be with you." This means that there is no point in trying to eliminate poverty, they insist. These pastors argue that when Lyndon Johnson said he would drive out poverty, when Bill Bradley puts forward a plan to eliminate child poverty in America by the end of the next decade, and when Bill Clinton declares in his final State of the Union speech that "no child shall live in poverty"—all that shows, they insist, is that none of them knows his Bible.

It's a catch-22. The political arm of the religious right want to take government out of the picture and give money to churches to help the poor. But the religious arm of the religious right, the conservative pastors themselves, then say: We're evangelists, social outreach is not on our agenda.

Everybody has his justification for directing the responsibility elsewhere.

It makes you wonder: Whose churches exactly are the religious conservatives talking about? The churches they don't frequent, perhaps? To quote a select, maybe telling, line from Bush's Indianapolis speech: "We will make a determined attack on need by promoting the compassionate acts *of others*." So government withdraws, other people's churches are encouraged to pick up the slack, and the poor are left twisting in the wind. If this is American compassion, it is not the kind that Tocqueville talked about.

It seems that as the word "compassion" comes into vogue among some conservatives, its meaning is distorted. Conservative Christians use the word but appear to exhibit little of the "suffering together with another" that it connotes. They withdraw, instead, behind the doctrine of evangelism and fail to reach out to fellow citizens who are materially less fortunate. Poverty, they say bluntly, is a sign of personal sin. The way to help the poor—white or black or Hispanic—is to convert them. Let God help them then. After that, it's up to them to help themselves. Other conservative Christians, such as George W. Bush, who say they want government to do less and the church more, appear surprisingly deaf to the isolationist views of their fellow Christian conservatives. They appear not to have considered that the compassionate church that Olasky refers to in the humanitarian and progressive era of the early 1900s may not be the same church today.

As inequality displaces equality as the dominating element of American society, perhaps the reason for the change of heart is not hard to fathom.

For as Tocqueville warned: "Thus the same man who is full of humanity toward his fellows when they are also his equals becomes insensible to their sorrows when there is no more equality."[37]

THE DOMAIN OF THE SHEEP

During my travels through America prior to my journey south, I encountered a story of remarkable bravery and compassion, but whose telling had not found its logical place in the narrative until this moment. It is the story of a Catholic priest, Father William Cunningham, who died in 1997, and more particularly of his faithful lieutenant, Eleanor Josaitus, a feisty, wispy-haired sixty-five-year-old woman whom I met in Detroit, Michigan.

I was told about Josaitus by Bill White, the chairman of the Flint-based Mott Foundation, whom I had interviewed for a marathon seven hours just before I hit the road for Detroit. At the end of the interview, White, sixty-one, who is a larger-than-life hippo of a man, gave me two pieces of advice: "Detroit is the same story as Flint, except on a larger scale," he said, and "Go and see Eleanor Josaitus—she has more *passion* than anyone I have ever met."

It didn't take me more than five minutes with Josaitus to realize that White was right. But she wasn't always this way, she wants you to know. She used to be an ordinary suburban housewife, married to a businessman, raising five children. On Sundays, they'd stroll down the road to mass, where they listened to a dynamic pastor—by the name of Father Cunningham—who had a tendency to sermonize on social issues; then afterward they would stroll back home and gradually forget, as one does, the inspirational words he had said. But one day in the 1960s, as she tells it, she had a revelation that changed her life.

"I was watching the Nuremberg Trials on television when they interrupted the broadcast to show coverage of the march from Selma to Montgomery," she recalled. "The police were attacking the black marchers with electrically charged cattle prods and I just started crying uncontrollably. What is the difference between Nazi Germany and what is going on in my country today? I asked myself. What would I have done if I lived in Germany? Would I have pretended I did not see the oppression?"

No sooner had Josaitus begun to educate herself about the civil rights movement when riots were upon Detroit, the worst America had seen. In the days after the riots ended, she found herself walking the streets in the burning heart of the city with Father Cunningham, with whom she had begun forging a bond. "The tanks were still there, but the whites were already leaving," she recalled. "A lot of them didn't even bother to sell. They just abandoned their businesses and houses, never to return." She held her head while she recounted this story to me, her face screwed up in anguish. "I had watched the buildup of frustration among the excluded of our society, and then, with the riots, I watched the dam wall burst. And now the result was going to be even greater separation and exclusion."

In June 1968, as the panic-stricken whites continued to flee the city of Detroit to the suburbs beyond the eight-mile perimeter, Josaitus and her husband, Donald, did the unthinkable. They sold their house in the safe suburbs and moved into the still-smoldering city, buying a home in the formerly mixed neighborhood of Sherwood Forest. Their youngest child was three, their oldest, eleven. "I wanted to raise my children in an integrated environment where they would be judged by their character, not the color of their skin, and I didn't want to preach anything that I wasn't prepared to live," she said. The response of her extended family was severe: her husband's father disowned them, removing all their photographs from his home; her husband's brother asked her to revert to her maiden name so that he wouldn't be embarrassed by association; and her mother hired an attorney to try and take her children away on the grounds that she was endangering their safety. (Her mother later dropped the lawsuit, Josaitus told me, and over time came to understand her daughter's point of view.)

Josaitus and Father Cunningham now began to dream up, and then activate, a coordinated response to the disintegrating social fabric around them. They formed a nonprofit organization which they called Focus: HOPE. Their aim, she said, was to bring the community together, black and white, rich and poor, Catholic, Protestant, Jewish, whatever their religious persuasion, and to break through the barriers that separated them and find their common humanity, their common spirituality.

First, they took fifty priests away on a retreat and brought every controversial group to speak to them, including the Black Panthers. Their aim was to expose the priests to the prevailing mood of society, and to educate them. Next, they had white priests opening their homes to blacks, and black priests to whites, in an effort to bring the separate communities together. In response to the hunger and malnutrition they saw around them, they started a food program for poor, nursing mothers. One day Josaitus got a call from a seventy-two-year-old woman who screamed down the phone: "So I have to get pregnant before you will help me!" She decided there and then to add senior citizens to their program, and Josaitus went to Washington thirty-two times to lobby for federal support. The answer was no and no and no . . . but she refused to take no for an answer and eventually she got the support needed from the Department of Agriculture. "Father Cunningham was the face of Focus: HOPE, I was the organizer behind the scenes, and together we made a dynamite duo," she said.

Today Focus: HOPE has 850 employees and 51,000 volunteers. Their food program is copied in nineteen states. But their flagship—for which they have received ringing endorsements and personal visits from Bill Gates to Bill Clinton—is their educational facility. They have built a state-of-the-art Machinist Training Institute that turns out what Josaitus calls "renaissance engineers" who learn to design on computer and are then placed with local employers like General Motors and Ford. Their Center for Advanced Technologies offers associate's and bachelor's degrees in engineering, operating in partnership with private enterprise, so that students study at night and work on the shop floor in the day to pay their way, and emerge into jobs with a starting salary of $47,000. Less spectacular, but arguably even more important, are their First Step and Fast Track programs, which take young adults with a sixth-grade education and upgrade them to ninth- and tenth-grade English and math. With that, they can either enter the workforce or elide into the Machinist Training Institute.

To watch these young students at work at their lathes, to see the block-long, state-of-the-art college rise out of the inner city, where poverty rates approach 50 percent and every tenth house is either abandoned or burnt out, is to touch hope in a city that, more than thirty years after the riots, still struggles against hopelessness.

That just one Catholic priest and one practicing Christian can achieve all this—fired with the zeal of pioneers to break through racial and class barriers and acting out of a moral commitment to the common spirituality of humankind—is something inspiring and miraculous.

And yet, as I travel through the South and make the acquaintance of Catholic and progressive Protestant clergy in Alabama, it becomes clear that the most inspiring thing about Father Cunningham's and Eleanor Josaitus's story is that it is far from unique. It is, in fact, one of many.

The Roman Catholic Church and many progressive Protestant sects—the Episcopalians (effectively the Anglican Church in America), the progressive Methodists, the Lutherans, and the Presbyterians among them—have adopted high-profile social commitments to the poor. The Catholic mandate, as set out by the National Conference of Catholic Bishops, is perhaps the most clearly articulated, and stands out in opposition to the conservative Christian approach.

The Reverend Michael Farmer, a Catholic priest and chancellor (administrator) for the Archdiocese of Mobile and Montgomery, explains the Catholic philosophy as passed down by the bishops: "We believe that poverty is the result of *structural* injustice in society, not personal sin," he says. "Poverty and inequality have to be understood in context. They arise due to a combination of factors, including discrimination against nonwhites, a regressive and unfair tax system, the powerlessness of the poor in the political arena, and the greed of the haves. These inequities are too large to be overcome by individuals themselves. They require society's intervention, both indirectly in advocating for political changes, and directly in getting our hands dirty and helping the poor ourselves."

Father Farmer acknowledges that not all Roman Catholics follow this doctrine. "There has always been a conservative element in the Catholic Church who believe that the primary focus of the church should not be social justice, but rather holy sanctification and religiosity," he says. "They are a minority, less than twenty-five percent among us, but it is true to say that they can be very visible and voluble. Within the Catholic Church, as well as within the Protestant Church, you find a continuum of attitude and behavior towards the poor. It's just that with us that continuum is more skewed towards the social justice side, whereas with the Protestants it's more skewed towards the evangelical side."

Oscar H. Lipscomb, the archbishop of Mobile, articulated the challenge to Alabama's Catholics in a pastoral letter in 1990. "While we strongly encourage efforts to provide food, shelter, and clothing to the poor, we with like emphasis encourage advocacy efforts on behalf of structural change," he wrote.[38]

The emergence of poverty as a high-profile public priority for the Catholic Church is, however, a relatively recent phenomenon. Father Christopher Viscardi, a Jesuit priest who holds the chair of theology at Springfield College, the oldest college in Alabama (founded the year before Tocqueville's visit), says that up until the 1960s, the ethos of the Catholic Church was primarily inward-looking.

"American culture had a very strong anti-Catholic bias, and so the Catholic Church became a fortress church, protecting itself against the dominant Protestant culture," he says. "It had always been part of the Catholic mission to help the poor—especially since so many Catholic immigrants were poor—but it is only in the last thirty years, starting symbolically with the election of a Catholic president, John F. Kennedy, in the sixties, that we have witnessed a new self-confidence in the Catholic Church. And with it has come the emergence of a self-conscious social agenda seriously addressing issues like economic injustice, racism, and poverty." (Tocqueville, also a Catholic, had mentioned the prejudice toward Catholics in dispatches. "In the United States, which [Protestant] sects are the most inimical to Catholicism?" he had inquired of a Catholic priest on board a steamship. "All sects join in the hatred of Catholicism," came the wry reply, "but only the Presbyterians are violent.")[39]

Ironically, the Catholic Church has deepened its commitment to social justice at a time in history when their own congregants are typically no longer have-nots, but have instead become highly educated members of the middle and upper-middle classes. As Catholics are swept into the mainstream, they have, it seems, neither forgotten their roots nor lost their social consciousness.

In my travels through Alabama, I have numerous occasions to witness Catholic compassion at work. In Mobile, for instance, although Catholics are a minority, 22 percent of the city population, they are regarded by all the faiths and sects there as the leaders in ministering to the poor. And off the beaten track in the desperately poor Alabama "black belt," so named for the rich black soil, the high proportion of African-Americans, and the poverty, Catholics are often the *only* philanthropic presence, despite the fact that they comprise less than 5 percent of the local population.

For example, at a bend in the road in a remote patch of Alabama sixty-odd miles southwest of Montgomery, there is a Catholic mission staffed by seven nuns of the order of the Sisters of Saint Joseph. To get there is to take a scenic drive through rural poverty in America. You head west on Route 10, past pine plantations and fallow cotton fields, past tiny churches with simple symmetrical structures painted white. And as you head west, turkey vultures circling lazily in the thermals overhead, you drive past the grand and not-so-grand mansions, the breeze-block homes, the mobile homes, the half-collapsed shacks, and you wonder: Who in this day and age in America could possibly live there? Then you whiz through a one-gas-station village called Pine Apple (whose main street—amusing touch, this—is Banana Street) and before you're in, you're out, and that's when you come upon the mission that used to be called the Rural Health Clinic, but these days does not even boast a name.

The no-name clinic serves the people of Wilcox County, population 13,500, of whom 70 percent are nonwhite, 45 percent live below the poverty line,[40] and many are illiterate. The ratio of physicians to the population is a pitiful four doctors per ten thousand people.[41] It is a demographic profile of deprivation that would not be unfamiliar in many parts of rural South Africa. The only local work comes from logging, which is low-density in terms of number of employees per square mile; from cotton, which is mechanized; and from the occasional fast-food store or grocery. There used to be a sewing factory, and a few paper mills, but most of them have closed down. The second-largest employer in the entire county, other than local government and schools, is a no-name fast-food hamburger outlet that hires only part-time workers and refuses to pay medical benefits.

Sister Mary Maloy, the clinic's outreach worker, tells me that the hardest hit in the county are the women in their forties and fifties, whose children have grown up, but who have no jobs and are too old for welfare and too young for Social Security. As a defense against hunger, some of them fish in the polluted local river for food, she says. The clinic is where locals come for their health checkups; but it also runs a nutrition center, a clinic for the elderly, and a preschool learning center for three- and four-year-olds whose parents lack access to bus transportation to get them to Head Start. (The children are picked up in the morning and taken home in the afternoon.)

It is only in the last few years that residents got water piped to their houses, she tells me. Previously they had to lug jugs of water from streams or wells. E. coli bacteria was a recurring problem. The clinic helped the people organize and put their case to local government at the county commissioners' meeting. "They asked and asked and asked, but got nowhere. Eventually we had 102-year-olds and 97-year-olds going to petition them.

"The water pipes finally arrived, but not all the houses were strong enough to support proper plumbing," she says. "To install a bath," she explains, "you have to have a floor strong enough to support its weight. That is simply not the case with many of the wooden shacks. The walls have separated from the floor, the floors are rotten and full of gaping holes from which you just might find a rat looking up at you."

The clinic works with other organizations, such as the University of Alabama and Alabama Arise, the main lobby group for the poor in Alabama. "There are plenty of wealthy whites who live in Pine Apple and surrounds, but they, and their churches, have nothing to do with the black population. It's like two separate worlds," she says.

The sisters who staff the clinic come from Rochester, New

York, and St. Louis, Missouri. Their work is low-profile, unheralded, unglamorous, and poorly compensated. Sister Maloy has been there for seventeen years. Why does she do it? She looks startled at the question. "There are people in this area that are destitute," she says, as if the answer were self-evident. And then she adds, matter-of-factly: "We're Christians—it's what we're about. It's very rewarding. The people tell us: 'Your clinic has changed our lives.' "

This ethos of active empathy is not just evident among the clergy. It trickles down to the lay Catholic population. For example, in a 1999 *New York Times* poll of Roman Catholics living in New York City, "helping the poor" was cited by respondents as the number-one problem that the church should address.[42] To put this extraordinary poll result in perspective, in all the dozens of Gallup polls of the population at large over the last twenty years, poverty rarely has made it into the top ten priorities, let alone to number one.[43]

This poll, and most everything else that I have observed in my journey through the South, begs the question: Where in this jigsaw of American Christianity does the true spirit of America reside?

THE SPIRIT OF AMERICA

That elusive thing that writers like to refer to as "the American character" is a manifestation of that even more elusive and evolving thing we call the American spirit. It is a spirit that, for both blacks and whites in this vast country, is still deeply Christian. While Tocqueville acknowledged the proliferating number of sects that make up the pieces of the jigsaw, and sketched out some differences between Protestants and Catholics, he described the spirit of the church as if it were a monolithic entity. To do so today would be misleading in the extreme. Today, two profoundly opposing Christian ethics—progressive and conservative—compete to be the dominant ideology. Which one is winning?

Let's follow the money. According to official records, Protestant church collections for the poor are dramatically down at the turn of the millennium, despite the strong economy. Total dollar benevolences from the church to organizations supporting the poor declined by more than $320 million between 1996 and 1998, despite the fact that total donations from congregants to the church itself soared by $5 billion. As a proportion of total congregational collections, Protestant church donations to the poor fell almost by half, from 21 percent to 12 percent. This aggregate concealed some wild variations. On one extreme, the Church of Christ (Rhoda's church) gave less than 1 percent of its church finances in benevolences, while the Southern Baptist Convention gave just 1.33 percent, whereas at the other end of the spectrum, the progressive United Methodists gave 20 percent.[44]

Only time will tell whether this is a blip or a trend. But as it stands, the fiscal bar chart looks like an expression of the conservative Christian ethic rather than the progressive one.

What about changing attitudes to the poor within the general populace? Are they hardening or softening? Gallup polls say that increasingly, Americans want to disengage from the problems of the poor. In 1998, 40 percent of Americans held the opinion that the poor themselves and their families had the greatest responsibility for helping the poor, up from 30 percent a decade earlier. Only 32 percent believed that the government should have the prime responsibility for helping the poor (down from 36 percent), and 14 percent thought the church should be the key agency (down from 19 percent).[45] Once more, the conservative isolationist ethic edges out the progressive one.

In the face of these statistics, I meet the Catholic archbishop of Mobile, Oscar H. Lipscomb, and ask him for his thoughts on the spirit of America and how he thinks it might have changed since Tocqueville's day.

"I have no illusions," he says. "The religious spirit of America takes a largely Protestant form and is primarily Calvinistic. It believes that God rewards the righteous and that if we are materially successful, that is visible evidence of God's favor. It is an individualistic and materialistic Christian ethos and it happily takes second place to economic interests. But I think that if you want to find the true spirit of America, you don't go to the churches. You go to the shopping malls and the stock market and you watch television. Those are the most pervasive elements in society today. They set the values, determine what people need, and decide what is good.

"Was it different in the time of Tocqueville? I think yes and no. Right from the beginning, nothing trumped economic drives. Maybe freedom, maybe freedom. But once freedom was obtained, the pursuit of wealth was primary. The difference between now and then is that unless you were a slave, there was ample opportunity for the have-nots to become haves. There is the story of the man who said to the servant: 'Sir, would you announce me to your betters.' 'Sir,' said the servant, 'I have no betters, and damn few equals.'

"There have always been a core group of Americans who have taken a socially progressive approach," he continues. "But they do not comprise the mainstream philosophical underpinning of the U.S." Lipscomb insists he is not being pessimistic, just realistic. "A good friend doesn't just tell you how nice you are. He tells you what is wrong. And there are a lot of things wrong with America," he says.

But the sheer demographics of the exercise—attempting to estimate the bare numbers of adherents to each side—yield room for hope. In the African-American church as well as the white church, there appears to be something like an even split between progressives and conservatives. Both groups look to win over the moderates who make up the complex middle ground.

Though Tocqueville was uncannily accurate in his subtle positioning of the influence and role of the church, what is equally clear today is that the early American experience was different. Then, for white Americans at least, the spirit of Christianity and the spirit of capitalism were in harmony. They breathed life into each other. They complimented each other. They facilitated each other. As long as equality was the creative element in society, the Protestant ethic acted mainly as a moral handbrake, correcting an excess here, nipping and tucking there, giving solace, but it traveled happily in the slipstream of capitalism.

Today the soul of America is deeply conflicted as to the causes of, and solutions to, poverty in America. Today America confronts head-on the legacy of segregation and racism in a way that it never did in the nineteenth century. Today inequality displaces equality as the norm, giving rise to opinions, feelings, and customs inimical to those experienced under equality.

Against this very different sensibility and backdrop, the church in America faces a much tougher challenge. And a choice. Either it can retreat into self-contained layers of evangelism and religiosity, distancing itself from the social gospel and leave business and government to address issues of social justice (if they so decide); or it can come out of the slipstream of capitalism to help heal the widening gap between the haves and the have-nots by actively advocating for political and social change.

Which broad "church" is winning this battle for the soul of America?

Nationwide, it seems too close to call. But here in the South, there is no doubt that the conservative perspective is dominant. To the extent that it succeeds in shifting the terms of engagement in the national political arena in Washington, D.C., to the extent that it infuses, shapes, and becomes the dominant ideology in the U.S.—that, Tocqueville would have had to admit, would be the true tragedy of American compassion.

6 CALIFORNIA

The America Tocqueville Never Knew

Oranges, almonds, olives, artichokes, pistachios, grapefruits, lemons, cherries, grapes. In neat, straight rows, as far as the eye can see, stretch orchards of almost every fruit, nut, and vegetable imaginable. Apricots, strawberries, garlic, lemons, walnuts, mushrooms, radishes, broccoli. The San Joaquin Valley—better known as the Central Valley, and sometimes called "the Salad Bowl of the Nation"—extends more than 250 miles, from Sacramento in the north to Bakersfield in the south. It is epic in its scale, munificent in its abundance, monumentally flat in its span, and strangely beautiful in its uniformity. It is also limited and slow. It must abide by seasons, wait for a combination of rain and sun to moisten and warm the ground, turn sand into fecund soil.

The silicon chip too is made out of sand: dry particles of sand called silica. But there the similarities end. The one breathes life into the slowly fattening seed of the fruit; the other is a semiconductor, the brain cells of computers, Ethernet networks, and the super-fast technological revolution.

There is sand and there is sand.

And in the time that it takes for an orange to ripen, a man could have made his fortune.

Subject: A Word, Monsieur?
From: David Cohen <dc368@columbia.edu>
To: Alexis@Tocqueville.org

Bonjour Alex! C'est Moi!

May I call you Alex? It's just that Alexis is so nineteenth-century. And monsieur can sound a little formal. I want us to be friends. And yet I hardly know where to begin. Perhaps with a good joke. I wonder, does humor travel across centuries? Let me say first, Alex, that reading your masterpiece, I can hardly believe that I am looking at this country through the eyes of a 26-year-old. Your confidence! Your prescience! Your breadth of vision! Your maturity!

But enough groveling. What, you may ask, gives me the right to think I can walk in your footsteps? I assure you, nothing. Except perhaps that I have the chutzpah to try, and what did you possess, Alex, if not chutzpah? And that like you, I am a foreigner, an outsider, and so if I have one virtue, it is that I might see the country as you did, afresh.

Convinced? Mais non? I did not think so.

Then perhaps the only reason of import is this: I read what you wrote when I was a young and impressionable college undergraduate, and I believed that America really was as you described it—a place of unparalleled equality, social mobility, and compassion toward the less fortunate. But when I got here, I found instead that this was a land of dramatic inequality, that the gap between the haves and have-nots was not narrowing, but widening, that the playing field was anything but level, and that the concerns of the poor struggled to make it onto the national agenda.

Do I have your attention?

Yes, I thought this was significant too. Especially since equality is the fulcrum on which your entire analysis of the American character turns. In your own words: "The more I studied American society, the more clearly I saw equality of conditions as the creative element from which each particular fact derived, and all my observations constantly returned to this nodal point."[1]

So curiosity got the better of me, Alex. I was tempted to find out if I was missing something, or whether you had simplified things, or whether America had fundamentally changed. You know, as they say, "shit happens" in

170 years. But what interested me the most was that the majority of Americans—from the President to the man in the street—still seemed to believe that things today were just as you described them all those years ago. They did not want to consider the possibility that someday, someone might have to do something about the millions of Americans who were being left behind. Is this what you meant by the "tyranny of the majority"?

So here I am. Writing neither to explain why I followed your route nor to lay out what I discovered along the way (see manuscript included as an attachment for all of that), but rather to explain why I have deviated from it.

In short: Why have I come here to California, the America you never knew? What do I hope to find out?

I could say simply that California has become America's most populous state and leave it at that. Its population is two and a half times that of the entire United States at the time of your visit, 33 million to 13 million,[2] and it comprises 12 percent of the country's current population. Right there, that is perhaps good enough cause for a detour, do you not agree monsieur? But that is not why I come.

I come because California occupies a unique place in the psyche of America. It is the frontier. And like you, I am interested in the power that the frontier exerts over the prejudices, habits, imagination, dominating passions, and all that comes to be called the national character. Had you lived today, you would have come to California as surely as you were lured to the wilds of Michigan and the barely populated outer reaches of the Mississippi River Valley. You recognized the pioneer mentality as a quintessential American phenomenon. And you believed, Alex, that it had a profound impact on the formation of the American character, the tendency toward equality, and the construction of the American Dream.

Yet unlike the present time, the frontier you encountered was reassuringly two-dimensional: it was all about conquering the length and breadth of the land. In 1831, the territory occupied or owned by the United States did not extend much beyond the banks of the Mississippi. Texas was still a part of Mexico, as was California, which at the time was sparsely populated by Franciscan missionaries, Mexican ranchers, Native American Indians, and a few hardy, leather-shirted beaver trappers. (The California gold rush was still eighteen years away and serious colonization had not yet begun.)[3] The United States itself was less than half the physical size it is now. You had no doubt, though, Alex, as to the temporary nature of that situation.

"The province of Texas is still under Mexican rule, but soon there will, so to say, be no more Mexicans there," you wrote. "In all the uncertainty of the future, one event at least is sure. At a period which we may call near, for we are speaking of the life of nations, the Anglo-Americans alone will cover the whole of the immense area between the polar ice and the tropics, extending from the Atlantic ocean to the Pacific coast." And so it is, that from ocean to sparkling ocean, all the land is conquered, occupied and spoken for.

But you could never in your wildest dreams, Alex, have predicted the complex form the frontier would take today. A technological revolution is underway in which the limitations imposed by time and space are all but eliminated. The whole world is becoming, how should I say, "wired," except that the word itself is already falling into obsolescence as wired technology is supplanted by wireless technology. Don't begin to ask me to explain! But what I will say is this: with a single keystroke you can reach anyone who has a cyberspace address in a second. Did you clock that? Not a month, or a week, or even a couple of days—we're talking instantaneous here, Alex! Whereas you experienced the lumbering beginnings of the Industrial Age, in which the wheels of production were of behemoth proportions, we are at the dawn of an Information Age where your entire office fits into the palm of your hand and where the working parts are either minute or invisible.

Mind-blowing, huh!

And here, right here in Silicon Valley, California, is the command center of this new revolution, this great disruption, this convolution that is, as I travel, transforming the way we communicate, do business, buy and sell, organize our lives—everything.

But let's pause a moment . . . catch our breath . . . for I would be misleading you to suggest that Silicon Valley is representative of all of California. The state's heartland is still the Central Valley, where thousands of miles of farms, employing thousands of new immigrants, feed the nation. Yes, we still have to eat. (A relief to me too.) The old geographic frontier sits alongside the new high-tech frontier in California, the old economy alongside the new, just as it does throughout America. Only here the two Americas are starkly delineated and so pathways of mobility between them can be more easily laid bare and distinguished.

I have to hand it to you though, Alex. The brilliance of your method was that you saw beyond transient details. You understood that however much the way we live changes, the passions of the people that make up a nation shift only marginally over time. The nature of the frontier may differ, I imagine you saying, but that is less important than characterizing the influence of the frontier mentality on the national character. It's the people, stupid!

Okay, okay. But that's my second piece of news. The people who populate the frontier!

In 1831, you marveled at the diversity of the immigrants who came from all of England, Ireland, Germany, Holland, and France.

Pah!

Today's immigrants to America come from more than one hundred countries and they pour in at a rate of a million a year. (That's just the legal ones.) More to the point, over 50 percent are Hispanics from Latin America, 30 percent are from Asia, and just 13 percent are from Europe.[4] Of course, within each group, there is enormous cultural and ethnic diversity. The Mexicans are as different to the Cubans as the Irish were to the Germans. But the point is—very few of today's immigrants are white. America may still be a majority "white" country—72 percent as of 1998—but on current trends, not for long.

Given, as you know, this country's less than pristine record on race, the fact that the avalanche from Latin America was unintended and unforeseen is perhaps the greatest irony of U.S. immigration policy.

Ha! Ha! Ha! Ha! Ha! Yes, I imagine it might make you want to guffaw too. But the change is all very recent, I assure you.

Permit me to explain, Alex. During the decades leading up to the 1960s, more than 80 percent of all immigrant visas had gone to people from Northern and Western Europe.[5] The legislation of the 1920s had established a quota system that aimed at keeping the "wrong" type of people from the "wrong" type of countries out. But in the civil rights cauldron of the 1960s, the quota laws were criticized as a discriminatory attempt to maintain the racial composition of America, that is, its Northern and Western European heritage. And so in 1965, Congress passed a law that abolished the national quota system and gave priority to the relatives of existing American residents. They called it family reunification. But they had no idea of the impact it would have.

Perhaps they should have read your masterpiece, monsieur. For I see on closer inspection that, even on this score, you were able to peer into the future with remarkable prescience. "One cannot doubt that the North Americans will one day be called upon to provide for the wants of the South Americans," you wrote. "Nature has placed them close together and has furnished the former with every means of knowing and appreciating the latter's needs in order to establish permanent relations and gradually gain control of that market."[6] If I may say so, monsieur, you are at times the master of erudite ambiguity. For I cannot discern whether you simply and prosaically foresaw that America, as the more advanced nation, would completely dominate the region economically, or whether your thoughts encompassed the then wild possibility that the Latinos would actually migrate and become American. Especially since, in your day, the Mexicans resisted the incursions of the Americans into their territory with vigor.

But back to my point, Alex, which is that nowhere is the browning of America more evident than in California, the prime portal of choice for new immigrants arriving in the United States. Today, whites make up just 50.5 percent of California's population, according to U.S. Census Bureau figures,[7] and first-generation immigrants comprise a quarter of the populace. Within two years, as the Hispanic population (presently 30 percent) continues to soar, due to both higher birth rates and immigration, California is destined to become a plurality, with no single racial group forming a statistical majority. Silicon Valley, which comprises the Santa Clara and San Mateo counties, has already passed this demographic milestone: in 1999 whites fell below 50 percent of the valley population, leaving no ethnic majority. Among school-aged Silicon Valley children, the trend is even more dramatic with only 39 percent white, 31 percent Hispanic, 26 percent Asian/Pacific Islander, and 4 percent African-American.[8]

By the year 2050, though probably sooner, America is predicted to look like California today. The US Census Bureau[9] projects that the national population shares will be 52 percent White, 24 percent Hispanic, 15 percent African-American, and 9 percent Asian/Pacific Islander. Politically, the implications could be profound. The Latino immigrants—who tend to be socially conservative, predominantly Catholic, poor, and as yet politically uncommitted—are the new swing voters. They already have a huge presence in the four key states—California, Texas, New York, and Florida—which, taken together, account for half of the electoral votes needed to win the presidency. Republican and Democratic strategists have begun to acknowledge that Hispanics are the new soccer moms (don't begin to ask me to explain!) and that whoever wins their support will win political power in America.[10]

So although there are those, monsieur, who still insist that California is the exemplar of everything the rest of America is not, I wonder whether it is rather the lead indicator of what America will soon be. In so many ways—demographically, politically, economically, socially—it showcases the future.

I wonder too: Does upward mobility still define the American experience? You wrote: "In America, most rich men begin by being poor."[11] Can you begin in Central Valley and end up in Silicon Valley? It would be nice to think that that little dream is still alive, monsieur.

I come then to California for a sneak preview of where America is headed. I come to travel, first to Central Valley, and then to Silicon Valley, to listen to the stories of America's newest pioneers, the immigrants, whether legally here or not. The newly arrived have an intensity of hope as well as a basis for comparison. Their heel is still fragrant with the aroma of their mother country. I want to grasp the impact of the frontier on the immigrant, and the impact of the immigrant on America. The frontier may shape the people, but here's the thing, monsieur—the people, too, may shape the frontier.

Until later, mon frère.

Click

CENTRAL VALLEY—LIFE INSIDE THE SALAD BOWL OF THE NATION

Pedro, twenty-nine, is a picker. Together with his partner, Hilaria, in her thirties, and their three children, aged nine, seven, and five, he lives in Visalia, a typical Central Valley town, where the population of 98,000 is half Latino, a quarter white, and where illegal immigrants are as thick on the ground as legal ones.

To enter Pedro's living room is to step inside the breathless frame of a still-life painting. Everything is meticulously in its place—carpet spotlessly clean, a vase of plastic red flowers, shelves adorned with a mix of kitsch and religious icons, from porcelain red swans and horses to white seraphs and angels. Biblical dioramas adorn the walls. And then you perceive the two people in the middle of this scene, sitting on two tattered sofas that face each other a few feet apart. She wears a shocking-pink top, her skin soft and dark, her eyes liquid. He is light-skinned, with a gaunt, hunted expression, and so thin it looks as if he has been flattened by a tractor. (Later I discover this is horrifyingly close to the truth.) They could be two characters out of a 1930s Walker Evans photograph. The only sound is the barely perceptible *click-click-click* of her knitting needles as she knits a sweater for her child.

I address Pedro and Hilaria—neither of whom speak much English—through an interpreter who knows them well. Pedro is responsive, but Hilaria is stubbornly silent. After listening impassively to her husband a short while, she turns toward me (it is considered respectful to let the man talk first in her culture, the interpreter later explains) and relates her story interspersed with his.

"Like most Mexicans, I came to America looking for something better," says Pedro. "My parents were pickers and I was one of eleven children. Our family made 15 pesos a day which is about $1.50. We were beyond poor. I came here in 1990, when I was nineteen, single, and fearless. There was a group of us. We waited until nightfall and then we crawled under the fence near the Tijuana border. I came with 200 pesos [$20] in my pocket, a change of clothes, my toothbrush. I even had soap. We walked for a few hours to a prearranged pickup point, where my friend's mother was waiting for us with cars to take us away. It was easy."

"I came in 1989, a year before Pedro," says Hilaria. "I was sad to leave my parents, and afraid, but I had heard that hard workers do well in America, and I have never been afraid of hard work. A few of us crossed the border where the river ran under the fence. We walked all night. I was scared we would bump into the border patrols with their dogs, and the sky was full of the noise of helicopters. The whole scene along the border is very dramatic, very frightening. Towards midnight, we saw that the helicopters, with their searchlights, were heading our way, and as they came closer, we dived under some trees beside the river. There was a terrible smell there, but we didn't dare move. When daybreak came, we saw why it smelled so bad—we had been lying next to two dead bodies. They were half rotting. I imagined they had died of starvation and exhaustion. I began to imagine that I was going to die like them."

Pedro made his way to Los Angeles, but it was difficult to find work without legal documentation. Fellow immigrants told him to try in Visalia, where many of the farmers wouldn't care if he had papers, he says, despite the fact that it is unlawful for U.S. employers to knowingly hire illegal immigrants. And so once again he found himself in the field, but now he was earning "a respectable $5 an hour" instead of $1.50 a day. Hilaria too found work, taking a job in a sewing factory, where she was hired to iron for 12 cents an item, around $4 an hour.

One day, Pedro and Hilaria happened to meet socially, hit it off, and soon thereafter Hilaria fell pregnant. They rented a small house in the northern, poorer part of Visalia and began to build their family. At first both worked, but as the family unit grew in size, Hilaria gave up her job to raise the children. Like many illegal immigrants, Pedro acquired false documents, including a Social Security number, he says, which he hoped would afford some protection and allow him to work. (At the local flea market, locals confirm, if you know the right person, you can still secretly buy false birth certificates for about $200, Social Security cards for $25, driver's licenses, and even green cards.) On the work front, Pedro put in twelve to fifteen hour daily shifts, earning about $50 a day, or $10,000 a year. His wages had initially seemed plentiful compared to Mexico. It was only later that he realized how much higher the cost of living was in America and that pickers never got a raise.

Like almost all pickers with families to support, Pedro was unable to haul his income above the poverty line, however hard he worked; and pretty soon, life on the bottom rung of American society had become an unrelenting grind. Lack of legal status, though, was to make him vulnerable in a dozen additional ways. One day, as a crackdown on illegal immigrants reached into Central Valley, Pedro and his fellow workers were rounded up in the field and deported to Mexico. "Without even letting us tell our families what had happened, they drove us across the border and dumped us there," says Pedro. "But know what? That same night, all nine of us, we turned round and walked straight back in."

He breaks into a grin. "Same damn hole in that same damn fence."

Hilaria too had a brush with the authorities. When her sister died, she traveled back for the funeral, once again crossing the border on foot. But this time she was seven months pregnant, and on her return into America, she couldn't run fast enough to elude the dogs or the helicopters. Luckily, she says, a lady from immigration took pity on her—and on her American-born children waiting for her return—and allowed her to stay.

Later it was the absence of medical insurance that threatened to sink the family. In a bizarre incident, Pedro was run over in front of his house and in full sight of his children. The car, driven by "a crazed woman," hit him at speed, then backed up and ran over him two more times. His lung burst, his liver, spleen, and testicles were crushed. Seven major organs were damaged. He needed nine operations to put him together. According to Josie Figueroa, the family's social worker at Visalia Youth Services, the "attempted murder" was a case of mistaken identity. The driver of the car had mistaken Pedro for his near-identical-looking older brother, who had followed Pedro to Visalia from Mexico and had been sleeping with the driver's mother. "There was some kind of family dispute thing, and the children had got together and decided to kill Pedro's brother," she says. Figueroa first met Pedro's family when his children were brought in for trauma counseling. At the time Pedro's life hung in the balance, they had no income and no means of paying the medical bills. Figueroa managed to convince an organization called Victims of Violent Crime to pay his medical fees and then arranged for the family to get partial welfare on the grounds that their children were born in America.

Although Pedro considers himself "extremely lucky" to be alive, and is grateful for the financial aid he receives for his children, he says that they cannot come out ahead on the welfare check of $596 a month, and that he is impatient to heal up and get back to work.

Their rent amounts to $390, which leaves a paltry $206 for everything else, he explains.

"How do you manage to live on that?" I ask.

"It's not how you live, it's the pain you feel when you do without," he says. "Yesterday was our eldest son's birthday. He asked us: 'Aren't you going to give me a party?' We had no money to even buy him a cake, let alone a present. We got in the van and drove around Visalia for a while. Then we came home. The look on his face was hard to bear. My younger children, they hear kids at school talking about their 'vacation,' and they ask me: 'Daddy, why can't we have a vacation?'"

Hilaria tilts her head ever so coyly and chuckles. "When you came from Mexico to here, Pedro, that was the last vacation you had." She pauses to savor her wry little joke. "And, we do go away," she adds, her eyes momentarily twinkling. "We go to the store down the road."

"Do you like Americans?" I ask them.

Pedro contemplates the question for a while. "I would have to say I honestly don't know," he says. "I don't know if I like them because I have never really communicated with an American."

"What do you mean?"

"To most Americans, I am basically nothing. I am basically to be walked on. Without papers, that's where you are and that's where you stay. I am not saying I am a nobody; I am a somebody, but in this country I am not worth knowing, so I am a nobody. Maybe it will be different for my children. They learn English and math. Maybe they can be a *somebody*."

"And if they do well, maybe they can make it out of here, perhaps even to Silicon Valley," I suggest, trying to insert a little optimism into the conversation.

Hilaria gives the interpreter a puzzled look. "Silicon Valley?" she asks.

"You haven't heard of Silicon Valley?" I reply, incredulous.

"No," says Hilaria.

"Have you heard of the Internet?"

"No."

"E-mail?"

"No."

"Computers?"

"I've seen one," says Hilaria.

Pedro nods. "Me too. They got one of them at the school."

Subject: Another word, monsieur . . .

From: David Cohen <dc368@columbia.edu>

To: Alexis@Tocqueville.org

. . . On the one hand, I want to bellow: "Thank God for America!" How rough life must be south of the border for people to do what they do to get here! At the same time, another voice inside me says: "This is America?" I am just four hours from San Francisco, yet I feel as if I am deep in the backwoods of a Third World country.

How is one to frame this family's experience? Is their lack of connection to mainstream society indicative of their own unique isolation? Or are they representative of a broader phenomenon? Of course, I will need to meet more immigrants to tackle these questions. But meantime, Alex, perhaps you won't mind if I use you as a sounding board. You know, like you used to do with your traveling companion, Gus.

I have to say, monsieur, that after scanning the contents of your diaries, you appear to have encountered a different kind of planter and picker immigrant on the rural frontier. Sure, their dwellings were more primitive, but their spirits were upbeat, they felt their prospects to be excellent, and they kept current with news from the rest of the Union. I seem to remember that you even found newspapers—newspapers!—in rustic log cabins on the outer reaches of Michigan.

Ah, but here it is, monsieur—your detailed description of a planter's house. Let me quote it back to you: "On the right of the chimney is stretched a map of the United States which the wind, coming in through the cracks in the wall, ceaselessly lifts and agitates. Near it, on a solitary shelf of badly squared boards, are placed some ill-assorted books; there you find a Bible whose cover and edges are already worn by the piety of two generations, a book of prayers, and sometimes a song of Milton or a tragedy of Shakespeare. Along the wall are ranged some rude benches, fruit of the proprietor's industry: trunks instead of clothes cupboards, farming tools, and some samples of the harvest. In the centre of the room stands a table whose uneven legs, still garnished with foliage, seem to have grown from the soil where it stands. It's there that the whole family comes together every day for meals. A teapot of English porcelain, spoons most often of wood, a few chipped cups, and some newspapers are there to be seen."[12]

You described, too, how the pioneers had a powerful sense of their own destiny, how with hard work, they regarded their economic success as inevitable.

Then again, Alex, back in 1831 there was no such thing as an illegal immigrant. America welcomed all comers equally and had a laissez-faire policy toward immigration. No fees, medical tests, language hurdles, or oaths of allegiance were imposed. It was only after 1819, when the federal government ordered ship captains to collect and report data on the immigrants disembarking at U.S. ports, that the nation even began to record who was here.

Perhaps I should conclude that there is no basis for comparison and I should simply write off the experience of the illegal immigrant as a red herring (poisson rouge?). After all, they are here illegally—how can their experience be relevant?

It is tempting to do so, Alex, but on reflection, I think it would be a mistake. Three reasons.

1. Their numbers are significant—there are six million of them. That's half the U.S. population at the time of your visit. They come into the U.S. at a rate of 5,000 a day, many turning over their entire life savings to the "*Coyotes*" who charge up to $1,500 per person to help guide them across the border. They say that 4,000 are caught just after they cross the border, but 1,000 a day elude detection.[13]

2. Their lives are completely entwined with legal immigrants: they work the same jobs; frequently share living quarters; their American-born children go to the same schools and can claim U.S. citizenship on turning eighteen. It is not uncommon for one half of an extended family to be legal and the other half not.

3. They are considered integral to the success of the U.S economy. As the *New York Times* puts it: "Were the nation's six million illegal immigrants expelled tomorrow, thousands of restaurants,

hotels, farms, poultry plants and garment factories and garden-ing companies would be forced to close for want of workers."[14] The *Times* went on to quote an economist who said that without these immigrants, the economy would have generated faster wage inflation, and hence higher interest rates would have been imposed which would have dampened the spectacular growth of the economy.

U.S. governments have to grapple with the problem of illegal im-migrants, including what to do with their American-born children. Presidents Gerald Ford and Jimmy Carter both appointed commis-sions to investigate the matter. The commissions concluded that the best way to deal with illegal immigrants who had put down roots was to grant them amnesty, which is what finally happened in 1986, when 2.7 million unauthorized aliens had their status promptly le-galized.[15]

But the present Congress takes a hard line, monsieur—interestingly toward low-income legal immigrants as well as illegal ones. In 1996, the Republican-led Congress enacted legislation[16] that bars legal im-migrants from receiving the same welfare and food stamp benefits as regular U.S. citizens until they have worked at least ten years in the United States. (In this respect too, then, low-income legal immigrants are placed in a similar category to illegal ones—another reason to think their experiences might not be that different.) In addition, there have been attempts to bar the children of illegal immigrants from attending public schools, most notably in California, where former Governor Pete Wilson rode to power in 1994 on the back of public support for this idea, which he used as the centerpiece of his campaign. The measure, known as Proposition 187, was passed by the California legislature only to be subsequently ruled unconstitutional by the courts and never im-plemented.[17] (Yes, as you observed Alex, "there is hardly a political question in the United States which does not sooner or later turn into a judicial one."[18]) But the fact that it won the electorate's support says something about the mindset of the Californians at the time, and most notably the mindset of the white majority toward the burgeoning pop-ulation of Latino immigrants.

So there you have it, Alex. It's not exactly a case of "Give me your poor," is it? Perhaps the fact that today's immigrants are not as "white" as past immigrants used to be may have something to do with it.

And yet, the immigrants continue to come. They come to better themselves economically, to partake of the American Dream.

I keep wondering—is this dream still accessible, Alex?

You know, maybe I have been thinking about Pedro and Hilaria all wrong. Maybe the trajectory of their lives isn't any different from that of the stereotypical immigrants down the decades where the parents make painful sacrifices in order for the children to advance.

Do the children advance? Voilà! That is *the* question. And perhaps easier asked than answered. Oh, how one yearns to be as certain as you were, Alex! Ah, but wait, there goes my telephone. (Another piece of technology[19] you were not acquainted with, monsieur, and no, don't begin to ask me to explain.)

. . . Good news. There is a Hispanic pastor who has agreed to see me. I have hopes that he can help put what I have seen in context. He lives in Lindsay, where I am staying, a town of 8,500 people about twenty minutes from Visalia. They tell me that this pastor is "a social worker, a translator, a mentor, an advisor, and a pastor, all rolled into one," and that he knows the local immigrant community as well as anyone.

On a personal note, Alex, I think you might feel at home here in Lindsay. It is on the original orange belt road that they dug for the wagons, and is the kind of old, sepia frontier town that still feels as if it should be ridden through on a horse.

Au-revoir, monsieur.

Click

Ruben Dario Sanchez does not strike you as your regular small-town pastor. Dressed in a black leather jacket, with tinted glasses, a goatee, and a grand bearing, he looks like a character out of *The Godfather* meets *The Name of the Rose*. It is only when you engage him in conversation that his soft-spoken voice and gentle eyes tell you otherwise.

Pastor Sanchez, fifty-six, came to America from Buenos Aires to get his master's in education thirty years ago. His intention was to return to Argentina, he says, but he stayed because he perceived a tremendous need for missionary work amongst the low-income Latinos. The position he currently holds, heading up the Seventh-Day Adventist Church in Lindsay, which he took five years ago, is one of several he has had administering to Latinos around the country, from Chicago, Illinois, to Oregon and southern California. (The Seventh-Day Adventist Church is a Protestant church that has 11 million members worldwide, 840,000 of them in America. Approximately 13 percent of the American membership is Latino, 30 percent African-American, and 55 percent Caucasian. Their growth is strongest among minority groups, and outreach and conversion often occurs through church schools—they claim to have the second-largest private education system in the world, after the Catholic Church, operating more than 5,800 schools and 95 colleges and universities worldwide.[20] Pastor Sanchez himself came from a Catholic family but converted to Seventh-Day Adventist after his parents sent him to one of their private schools in Buenos Aires.)

"The degree of alienation that the Hispanic immigrant feels is profound," Sanchez begins. "Culturally they are lost, language-wise they hardly speak English. Unless they arrive with college degrees, they have very little traction or connection to the mainstream job market."

He points to an aging Macintosh on his desk. "They are scared of that," he says emphatically. "They have no idea—no idea—about the Internet or Wall Street. I doubt whether there is a single person in this town who invests in the stock market. And you can count on one hand those who have e-mail."

"America offers these immigrants many advantages," he continues, "but at the same time it takes advantage of them. They are paid less than minimum wage, and they may work twenty years in the field and never get a raise. To survive, they live in barns and garages, wherever they can find a place to sleep. Sometimes three families share one house."

I interject. "You are talking about illegal immigrants, I assume?"

"No. I am referring to legal immigrants as much as illegal ones. Their ability to progress is determined only partly by their status, much more by their lack of English. Many would return to Mexico, but conditions there are worse, and it becomes harder to go back once they have American children."

"It is the children, do you agree, who carry the potential for transformation?"

"Ah, yes," he adds soothingly. "But therein lies both the greatest hope and the greatest pain for the new immigrant."

Sanchez explains that the children go to school where they learn English and are exposed to the American culture. The parents encourage this, he says, but they also try and impose the Latin American values and way of life—like no dating without a chaperone, live with your parents until you are married. They find their children's music "noisy and rubbish." The children, however, prefer the modality of their peers and so they end up in conflict with their parents over everything. "It's the biggest topic of conversation here. It can be a high price to pay for parents—disconnected from the society around them, and at war with their children."

"So the parents suffer alienation, which to some extent is inevitable, whereas their children are educated, go to college and progress. That's really the story of U.S. immigration down the decades, isn't it?"

"That's the other painful part," responds Sanchez. "The facts are that half the Latino children don't even finish school. Very few—and I mean very few—go on to college."

According to the Current Population Survey, only 53 percent of Hispanics aged twenty-five or older (nationwide) had completed high school in 1997 compared with 74 percent of African-Americans and 83 percent of whites. And less than 10 percent had a college degree, as compared to 25 percent of Whites.[21]

Part of the problem, the social worker, Josie Figueroa, tells me when we meet up, is that public schools in low-income neighborhoods are totally underresourced compared with public schools in affluent areas, and compared with private schools. It is a well-known statistic, I discover, that California spends fewer dollars on aggregate per student than forty-five of the other fifty states.

Lois Salisbury, president of Children Now, a nonpartisan policy and advocacy group for children with a particular focus on California, later tells me the following astonishing fact. In terms of the numbers of computers in schools, California is ranked either forty-ninth or fiftieth, depending on the method of calculation used. "How do you like that!" she exclaims. The state that is home to the single largest legal creation of wealth in the history of the planet—built entirely on computers—cannot be bothered to invest in the education of its children!

To understand why things got this way in the first place, you have to go back to the late 1970s, when a measure called Proposition 13 was passed. Prop 13 put a tight cap on increases in property taxes—for good reason, given the runaway housing inflation of the time—but as these taxes are used to finance schools, school funding has been woefully unable to keep up with inflation and the burgeoning influx of new students. To grasp why the situation has not been remedied for so long, many commentators point simply to the fact that Californian public schools stopped being majority white some time ago. At that point, concern for the schools' well-being by the white-majority electorate and their representatives in the state legislature slipped away like sand through an hourglass. It's not overt racism, but it's racism by omission and neglect. (I had encountered a similar malaise on the East Coast, where chronic underfunding of public schools in New York City is said to be linked to the fact that few whites go there anymore.)

Yet lack of funding, Figueroa adds, is only part of the story. Some of the problem seems to be with the Latino immigrant children themselves. You see it clearly in that the national high-school graduation rates of Hispanics are much lower than that of African-Americans (53 percent compared with 74 percent, as noted earlier), despite the fact that the latter are also products of the public school system.[22] "You get two types of Hispanic immigrant child," says Figueroa, "one who works hard, takes advantage of what America has to offer and makes something of him or herself, and another who wastes the opportunity. Unfortunately the second type predominates. Only a few dig deep academically. The rest end up in the fields, dishwashing at McDonald's, or if they're lucky, following Dad into the fruit-packing plant. The reasons are probably complex—to do with language deficiency, and perhaps a general sense of alienation—but I think it's also the Hispanic culture, which is not historically that academically inclined.

"But don't take my word," she says. "Go out and meet some teenagers for yourself."

The sisters Liz and Guadalupe Ramos are "hanging" with their friend Lupe Navarro in their driveway. They perch on plastic chairs arranged in a crescent, with a burnt-out shell of a car behind them in the yard. All three are legal immigrants of Mexican parents, they say, and between them they were either born in America or raised here from a young age. Liz, who has just turned eighteen, balances her ten-month-old son on her lap. Lupe, nineteen, cradles her one-month-old, while her three-year-old child tugs at her shoelaces. The two of them talk and laugh about "sucky" diapers and baby vomit, their conversation spiked with the cool bravado of youth.

Guadalupe, age seventeen, looks on and says, "I got better things to do with my life than have babies while I still a kid."

"Oh yeah? Like what?" challenges Lupe.

"Like, er, finish school?" I interject.

"Naa," says Guadalupe. "I dropped out back in ninth grade."

"Why?" I ask.

"B-b-b-b-borrrring."

"Huh?"

"Because it's boring, and a waste of time. I went to pick walnuts instead."

"That was more interesting?"

"You know, if it wasn't for us Mexicans, Americans would have nothing to eat."

"Oh? And how's that?" I say.

"Well, you won't find white people picking walnuts and grapes."

"And you won't find Guadalupe picking walnuts either!" shrieks Lupe. "She didn't last one week!"

"Hey, I got the fever. I couldn't breathe," Guadalupe protests, mock huffing and puffing as she talks.

"The hospital couldn't find nothing." Lupe and Liz laugh raucously.

"They treat you like shit in the fields," shrugs Guadalupe. "I'd rather baby-sit. I get seven dollars an hour. That's more than the pickers. And in a few years' time, if I still want, I can still go back to school."

"Most children in our school drop out," explains Liz. "I dropped out too, but now I'm back at night school doing business classes. I want to work with computers. I want to make a lot of money."

"What's a lot of money?" I ask.

"Twenty dollars an hour," replies Liz. "My husband, Alfredo, he works in a packing factory and he earns six dollars an hour. He says his boss screams and swears at them all the time. 'Hurry the fuck up!' 'You guys don't know shit!' 'There are more Mexicans to take your job if you don't like it!' "

"What do you expect? It's a racist country," says Guadalupe. "Look who's running for President—they're all white. The President's white, the government's white, the senator's white, they're all white. They act like they care about us, but they don't care."

Guadalupe's mother, Maria Ramos, wearing an apron and a frown, has been hovering on the fringe of the conversation and now bursts forward, unable to restrain her agitation. "If you were to study—" she jabs her finger at Guadalupe—"if you were to go back to school, *you* could be President!"

"As long as I live, I'll never see a Latino-American President!" Guadalupe shouts back. "Who has power in America? It's all whites."

"But if you were to study," her mother counters angrily, "you would better yourself, and with it the whole Mexican race."

They argue on in Spanish, the layers of complexity of their relationship slipping beyond the reach of my short visit. When the tension subsides, I drop what has become my pet question.

"Have you heard about what's happening in Silicon Valley?"

"Silicon Valley?" Lupe frowns. "Silicon Valley?"

"It's where white women go to have their breasts enlarged," smirks Guadalupe, pushing out her ample bosom provocatively as she talks.

"Those are silicon *implants*, you ass," says Liz.

The three girls crack up. It's a revealing slice of life. And sometimes there is nothing funnier, I muse, than the acute pleasure of one's own ignorance.

I have one more set of interviews to do—with perhaps two of the most highly educated immigrants in Lindsay. I am interested to hear how life might differ when you arrive in Central Valley already armed with a profession or a college degree. We have arranged to rendezvous at their family-owned restaurant, called Robles.

To get there from the Ramos house in Visalia, I take the backroads through nearby Tonyville, a pickers' village where mangy dogs and chickens run in the yard among old bedframes. Some of the houses here are no bigger than enlarged sheds, their gardens littered with discarded Pepsi bottles and chip packets. Everywhere cars are up on bricks with men lying under them. Everyone seems to be a part-time auto mechanic.

As I drive, I listen on the car radio to a phone-in talk show debating whether George W. Bush really is a compassionate conservative and whether it was the religious right who downed John McCain in the South Carolina primary. Another channel covers a report, just in, about how according to California lottery data, the poorest Californians (those earning under $35,000 a year) are the ones buying the most tickets. They also discuss the impact of the new proposition put before voters (subsequently passed) to legalize Vegas-style casinos on Indian lands throughout the state, which, pundits predict, will turn California into a major gambling destination.

Compassion, religion, gambling, inequality—many of the themes I have visited in other parts of the country repeat themselves here.

The road from Tonyville bisects orchards of grapefruits, lemons, oranges, and tangerines and then eases into the wide, almost deserted main street of Lindsay. I pull up outside Robles Restaurant. Over the road, the shuttered Lindsay Theater advertises the forthcoming attraction: the U.S. Air Force Band, which will be performing in two months time. Robles Restaurant is run by two sisters, Gloria and Margarita, and they tell me that the people I have come to interview, their sister, Ana Rosa Celaya, and Gloria's husband, Aaron Estrada, will be over in an hour or so. In the meantime, they bring me a burrito, on the house, which I notice is one of the main-course items. It sells for just $2.50.

Aaron Estrada, forty-five, is a public accountant. Ana Rosa Celaya, thirty-nine, is a medical doctor. Estrada came from Mexico City when he was twenty-eight because his wife and her family had permanent residence in America. Celaya, who had lived her youth partly in America and partly in Mexico, but was educated in Mexico, came because she hoped to make a "decent" living. "In the part of Mexico where we lived, my patients would pay me with food because they had no money," she explains. But, as it turned out, neither has been able to practice his or her profession in America.

Estrada has spent the last fifteen years working, not in a suit and tie as he was accustomed, but as a laborer on a farm. His job is to collect honey from beehives. "You work sixteen hours a day in the sun," he says, in halting English. "You're covered head to foot in a beekeeper's uniform. It's hot in there, up to 105 degrees. And there are the bees. My job is to pull honey from their hives, but the gloves get wet from the honey and I get many stings. I get forty to sixty stings in my fingers in one day. It's not a full sting, because it's through the glove, but still, I get afraid. Obviously, it's a frustrating life for me. Very bad, to be honest."

Celaya's opinion is that Estrada's situation is somewhat of his own making. "You need to have vision when you come here," she says. "You need to have a dream—and most important, you need to learn English. I was a doctor, but all I could get when I arrived was a job picking olives. So I learned English and I got a job as a physician's assistant. Life is not easy for us here . . . I'm not working as a doctor. But at least I'm working in a job related *to* my field, rather than Estrada, who is *in* the field."

"Do you know any immigrants who have *really* made it financially?" I ask.

Celaya thinks for a moment. "Only one," she says.

"Who's that?"

"My youngest sister, Imelda."

"How did she manage it?"

"The oldest way—she married a rich guy. They live in a place called Campbell—like the soup—near San Jose."

"Of course. That's in Silicon Valley," I say.

"Silicon Valley?" She looks at me quizzically. "Silicon Valley?" she repeats. "I've not heard of it. No. I didn't hear that name."

SILICON VALLEY: WOODSTOCK FOR CAPITALISTS

They call it "Ground Zero." "The Center of the Universe." "The Land of Milk and Honey." "Woodstock for Capitalists." Locals reach for the ultimate metaphor to capture the essence of this place, but no superlative can convey the enormity of what is happening here; and so, in the end, they just settle for Silicon Valley or *the* Valley.

To make the journey to the center of gravity of the New Economy, you take Highway 101 from San Francisco and follow the glut of dot-com billboards marching south. They profile a dazzling array of online products, from music to mortgages, but mostly they trumpet services both mystifying and incomprehensible to the passing motorist: "gesundheit.com," "vstream.com," "marketfirst.com." Within twenty minutes, you're passing a ticker tape of road signs— San Mateo, Foster City, Redwood City, Menlo Park, Palo Alto, Sunnyvale, Santa Clara, and finally San Jose. Take any one of those exits and, voilà, you've arrived. But if you're expecting the futuristic essence of the place to be reflected in its architecture, if you're hoping for some kaleidoscopic postmodern exterior to symbolize the macroscopic fortunes being minted on the interior—you will be sorely disappointed.

As has been said before, there is not much there, there.

But then, when you think about it, it's entirely apt—because Silicon Valley makes its money on things invisible to the naked eye. It is the temple of the bit and the byte, not the clunky old atom. And so what you find instead are amorphous, low-slung office parks, indistinguishable one from the other but for their tinted windows of varying hues. Only the hallowed names out front—

Cisco Systems, Intel, Yahoo!, Excite, Hewlett Packard, National Semiconductor, Kleiner Perkins—arouse your curiosity and signal your arrival.

My journey through Silicon Valley begins with a telling mistake. I arrive a day earlier than planned and find that there is not a single available hotel room in the whole of the Valley. From Holiday Inn to Super 8, from San Jose to Palo Alto, in each case it is the same story: "You not prebook? Sorry, we have no vacancies—nothing."

One has to have traveled in America to know how extraordinary this is. No, there's no major convention, I am informed, it's just business as usual with tens of thousands of businessmen coming and going. Boy, if ever there was a barometer as to how HOT this place is, this is it!

Sleeping in one's car, I discover later, is not that unusual in the Valley, especially among low-income workers who cannot afford the astronomical rental accommodations. But, as I say, I only think about this later, because the travails of the low-income segment of the population magically fall off one's radar as soon as you enter the Valley. You just don't think about them. Nobody reminds you. They are not part of the conversation.

The Valley keeps you focused on what, to it, matters most— the insanely *fasssst* creation of unimaginable wealth. And it tortures you at every turn, reminding you that you are being *left out*. It's like participating in the ultimate mind-altering drug-trial experiment and discovering that you're the only person in the control group. It should carry a health warning: "Enter at your own risk— may seriously destabilize your mental well-being and image of self." When columns of sports utility vehicles (SUVs) pull up beside me at traffic lights, set so high off the road that I make eye contact with their tires, I find myself thinking: Why am I the only guy driving the dinky toy? The Valley challenges your value system. It makes you justify who you are, laughs at your stupidity if your prime motivation is *not* the pursuit of the dollar. And it sets up a racket in your brain that soon becomes a painful, deafening roar, that maybe—just maybe—in this unique window of time . . . how can you afford not to be about making money? You cannot pretend not to be thrown off-balance by the culture of the place. It repulses you, it attracts you, it's infectious, and it washes over you in waves. It takes time, though, to decipher what the culture is really about, how it weaves its magic and how it leaves its mark on society.

First there are the stories—everyone has at least one—told by people who have watched other people make it bigger than they have. (No one tells stories about the people who have made less than they have. The emphasis is relentlessly on bigger, better, larger, higher, onward and upward, so much so that looking downward almost feels antithetical to the culture.) What is most discombobulating about these stories is that the wealth created is so vast, so immediate, and so apparently accessible. Fortunes that once took twenty years to amass are achieved by callow twenty-one-year-olds in their first year out of college.

Lawrence Stone, the former mayor of Sunnyvale in the heart of Silicon Valley and currently the assessor for Santa Clara County, tells me this story about his pal Steve Westly, who had had, he insists, "an unremarkable career" kicking around from job to job. "Finally Steve gets a job earning $60,000 a year in a department in San Jose local government," he says. "Some months later the top job in the department becomes vacant, Steve goes for it, but he loses to a female colleague, and so he leaves, licking his wounds, to go work for a small high-tech start-up. A few months later he leaves that company to become a vice-president in charge of marketing at another small start-up. A year later, this company—which just happens to be called eBay—goes public. Suddenly, this guy who earned half of what I do, and who I used to feel a little sorry for, is worth $400 million! I said to him, 'Steve, you should give that woman who got that job ahead of you $10 million and tell her: Thanks! That was the best job I never got in my life!' "

But it is the tidbit that Stone drops at the end of our conversation that really gets the blood up. "You have secretaries and back-office staff rolling in millions of dollars of stock options. Take my wife. She's the personal assistant to the CEO of a high-tech company. She has stock worth, oh . . . half a million dollars."

Then there are the anecdotes that convey how frenetically everyone is on the make. Joan Hamilton, a columnist for *Business Week* who lives in the Valley, tells me the story about a guy who lost concentration for a minute and drove into the rear end of a Ferrari. "They are exchanging details, in the form of business cards, when this guy notices that the man he has just crashed into, the man in the Ferrari, is a venture capitalist. 'You're a VC!' he exclaims, unable to contain his excitement. 'I have a business plan! Would you be willing to read it?' "

Even car accidents are viewed as an opportunity to network.

Venture capitalists say they receive sixty business plans a day, adds Hamilton. "From priests to prisoners . . . everyone here is a budding entrepreneur with their own little-idea dot com. Dinner parties, weddings—they're all about networking. The hostess will explain: 'That's so and so, he's head of X company, just went public for eighty million dollars.' But don't look for deep reflection or intellect. Most of these Internet guys are positively sophomoric. They get away with it because they're worth $13 million. So they're legends in their own minds. Some of them like to say that it's not about the money. But it *is* the money. The money here is so extraordinary, it cannot *not* be the money."

The youth of the place—brash, confident, barely postadolescent, and ahistorical—smacks you in the face. Chip Bayers, a thirty-five-year-old senior writer for *Wired* magazine, tells me that a few years ago he looked around and realized that everyone in the office was younger than he was. "You're in your early thirties and you feel you're a jaded old-timer," says Bayers. "In this place, the future is everything and no one is interested in the past. It's all about what's happening here, today. What happened last year is ancient history."

The workplace itself is set up to resemble the playground. I visit the offices of the Internet portal Yahoo!, decorated in bright purple and yellow, and I am struck by how each employee's cubicle (they call them "cubes") is decked out like a teenager's bedroom. Tim Koogle, presently Yahoo!'s chairman and, until recently, its chief executive officer, has four gleaming red and white electric guitars in his cube. A huge poster of Kurt Cobain, the lead singer of the rock group Nirvana, who committed suicide in 1994, dominates

244 | CHASING THE RED, WHITE, AND BLUE

the cube of one of Yahoo!'s lawyers. Everyone has decorated his or her little space with posters, toys, and tchotchkes, from model planes to water pistols. Jerry Yang, the co-founder, has his own little sofabed to complete the office-as-bedroom getup. When I am introduced to Yang, a Stanford University graduate born in Taiwan, he is eating what look suspiciously like homemade sandwiches. He greets me but stares like a gawky undergraduate at his sandals. If I had to bump into Yang on the street, I would never guess that this guy is one of the biggest hitters of Silicon Valley. In fact, as I later discover, he is one of their elder statesman—the average age here is under thirty. Yahoo! has something of the feel of Willy Wonka's chocolate factory: conference rooms named after ice cream flavors; foosball (table soccer) in the canteen; oversized Alice-in-Wonderland type chairs in the reception area, with bowls of free "red-hots" candy; and who knows what secret new recipes being dreamed up just a few cubes away.

A story making the rounds is that Home Depot has run out of doors: the dot-com companies have apparently been buying them by the truckload to lay on top of filing cabinets in order to make desks. "Who has time to waste setting up an office the old-fashioned way?"

These giddy anecdotes would not be so powerful were they not underpinned by one startling statistic. As almost every newspaper and magazine article about Silicon Valley reminds you, "an estimated 60 new millionaires are created here on average every day."[23] The fact that a good deal of them are only millionaires "on paper," whose stock options will only vest in a couple of years' time, by which time they may not be worth anything at all, does not hamper the bandying about of this mind-bending statistic.

Then you start to meet some of these success stories yourself. Within five minutes, you know what they do and their net worth. "I'm worth eight digits," one Taiwanese immigrant "angel investor" tells me over our first drink. I respond with a blank stare that makes him uneasy. He's not sure now whether I think this a little or a lot. For all he knows, I may be worth *nine* digits. (Actually, I'm just computing whether his eight digits are meant to include the two for cents, and wondering at the same time whether he has given new meaning to the phrase "digital divide.") In the midst of my temporizing, he cannot help jumping in. "Around twenty million," he announces. He is about as coy as they get.

The most revealing thing, when you think about it, is that these people actually *know* their net worth. They carry it around in their pockets like a calling card, able to produce it on demand.

It's as if their *net* worth and their *self*-worth were one and the same thing.

At local hangouts, like the trendy Tied House brewery, clusters of young, single guys stand around schmoozing. It is a Friday night and the beer is flowing, but the fascinating thing is that their interest in chatting up the opposite sex is nonexistent. (Matchmakers say, I learn later, that the dating scene in Silicon Valley is a lost cause.)[24] The talk is relentlessly focused on technology, dot coms, and stock options. After a while, the fragments of conversation swirling about me meld and start to sound the same: "Think equity . . . *burp* . . . keep it quiet . . . *burp* . . . dot com."

But these are merely my first impressions of the frontier. Perhaps, when you actually live and work here a while, things start to settle down and people are motivated by things other than money. There are those who insist that the money is incidental, that the money is just to "keep score":

"It's the excitement!"

"It's the chase of the deal!"

"It's the technology!"

To be sure, the spirit of innovation is a leitmotif of the Valley, as is the busting of the traditional business model, and the opportunity to be a part of history.[25] There is also the feeling—by turns strange and exhilarating—of living in a place of almost totalitarian optimism and confidence. There will be boom and bust cycles in the economy; but the Internet revolution itself—that is unstoppable.

How, I wonder, does the new immigrant fit in to life on the new frontier? Of the Valley's population, a whopping 32 percent are first-generation immigrants, versus 10 percent in the country as a whole.²⁶ What can they tell us? And does their comparative perspective throw some light on the values, culture, and character of America itself?

"ONE DAY I'LL BE WORTH SOMETHING. RIGHT NOW, I HAVE ABOUT A MILLION DOLLARS."

Campbell—like the soup—on the suburban outskirts of San Jose in the Santa Clara Valley, is where Imelda Lozano and her husband, Elias, recently bought a house for $407,000. At first sight, it appears to be the kind of unremarkable, cramped home she might have lived in were she still with her family back in Robles Restaurant, Lindsay, Central Valley. Except that to dwell on this observation would be to miss the point: they have bought it to demolish it. "We're tearing down the house and building a five-bedroom one in its place," Imelda tells me over herbal tea as we sit in her living-dining room. The whole deal will cost them almost a million dollars—a bargain, apparently, for Silicon Valley, where housing prices are shooting through the roof Manhattan-style, and where this week the *San Jose Mercury News* carries a story about a rather ordinary, plain house that went for *double* its asking price.²⁷

Imelda, twenty-nine, and Elias, thirty-four, have been married four years. They are both Latino, but they stem from wildly different worlds and would never have met but for the young-adult program of the Seventh-Day Adventist Church, of which they are members.

Imelda has almond eyes framed by dark hair, a delicate bone structure, and a vivacious smile. She grew up the seventh child of pickers who followed the crop on the West Coast. Her parents had emigrated from Amtitan, a small town in the state of Jalisco in the rural center part of Mexico, when she was two years old. From the age of nine, when she was big enough to carry a bucket, she would join her family in the orchards over the summer months, picking from four A.M. until sundown. First they went to Oregon in June to pick apples, then to Washington State to pick cherries, and from there to the Modesto area of California and on to Lindsay in Central Valley to pick olives. "I hated it—I hated it so much," Imelda recalls, bunching her hand in a tight fist and thumping the table. "We'd have to get up when it was still dark and cold, and at night, we'd be living in these makeshift labor camps where the accommodation was never big enough to fit our whole family. I was the baby of the family, so I was allowed to sleep indoors, but many nights my brothers slept out in the orchards. I remember one summer someone from the church heard that there were children sleeping in the field and they lent us a house that was empty for the whole season. 'We have a house!' my mother told us. Ah, it was so exciting! So special!"

During the rest of the year, Imelda went to school—sometimes in Mexico, sometimes Los Angeles—though never to the same one for long. She went to more than fifteen schools in all, she says, up to four in one year. "Many of the landlords did not want children on the premises, and when they discovered that my mother had kids, they would throw us out, and we'd have to find another place in another area to live, and that meant another school. I was moving around so much that I never learned to write good English or good Spanish. I rebelled, ran away from home at one point. My life was a mess. I knew one thing—I didn't want a life like my parents', but I didn't know how to change it."

Elias wears loafers, tracksuit pants, and an old T-shirt. He is not as svelte as he once was and his hair is beginning to thin a little on top, but his eyes twinkle with a keen and youthful intelligence. He grew up in Medellín, Colombia, the son of a preacher, where he had a comparatively normal middle-class childhood. He played soccer, took piano lessons, did well at school. "Life was a lot of fun," he recalls. He came to America, age eighteen, to take his bachelor of science and followed that up with a masters in electrical engineering at Washington State University.

At twenty-four, he came to Silicon Valley, a qualified engineer, and went to work for LSI Logic, a semiconductor company whose business it was to develop silicon chips for the computer industry.

He was still very much single when he joined a church trip to visit a congregation in a part of the country he could only imagine— Lindsay in Central Valley—and there he met a dark-haired, young rebel who was working as a hairdresser and a beautician. The rest, as they say, is history.

By the middle of the nineties, Elias found himself, like most ambitious hardware engineers in the Valley, a man in high demand. "I sat down and said to myself: I want to be a millionaire by the time I'm forty." He wasn't going to get there at LSI, so for $80,000 a year plus stock options, he joined a start-up, 3DFX, that does silicon chips for computer games, and where an initial public offering (IPO) was in the cards.

He was employee number 77 to join, he says, but the roller-coaster that is Silicon Valley was only just beginning. He worked unconscionable hours—seventy-hour weeks were the norm. And his marriage began to feel the strain. But it was not forever, he would tell Imelda, and it would be worth it: their stock options alone would transform them into multimillionaires overnight.

But just before the IPO came, the company did a reverse share split that halved his windfall. "That was a big bummer," he says. "I didn't make what I considered *real* money. I started to feel like I was being left behind." This feeling only intensified when a good friend whom he had recruited to 3DFX left to join another start-up, called Growth Networks, a high-speed networking company that hit the jackpot when it was bought out twelve months later by Cisco Systems. "She became an instant millionaire," says Elias. "Probably a few times over! Okay, she has to wait four years to get fully vested . . . But it's happened to me a few times already—I join the wrong company, I miss the boat."

"Elias was so upset," says Imelda. "You should have seen him punishing himself: 'That job was offered to me! Why didn't I take it? I could be a millionaire.' "

"Elias," I said to him, "you should be happy for your friend. Besides, I thought you told me that we already are millionaires."

"We are," he says, "but only on paper." He tells me he wants to "double up." I'm happy as long as I've got ten dollars in my pocket and he wants to double up. I had to say: "Hey, wait.

There's some reason God didn't want you to have all that money right now."

"How much *are* you worth, Elias?" I ask him.

"One day I will be worth something," he says. "Right now, I have about a million dollars."

"That's pretty good. You're only thirty-four—that's six years ahead of target," I say.

"Oh, I don't think so. A lot of people have a lot more. But I am planning my own start-up. I have a lot of ideas. I can't tell you what they are. Secrecy is everything. And timing."

"You mean if you tell me, you'll have to kill me," I quip, trying to make light. But he does not laugh.

"It will be in the high-speed Internet access field," he continues, poker-faced, "but beyond that I cannot tell you. And then, after I've taken my start-up public, I want to sit back and be a venture capitalist." Elias, it seems, dismisses his million partly because it is the product of the "slow," unspectacular accretion of wealth from a combination of thrift, stock options, and an old-economy packaging business that he started on the side with a friend some years ago. He has not made it the Silicon Valley way—with a bang! And until he does, part of him feels like a failure.

"I'm no different from anyone else in the Valley," he says. "Everyone here is trying to get as much as they can as fast as they can. I include myself in that. It's hard to escape. You know someone, he has an idea, he goes public, he makes millions. You feel weird. Why can't I have the same too? It's the Silicon Valley influenza."

"Money is everything here," agrees Imelda. "People can't sleep for worrying about it. I guess we all like money, that's normal, but I want to make sure I don't end up obsessed by it like them. That's my challenge."

Recently Elias decided to take his foot a little off the gas. He left 3DFX and joined National Semiconductor, a company listed on the Nasdaq Exchange and one of the largest silicon-chip makers in the Valley. His salary is more than $100,000, he says, but since the company has already gone public, it is "just a job" and so he works normal hours. "You can lose perspective in the Valley very rapidly," he sighs. "You can get caught up in all the materialism and lose your family. The rate of divorce here is very high. When I worked long hours it was very difficult on our marriage. If it wasn't for my religion, and my wife, I'd be a complete mess."

"Do you call yourself an American?" I ask each of them.

"Oh, I'm Mexican. One-hundred-percent Mexican," says Imelda. "A piece of paper doesn't change your identity. I was actually sad when I had to swear allegiance because I felt that I was saying I didn't want to be Mexican anymore. But I am pleased to be *in* America. This country has offered me a great life. I can be myself, I can dream, I have the opportunity to become whatever I want. Right now I am studying business administration. If I want to be a successful businesswoman, I can get a lot of help to achieve that. That wouldn't happen in Mexico—there you have to know the right people to get ahead. This is a fair country."

"My dad taught me to admire America," says Elias. " 'Learn as much from the gringos as you can,' he always told me. But now I don't just admire. I see that we make this country just as much as America makes us. *We* make Silicon Valley. *We*—the new immigrants—are defining the identity of America."

Subject: Let's wrap this up
From: David Cohen <dc368@columbia.edu>
To: Alexis@Tocqueville.org

Okay, Alex, so you were right. So the frontier is—as you pointed out—primarily about making money. Sure, it is also about risk-taking, reckless speculation, and keeping your hand on the wheel of progress, but ultimately it is driven by economic imperatives.

Did I mention the giant billboard advertising E*Trade on Highway 101? It looks like this:

TRYING TO MAKE MONEY IS ONLY HALF THE FUN.

NO . . . THAT'S PRETTY MUCH IT.

Your diaries on the frontier said something similar: "To cross almost impenetrable forests, pass deep rivers, brave pestilential swamps, sleep exposed to the damp of the woods: these are efforts the American has no difficulty understanding if it's a question of gaining a dollar, for that's the point."[28]

I wonder too whether you will recognize these immigrants from Silicon Valley a little better, monsieur. I mean, compared to the ones from Central Valley. I am not talking about their seemingly instant wealth (yes, it took longer to make it back then); neither am I referring to their apparently ambivalent national identities (ties to homelands are indeed closer than ever before), but rather to the tremendous sense that these immigrants have of empowerment. They feel that they are actively fashioning their own path, and with it the future of this country. That was the spirit of the frontier back then, monsieur, and it is, quite remarkably, the spirit of the new frontier now.

But here's my question: The Frontier may be still about money, but is it also still about equality?

Intuitively you expect that it must be. The place that has created more wealth in a shorter time span than anywhere in history, where even secretaries and back-office staff can become millionaires, must surely have led to a vast widening of the middle class and a dramatic increase in equality. If not here—you ask yourself—then where?

But the statistics tell a sobering story. Because despite the fact that the new money has indeed created a whole slew of new millionaires, the income gap between the haves and the have-nots has widened dramatically in Silicon Valley. (Yes—I said in Silicon Valley, Alex. I am not even beginning to talk about the gap between Silicon and Central Valley.)

The graph looks like this. Between 1992 and 1998, the most affluent fifth of Santa Clara Valley households saw their income (adjusted for inflation) rise by 38 percent, whereas the least affluent fifth of households saw their incomes decline by 10 percent. Quite astoundingly, the adjusted income of the lowest quintile of the Valley's population is still below 1992 levels, the year that President Clinton took office.[29] When you bear in mind that this measure of income takes no account of stock options—the remuneration of choice for top-tier employees—you begin to appreciate just how significant the disparity has become.

But the story doesn't end there, Alex. The income divide is mirrored by an equally severe education and digital divide, which bodes poorly for the prospects of the next generation.

Here are a few statistics to get your head round. In Silicon Valley, only 57 percent of Hispanic students and 60 percent of African-American students graduate high school, compared with 86 percent of white students and 97 percent of Asian students. And in the broader San Francisco Bay Area, 46 percent of people with household incomes of less than $40,000 have access to the Internet compared with 81 percent with household incomes of more than $80,000.[30]

The reason for the widening income gap is not hard to fathom: two of the fastest-growing jobs in Silicon Valley—as in the rest of America—are:

- Software engineers (average Valley salary $96,000 and rising), and
- Cashiers (average wage $23,000 and stagnant)[31]

The expansion of the high-tech industry on the one hand and the food and hospitality service industries on the other is leading to a top- and bottom-heavy economy with limited access one to the other.

You might say that, in shape, it's an economy that increasingly resembles an egg timer. (I trust you are familiar with the item, monsieur.)

In the last three decades, Alex, there has been a fundamental change in the nature of work in America, a change that is structural, not temporary, and which this country has yet to fully face up to. Simply put, as a result of the shrinking industrial base, the traditional way of accessing a middle-class lifestyle, through a secure blue-collar job, is all but over. Where once hard work, skill, and ingenuity alone were sufficient to access the fabled American Dream, today, as local and national job-growth findings make clear, education has become the best predictor of a person's earnings. A postsecondary education—ideally a college or some sort of technical degree—is the key to playing hopscotch from the low-paying sector of the economy to the high-paying sector.

America may still be thought of as the land of the self-made millionaire, but as a recent demographic profile of these self-made millionaires makes clear, an overwhelming number of them—nine out of ten, in fact—are college graduates.[32]

You may wonder, Alex, where immigration—once the great equalizer—fits into this picture of inequality. In your day, most immigrants came with nothing but a suitcase of clothing and enough cash to tide them over while they looked for a job. They all started, metaphorically speaking, on the same whitewashed line drawn in the dirt. "Ready—steady?—go! . . . Run, boy, run!" the country encouraged them. There was, to be sure, a robust air of great equality about those white immigrants and about those times.

But today's immigrants arrive anything but equal. Some jet in to take up places at the great American universities; some crawl under the fence; others arrive with little more than the promise from a relative of a roof over their head. There are distinctly two categories of immigrant coming to America at the turn of the millennium—the highly educated and the highly uneducated. According to the U.S. Census Bureau, 30 percent of foreign-born adults have a college degree, whereas 34 percent did not finish high school. Of the U.S.-born population, 24 percent have a college degree and 16 percent did not finish high school. So the foreign-born tend to be bunched more radically in the top and bottom educational levels than even the U.S.-born. As a result, concludes the Census Bureau report, "Immigration is contributing to inequality."[33]

So there you have it, Alex: rising inequality—not equality—has become a fact of life here. And not just in Silicon Valley. According to a recent joint report by the Center on Budget and Policy Priorities and the Economic Policy Institute[34], the income gap between high- and low-income families has widened in forty-six states since the late 1970s. (California, by the way, is one of the states where income inequality grew most.) The report, which analyzed the latest census data, found moreover that in forty-five states, the gap between the incomes of middle-income families and the richest 20 percent of families expanded between the late 1970s and the late 1990s. The middle classes, they discovered, are losing ground as well.

The primary cause of the growth of income inequality, notes the report, is "wage inequality." "Factors generally identified as contributing to increasing wage inequality include globalization, the decline of manufacturing jobs and the expansion of low-wage service jobs, immigration, the lower real value of the minimum wage, and fewer and weaker unions."

But what we don't know is this: Will Americans—the people and the politicians—act to reverse this trend? Where there is a will, there is a way.

But is there the will?

It is in the pursuit of an answer to this question—a question that tells us so much about modern American values, monsieur—that I raise two others:

1. Is inequality—and the plight of the have-nots—a concern of Silicon Valley residents and politicians?
2. How does the frontier mentality impact attitudes to the have-nots?

To the extent that the frontier mentality seeps (or leaps) into society as a whole, we may yet throw light on deeply and even unconsciously held attitudes to the have-nots throughout America.

I will be thinking of you as I make my way to Washington, D.C., monsieur. For barring a sequel, this is my last communiqué. I have to wrap things up. The time of my departure from the United States is drawing near. You have been, in a somewhat unique way, both the backbone of my venture and a wonderful traveling companion.

Did I mention that my original working title for this book gave you a starring role?

A Frenchman, an Englishman, a Country Called America, I called it. Okay, I fib a little. "An Englishman" came before "a Frenchman." What do you expect?

No matter—my publisher discards it anyway. They think that it sounds like a bad Irish joke.

Click

THE FRONTIER MENTALITY AND ITS INFLUENCE ON AMERICA

Speak to enough politicians and journalists in Silicon Valley and two facts become unanimously clear. They are:

1. *The Silicon Valley have-nots are not part of the conversation.* In fact they are completely off the page. (As regards the immigrants in Central Valley—forget about it. Just as Silicon

Valley is off the map to many immigrants of Central Valley, so the reverse is also true. The immigrants of Central Valley are out of sight and out of mind to the residents of Silicon Valley.) The closest one gets to a conversation about in-equality in Silicon Valley is a rising concern about the "have a little" civil servants—the teachers, policemen, and firemen—who are essential to the community, but who can no longer afford to live in the community. Teachers are ei-ther leaving the Valley or leaving the profession to do some-thing more lucrative, resulting in a worrying shortage. (Salaries of these civil servants range from $31,000 to $53,000—a typical lower-middle-class income for most parts of America, but not enough for the Valley, where the cost of living is the highest in the nation and where the median price of a home is $410,000.)[35]

2. *The defining hallmark of the frontier mentality is its* optimism.

Is there—I wonder—a connection between these two obser-vations?

The supercharged optimism of American society is something I noticed immediately upon my arrival in America. Perhaps this had something to do with my comparative perspective—the fact that Britain really is, as the cliché has it, more pessimistically inclined—but whatever the reason, I was immediately introduced to both its vices and virtues. To me the great gift of this national optimistic streak is that it is enormously inspiring. It entreats you to chase your dreams and to rise to your full height, insisting that anything is possible. It's a snort of freedom that gives you more of a high than seems legal, and which I had not experienced in Europe.

The flip side, which to me is as maddening as the upside is enchanting, is that it tries to put a *positive spin* on everything, from the personal to the political. On an individual level, it makes Amer-icans more likely to want to hide their vulnerability—both from themselves and from others—and leads to less intimate personal relationships. True intimacy in friendship is not possible—and is certainly not sustainable—without an ability to be relaxed around vulnerability. On the other hand, economically based relationships—the kinds you make networking, for example—are in no need of "vulnerability" to keep them watered.

But it is on a communal level that the effects may be most damaging. I am referring to a stubborn reticence to look into the shadows, to face up, without sweeteners, to the darker (I was going to say "real") side of life in America. Again (and this is a comparative perspective, drawing on my life growing up in another country—this time South Africa), no report card on that country will be taken seriously if it attempts, thirty-five years from now, to measure its success by how well the top third, or even top half, of the population are doing. Yet America, thirty-five years after the civil rights movement of the 1960s, habitually assesses itself in precisely this way.

Tocqueville picked up on the optimism of Americans too and noted that it was a quality born on the frontier. He believed that their optimism was the result of their successful battles with nature, which receded under their onslaught year after year. These victories not only rolled back the frontier, but gave Americans a great sense of forward motion, of progress, and ultimately instilled in them an enormous confidence and belief in themselves that became part of the oral history of the country, passed from generation to generation.

In Silicon Valley, this trait of optimism has reached its apotheosis. Here "positive thinking" is not just an option but an injunction. Optimism rules in an idealized, almost totalitarian way. It is here, therefore, that its effects can most clearly be seen and analyzed.

The glossy magazine *Wired* has been at the heart of the new frontier experience and is regarded by some as the classic window into the zeitgeist of Silicon Valley. I arranged to meet some of its journalists and editors to sound out their perspective.

Chip Bayers describes the optimism as "double-edged." "Coming to California has allowed me to do things with my career that I didn't feel I could do on the East Coast," he says. "It appeals to your sense of justice and equality that you can build something so fast and from scratch—and that is incredibly attractive. On the other hand, that same optimism rapidly begins to feel like an enforced optimism, like a commercial ethic devoid of spontaneity. It's the optimism of the salesman, the optimism that does not want to be a victim because no one will give anything to a victim. It's the idea that *this moment*—smile—could be the crucial moment where your life changes. So smile, damn it! Smile!"

Martha Baer, the former managing editor of *Wired* and presently a senior contributing editor, goes further in making the link between optimism and the attitudes to the have-nots explicit. "The trait of optimism reigns supreme in Silicon Valley and in California," she begins. "Part of what that optimism means is that you've got to embrace a forward-looking mindset. The focus is relentlessly on the next next thing. You don't *ever* look backward. Talk about poverty and inequality is a double no-no because not only is it pessimistic, but it's backward-looking as well. It's seen as old world, old economy, European—exactly the opposite of what this place is meant to be about. So inequality can't even get on the agenda. You're seen as hopelessly 1960s and left-wing (a word that has become derogatory out here) if you bring it up. So the conversation doesn't even happen. And if you insist, you're dissed. You're an embarrassment. You're the subject of intense eye-rolling. On the other hand, if you adopt the forward-looking and optimistic mindset, if you conform to that, you tend to be rewarded. So the attitude is entrenched."

Another former *Wired* journalist, who gives me her name but insists I not use it, tells me that she cannot say what she "really thinks" unless she remains anonymous. "It's a dangerous thing to say this and still expect to get work out here," she says, "but in the magazine and media world, and especially within *Wired* (which in many ways both reports on *and* mirrors Silicon Valley), the ethos is that we're done worrying about poor people. People who talk about social programs and inequality don't get it. Looking at who's being left behind is boring. The problems of some decaying housing project is about as far as you can get from the sleek, fleet, and efficient promise of technology. Technology is what promises change. The people are incidental."

It's optimism run amok.

Tocqueville warned that the willful social exclusion of a minority portion of the population was the Achilles' heel of democracy in America. In his most famous chapter, "The Omnipotence of the Majority in the United States and its Effects,"[36] there is an intriguing subhead that could have been written by Karl Marx: "The Power Exercised by the Majority in America over Thought."

Tocqueville was concerned that just as an individual vested with omnipotence could abuse it against his adversaries, so might a majority behave in the same way. He was not asserting that America was a land where tyranny reigned, but rather that "the germ of tyranny is there" and that despite it being a democracy, he could find "no guarantee against it."

Such a tyranny, he added, may take a subtle form. "It is when one comes to look into the use made of thought in the United States that one most clearly sees how far the power of the majority goes beyond all the powers known to us in Europe," he wrote. "Thought is an invisible power and one almost impossible to lay hands on, which makes sport of all tyrannies . . . In America, while the majority is in doubt, one talks; but when the majority has irrevocably pronounced, everyone is silent, and friends and enemies alike seem to make for its bandwagon."

"In America the majority have enclosed thought within a formidable fence," he explained. "The writer is free inside that area, but woe to the man who goes beyond it . . . He must face all kinds of unpleasantness and everyday persecution." Unlike a monarchy, he continued, society as the master no longer said: "Think like me or you die." Instead it said: "You are free not to think as I do; you can keep your life and property and all; but from this day you are a stranger among us. You can keep your privileges in the township, but they will be useless to you, for if you solicit your fellow citizen's votes, they will not give them to you, and you only ask for their esteem, they will make excuses for refusing that . . . When you approach your fellows, they will shun you as an impure being, and even those who believe in your innocence will abandon you too, lest they in turn be shunned . . ."

"No writer," added Tocqueville, "no matter how famous, can

escape from this obligation to sprinkle incense over his fellow citizens. Hence the majority live in a state of perpetual self-adoration. Only strangers or experience may be able to bring certain truths to the Americans' attention."

Local politicians attest to how difficult it is to get Californians to focus "attention" on the problems of the have-nots. An attempt to get a "living wage" ordinance onto the ballot in the late 1990s failed miserably, whereas a motion sponsored and funded at great expense by a Silicon Valley millionaire to ban bilingual education in California—part of making the immigrants "more American and less Hispanic" to the white, English-speaking majority—succeeded.

In the meantime, California's child poverty rate[37] continues to be stuck at around 24 to 25 percent for children under eighteen, and at almost 30 percent for children under six years of age, despite a decade of unprecedented wealth. The fact that a disproportionate number of these children in poor families are Latino and African-American may also have something to do with the lack of "attention" they receive.

But change—dramatic change—may be just around the corner in California. The shifting demographic is leading, inexorably, to a new majority over time.

Today's poor Latino children are not just tomorrow's poor Latino adults—they are part of tomorrow's majority. If they grow up written off and socially excluded, will they remember the way they have been treated? Will they seek some sort of retribution? For when they come to exercise their vote as fully grown adults, they will find that decisions regarding the Social Security arrangements of the white elderly—who are none other than today's young adult voters—are in their hands.

The irony is that by the year 2030, the aging white population will be increasingly dependent on the goodwill and good governance of the so-called ethnic minorities. "There's got to be a backlash coming," says Lawrence Stone. (Stone claims to have been Bill Clinton's first contact in Silicon Valley, having hosted him as the mayor of Sunnyvale two years before he became President of the United States.) "You just can't kick these Latinos around like we do forever," he says. "There will be consequences one day. Right now they are not unified politically. But one day they might be. Then the price to pay in California may well be extreme."

A FINAL SALUTARY TALE OF HOPE

Okay, call me a coward. Before I go to Washington, D.C., to sum up, I too want to sprinkle a little incense. But truth is—I would not be telling the full story of the frontier were I to stop here. For there is one quality of Americans—especially those who inhabit the frontier—I have not touched upon. I am referring to their restless capacity to reinvent themselves, to change, to adjust to new realities, more specifically, to realign their values beyond mere self-enrichment in a way that confounds our expectations.

Consider the story of Anthony Elgindy, a thirty-two-year-old immigrant I meet in San Diego, whose story, though unique in its detail, captures something about the search for meaning that is also very American.

Anthony Elgindy was born Amr Ibrahim Elgindy in Cairo, Egypt. In 1971, when he was four years old, his parents moved to Chicago, where his father—who had graduated top of his class at the University of Cairo—came to complete his engineering degree, and his mother to complete her studies in medicine. The plan for Anthony (his adopted name) was that he too would become a doctor, but to his parents' dismay, he quit college after two years because, he says, he became "more gripped to operate on money than on people."

His father told him that he'd be "a bum" and "never amount to anything," but, as Elgindy points out, he was just buying into the American culture, and indeed, the values of his father, who had quit his profession to become an import-export businessman. Elgindy became a car salesman, and then, soon as he was old enough, he took the exams to become a Wall Street stockbroker, "the former being perfect training for the latter," he claims.

In 1991, aided by his high-energy, fast-talking, and outgoing personality, Elgindy made his first million on commissions. He was twenty-four years old. Two years later, he quit trading for other people and began to trade strictly for his own account. He turned one million dollars into two million, parlayed that into four, and just kept on doubling his portfolio, he says. In the meantime, he had married Mary, the daughter of a Tennessee preacher, had become a father of the first of three children, and had begun to live life quite literally in the fast lane, indulging his love of fast cars.

I meet Elgindy in his private office in the early months of the year 2000. Dressed in blue jeans and a black leather Harley-Davidson jacket, he sits fidgeting with his hands and breathing loudly (more like snorting like a bull, actually), surrounded by flat-screen, state-of-the-art Bloomberg systems. "What can I say—I'm an incurable hyperactive," he apologizes, with a flaring of his nostrils and a slight raising of his eyebrows. Elgindy has become a trader with a cult following. More than 350 individuals pay $600 a month for membership of his Internet Web site, for which they get to see, online, the trades he is making in real time. His personal portfolio is worth "between $20 million and $30 million," he tells me, as he drives me in his humvee—the obscenely wide military-type jeep with onboard TV, VCR, and satellite tracking system (the same kind of vehicle that Stormin' Norman Schwarzkopf used in Operation Desert Storm)—to his secluded million-dollar mansion. It is set on two acres, with Italian marble floors, a zero-edge swimming pool, and a ten-foot waterfall. On any given day, the following vehicles line his driveway (in addition to the Humvee):

- An F1 Ferrari Spider (bought in 1999 for $180,000)
- A two-door Mercedes CLK320 (bought in 1999 for $70,000)
- A Jaguar XJR (his wife's, bought in 1999 for $80,000)
- A Sandrail (an off-road car bought in 1999 for $65,000)
- A Harley-Davidson motorcycle

When I ask him why they need five cars, he tells me that he has cut down, that he used to own ten. His cars, he says, dark eyes flashing boyishly, are his "toys," and that's why they are all convertibles and all red, "because toys should be red." Driving the Humvee, he adds, grinning broadly, is like driving around in the world's biggest Tonka truck.

Elgindy has everything the American Dream can possibly offer. He is proud of what he has built up and displays it flamboyantly. And yet, as he will also tell you, this voracious and too-narrow pursuit of the American Dream was very nearly his downfall.

Elgindy says that his "coming to his senses" was provoked by two dramatic life-changing events.

The first was that his wife filed for divorce. "Mary left me because I had emotionally neglected her and the children for years, and because of my selfish work-work-work, me-me-me lifestyle, and for the first time I was forced to look at who I had become," he says.

"I began to realize that money gives you one thing—the ability to express who you really are. If you're a jerk, that jerk will come out big-time. I discovered in the nick of time that I was an incredibly big, obnoxious jerk and that I didn't like myself much, either. . . ." He trails off. "I realized that if I died there and then, I was headed for a very small funeral. I promised to change. I asked Mary for another shot."

The second event took place a few years later, when Elgindy and his family were vacationing in Hawaii. One day, from his suite at the Sheraton, he was watching the Kosovo crisis unfold on CNN. "I saw people putting children on trucks," he says. "I thought: What kind of terror would provoke a parent to send their kids away on a truck? I was curious. At the same time, I had a vague notion that maybe I could do something to help. I decided to go and see for myself."

Next thing, Elgindy flies into Greece, and from there, together with an interpreter, he drives to the Macedonian border and walks across. Within two days, word had spread through Skopje that there was "a crazy American" running around town looking to help the orphans. Elgindy found himself wearing a too-small, borrowed suit and being interviewed on local television.

He plays me the videotape footage. The interviewer is clearly skeptical of Elgindy and asks him in a dispassionate tone: "So what brought you to Macedonia?" Elgindy finds himself making it up as he goes along. He has no history in this work, no thought-out plan to help, no real idea why he is there beyond his own intuition and curiosity, but he gathers his thoughts and speaks anyway. "I saw kids with no parents," he begins. "I put my life on pause to try and help . . . Individuals need to take themselves out of their own little world . . ." What Elgindy eventually told the interviewer was that he wanted to help the orphans by arranging visas, financial support, and safe passage for those who had relatives back in the United States.

Elgindy managed to arrange a visit to Camp Stenkovich II, where thousands of refugees were being held. Elgindy recalls: "I went to the Skopje McDonald's and bought 250 McFresh sandwiches, which I had to hide in a sack, because we weren't supposed to take anything in. We went from tent to tent meeting the refugees and handing out food. In addition to that, I gave each tent $400. I handed out $50,000 in one night."

"So all your life," I say to Elgindy, "you have helped only yourself. And suddenly you're in Macedonia handing out $50,000 to refugees. I don't get it."

"My whole life, I had been driven just by dollars," he says. "I cannot say really what made me go there—a search for something deeper, maybe—but when I was there, for the first time in my life I felt that I was doing something more valuable than just trading."

Quite extraordinarily, Elgindy managed to help bring twenty-three people back from Kosovo, he says, including a judge whose life was in danger and his family of ten, whom he continues to support financially. I meet the judge, Hassan, and his son, Valton, a wide-eyed twenty-one-year-old, whom Elgindy now employs and whom he is training to become a stockbroker. Valton cannot stop singing the praises of his mentor. "He is more than a role model to me," he says. "He is my idol. He has helped more people than you can imagine."

Elgindy may be murky as to why he went, but he is clearer on the impact that the madcap mission has had on his worldview.

"In this country," he says, "you're taught that other people are the competition, the enemy, and that in order to win, you have to step on them. Everything is a competition here. But when I went to Kosovo, my whole worldview was turned upside down. I would go into tents where people were starving and they would offer *me* what little they had. It just blew me away. I saw then that I wanted to serve people, not crush them.

"I never loved people like I did after going to Kosovo," he continues. "I realized that you cannot be happy simply because of the zeros in your bank account. It ain't about money, man. As an immigrant, you start of with zero inheritance and so you go after financial success. I grew up, in that sense, typically American, but I realize now that life is not simply about materialism. You cannot make a million dollars a year but neglect your wife and be called a success. You cannot make a million dollars a year but ignore the suffering of the have-nots around you and call yourself a success. Success involves love. Otherwise it's a meaningless existence."

So has Elgindy translated his epiphany in Kosovo into action in America?

Elgindy acknowledges that he is confused about how to help beyond his support of the clutch of immigrants he brought over. All the negative publicity about social programs has left him wanting to do more, he says, but untrusting of anything other than things he can do, touch, and measure for himself. He wants to be able to see "a societal return on his investment."

On this score, Elgindy is not alone, and in fact represents something of a trend. Philanthropy is on the up in America, with the number of family and community foundations having doubled in the last fifteen years,[38] with particularly notable growth in California and in the high-tech industries. Increasingly, say the experts, the new philanthropists are looking to "invest" their money rather than just "give it away." They call it "venture philanthropy" and "social investment" and they want to be able to measure a return on their investment.

"I don't want to give the have-nots a helping hand, I want to give them an opportunity hand," says Elgindy. "I think that being American means being given the opportunity to express yourself, and to use your God-given talents to afford other people the same equal opportunity."

How to achieve that equal opportunity?

He throws up his hands. On that front, he admits, the spirit is willing, but his education is only just beginning.

7 | WASHINGTON, D.C.

The Sum of the Parts

I blow into town expecting some answers. Like a cowboy come riding out of the west, who's been gone awhile and seen some things, I enter the capital ready to shoot some hard-hitting questions at the people who sit at the center of power.

On the news, Gore is saying that he wants to hold open town meetings to hear what the people really want. Bush is trumpeting the virtues of compassionate conservatism. Both men want to win over the group of Americans who have not yet enjoyed the benefits of the economic boom by promising to connect them to the full spirit of the American Dream. It's potentially good news for the sizable portion of society who have been left behind, but time will tell whether the candidates are sincere—and, importantly, whether the new president will have the support to push such an agenda through Congress.

My first instinct is to lasso congressmen with the full force of my findings and challenge them to respond. I want to begin by telling them that I have sojourned in the East and in the West, in the North and in the South, that I have listened to the testimony of ordinary people, that I have formed my understanding of America from the ground up. I want to say that I have encountered a very different America from the one-dimensional portrait of prosperity and contentment that is typically painted.

But to pursue a confrontational strategy, or to sum up, would be premature. For there are key pieces of the puzzle that still need to be filled in.

So let me back up a minute. Why have I come to Washington? Why have I chosen to make my last destination here on the verdant banks of the Potomac River?

Part of the answer is simply because Tocqueville finished here and the historical symmetry is aesthetically appealing. Yet there is a more substantive reason. As I have traveled, I have tried to explore the unique flavor of each region and to connect it with deeper nationwide trends. For me, California epitomizes the spirit of the frontier, the South carries the conscience of the nation, Ohio is the Bellwether State, Flint is the face of deindustrialized America, New York epitomizes the trend to increased inequality and social exclusion. But Washington represents the political union of all of these places. It is where elected politicians from all fifty states gather to pass laws that impact the lives of people throughout the Union—in both the parts of America that Tocqueville visited and the parts that developed later and that he never knew.

Washington is the sum of the parts. And what happens here impacts everywhere else.

The idea that all roads lead to Washington was imagined by the founding fathers and is encapsulated in the street plan of the city. The city is a grid with numerically numbered streets running north to south and alphabetical streets layered east to west, but superimposed over this alphanumeric grid are the broad diagonal avenues that give the city its elegance and which are named after states. So it is that Pennsylvania Avenue slides in from the northwest, New Jersey Avenue and Delaware Avenue arrive from the north, Maryland Avenue sallies in from the northeast. These avenues converge on the white-domed Capitol Building, the magnificent focal point of the city and, since Abraham Lincoln, symbol of the Union. It is here, under the portico of the Capitol, that the axes of the city cross, dividing Washington into its four geometric quadrants. It is here, on this central nodal point, that the great debates that shape the nation take place, and where the compass by which America charts its course is set.

In 1832, Tocqueville ascended the stairs of the Capitol—its foundations embedded deep in this identical plot of land known as Jenkins' Hill—to meet with politicians and to listen to arguments on the floor of the House and the Senate. At the time, horses and other farm animals grazed on the grounds, and inside, the Capitol was lit by gas-burning chandeliers. The senators dressed in long tailcoats and wrote with feather quill pens, and the public, who came to listen to the skillful oratory, draped themselves from the elegant visitors, gallery dressed in their Sunday best. One hundred and sixty-eight years later, I climb the well-worn steps of a Capitol that has been significantly modernized and extended—the famous cast-iron dome (painted white to resemble marble) was completed in 1863, the terrace added ten years later. In the early 1900s, the building was wired for electricity. Air conditioning was installed in the 1930s.

As I had done in Manhattan, Flint, and Pittsburgh, I retrace the Frenchman's footsteps and half wonder whom I might find. But serendipity, the magical companion of the travel writer, is less useful here. Everything in Washington happens behind closed doors. You have to make appointments.

I have arrived, to be honest, a far-from-neutral observer, my ears ringing with the criticism of a nation grown cynical of its politicians and wary of the corrupting force of soft money contributions. I wonder: Was Tocqueville fresh to what he would discover here, or did he arrive with biased preconceptions as well? I root through the text of his diaries and find the following entry as he took his bumpy ride toward the capital.

"Conversation with a lawyer of Montgomery (Alabama), 6 January 1832," Tocqueville began. "I've travelled two days with this young man. I've forgotten his name, which is an obscure one anyhow. Yet I think I should make a record of his conversation. It is stamped with great practical common sense." Tocqueville went on to pepper his companion with a series of questions, one of which was to inquire: "Do the people choose good representatives?"

"No," replied the lawyer, "generally they elect men of their own capacity, and flatterers."

"But there must result from these poor selections poor laws and a poor government," Tocqueville then suggested.

"Not nearly to such an extent as one would at first believe. There are always, in our assemblies, some men of talent; from the first days these overwhelm the others and dominate business entirely. It's really they who make and discuss the laws; the others vote blindly. We have had representatives who didn't know how to read or write."[1]

The idea that quality trumped ignorance would have been a comforting thought to Tocqueville, who agonized constantly whether American democracy would work in France. On arrival in the capital, though, Tocqueville was underwhelmed by the physical spectacle of Washington (then a small town of just twenty thousand people) and seemingly conflicted by what he thought of the politicians. Of the first, he wrote: "Washington offers the sight of an arid plain, burned by the sun, on which are scattered two or three sumptuous edifices and the five or six villages composing the town. Unless one is Alexander or Peter the Great," he added sarcastically, "one must not meddle with creating the capital of an empire."[2] Later that week, he wrote his father: "Washington contains at the moment the outstanding men of the entire union."[3] And yet elsewhere he opines: "To win the votes of the electors, one has to descend to manoeuvres that disgust distinguished men."

But as soon as I begin to take in my surroundings, I find that my predisposed state of mind starts to shift quite radically. The Mall, which runs from the Capitol Building to the Lincoln Memorial, is a vista of breathtaking color, grandeur, and beauty. It runs via the soaring, needle-shaped Washington Monument and the long, shimmering Reflecting Pool and is lined by grand government buildings and monumental museums. Its blend of classical European lines, American symbolism, and unostentatious simplicity evokes an emotional response of which its architect, Frenchman Pierre-Charles L'Enfant, would have been proud. It humbles. It inspires. It makes me believe that the high-flown ideals—of equality and inclusiveness—engraved on the walls of the Lincoln Memorial are what this country is about. It is an open urban space to rival any, and enough to convert a cynic into a patriot.

Then I enter the lobby of the Capitol, the belly of the beast. And I discover that neither of my bipolar expectations matches up to the reality.

What I find instead is a marketplace. In this marketplace, there is no single idealistic truth and damn few outright lies, just a plethora of competing points of view jostling for the attention and support of the politicians. Of course, some of these points of view have a lot more money behind them than others. But it is not as simple as that. It is a fiendishly complex marketplace with its own rules and regulations. And the people who sit at the nexus of all this money and power and who know the rules better than anyone else are a ubiquitous group of people that Tocqueville, in all his talk about the division of powers and checks and balances, never mentions once. They were simply not around in the Frenchman's day.

They are the lobbyists.

In his 1995 State of the Union address, President Clinton referred disparagingly to the growing role played by lobbyists. "Three times as many lobbyists are in the streets and corridors of Washington as were here twenty years ago," he said. "The American people look at their capital and they see a city where the well-connected and the well-protected can work the system, but the interests of the ordinary citizen are often left out. As the new Congress opened its doors, lobbyists were still doing business as usual—the gifts, the trips, all the things that people are concerned about haven't stopped . . . Tonight I ask you to just stop taking the lobbyists' perks. Just stop." (Applause.)

But five years on, lobbyists are even more integral to the way the capital appears to function.

Lobbyists, I surmise, are the underbelly of Washington. They are the connective tissue between the key constituencies that have the run of the capital. As such, they are perfectly positioned to reveal how power operates in America.

I spend a few days setting up appointments. Then I grab my jacket and head for the door.

THE CANNON AND THE PEASHOOTER

K street is the Wall Street of Washington. It runs parallel to the Mall, passing a few streets up from the White House, and although it bears no physical resemblance to Wall Street—being longer, wider, and not at all cloistered—it too harbors the reputation of housing the firms that employ the highest-paid brokers in the city. I am referring, of course, to the lobbyists, most of whom are lawyers by training, or former staffers on Capitol Hill who have decided to cash in by turning their extensive network of political contacts and insider knowledge to profitable advantage. And yet, like Wall Street, K Street exists as both metaphor and physical reality. The lobbying industry has grown so fast that it long ago slipped its moorings, and these days lobbying firms are to be found throughout the city.

One of the first lobbyists I have arranged to meet is Howard Vine, the managing partner of a high-profile lobbying firm, Greenberg Traurig. They are situated on Connecticut Avenue, across the street from Lafayette Square, which, as he later explains to me, "is as close as you can get to the White House without actually being in the White House."

Vine is on a phone call when I arrive, and so I am ushered into a nondescript conference room on the fifth floor with a view of the Washington Monument. The room has a round wood table in the center, and a side table groaning with leftovers from a prior lunch meeting. I am encouraged by Vine's secretary to help myself to the triple-layer sandwiches, pickles, sodas, and bags of Cape Cod king-size potato chips while I wait. "Howard will be through in a few minutes," she says.

But forty-five minutes later, having sated myself on pickles, there is still no sign of Vine. I am growing impatient, torn between leaving and grabbing a postlunch nap as the sun rays slant warmly through the glass patio door, when Vine breezes into the room, apologizing profusely. "I had to take that call," he says. "It was about my divorce."

Vine perches opposite me, dressed in a tailored suit, and good-looking in a swarthy, ruddy-faced way. He is in his forties and he settles down to explain what he does to justify his salary of $750,000 a year. What exactly are you trying to get for your clients? I ask. Is it simply access to the ear of a politician? The wording of my question is spurred by an earlier conversation that I'd had with David Broder, a political journalist at the *Washington Post*.

"For people to be represented in this democracy takes much more than simply voting for their congressman every two years. To be represented, you have to be *represented*," Broder had told me.

"And that takes?"

"Access," he had replied.

"And to get access takes money?" I had suggested.

"Well, access doesn't necessarily take money—the media have access, grass-roots organizations have access, intellectuals who have policy ideas have access—but money is one route to access. For policymakers, the commodity most valuable to them is their time, and someone who gives them money has a claim on their time. Access is the key. Without access, you won't be represented."

Broder had been making what I thought was a subtle point, that money bought a donor access but not necessarily more than that because of offsetting nonmonetary forces.

I expect Vine to be more circumspect than Broder, but his response is unequivocal. "My clients want *much* more than access," he begins. "They want a result. I am paid to produce . . ." he pauses, searching for the right word, "to *engineer* the right result for my client."

Vine describes the relationship between K Street and Capitol Hill as symbiotic. "The lobbyist is dependent on the member of Congress to advance the cause of his clients. The member of Congress is dependent on the lobbyist to help raise the money he needs to be re-elected." A member of the House of Representatives needs $700,000 to run for office, he tells me, which means a thousand dollars a day for two years. With the prohibitive cost of airtime on television, it's only getting more and more expensive. "It comes down to what Congressman Richard Gephardt, a good friend of mine, says: 'Money is the mother's milk of politics.' Money preoccupies congressmen in their judgment, in their philosophy, and in their approach to politics. We help them overcome their fundraising problems and we ask them to help us with our client's problems. It's all about building relationships."

Vine has an eclectic mix of clients. He represents megacorporations such as Unilever as well as the Department of Agriculture for the state of Florida. "The Mexicans were dumping tomatoes into the U.S., killing the Florida tomato industry, and I engineered an action to stop them and won," he says. He also represents, for example, the largest ball-bearing company in America and an Internet-based health-care provider called WebMD. He explains how WebMD, an Internet start-up worth $12 billion, have been smart enough to realize that government legislation is at the core of their future stream of profits. "They realize that as a health-care provider operating through the Internet, they are at risk of being heavily regulated," he says. "Government is going to shape their reimbursement rate, their taxes." They pay Vine $250,000 a year to help them figure out "where they need to bond long-term in order to ward off adverse legislation." So far, in addition to his own fees, he has them contributing $100,000 to the Democrats and $100,000 to the Republicans ("We always play both sides") as well as contributing computer equipment to the Democratic Congressional Campaign Committee for House of Representative members. "We're still working on what to do for the senators," he adds.

Vine has been in the lobbying business twenty-three years. In that time, he has seen it become infinitely more complicated. "It used to be that lobbyists worked on behalf of a handful of powerful trade associations," he says. Foremost among them was the Business Roundtable, which comprised the CEOs of the largest corporations in the U.S. "It was the voice of big business, and when they spoke as an organization, they changed law." What has happened since, he explains, with the proliferation of individual leadership committees and political action committees (PACs)—which individual congressmen use to raise their own funds—has been the fragmentation of power so that now you have businesses competing with each other for the time and attention of the congressmen.

"In the old days," he adds ruefully, clasping his hands together, "you went to one or two key people and if you took care of them, you were okay. Now, with all the money sloshing around Washington, you're barely covered."

"In this cacophony, who represents the have-nots?" I ask.

"Well," replies Vine, "they're losing one of their greatest champions when Daniel Patrick Moynihan leaves the Senate. There's still Kennedy, and Gephardt, who is one of my closest friends," he reminds me, "and one or two others. But overall, there are fewer and fewer congressmen willing to take on their cause."

"Why is that?" I ask.

"Because," he says, "it just doesn't sell."

"At the end of the day," Vine explains, "congressmen need a message that resonates with the people who fund their campaign. And obviously, since the working poor don't have money to contribute, you won't find many politicians taking on their concerns. You see this particularly in the House, because the short two-year election cycle means members are always thinking about the next election. Helping the poor is something they're not going to do unless their pollsters tell them it's popular. For example, with the economy so buoyant, raising the minimum wage another dollar has become a safe thing to do, so it will probably pass. But otherwise, they're not going to touch the issue, because they can't afford to."

"Is this democracy you see working?" I ask.

"Yes, I think it is," he says, without a flicker of hesitation.

I laugh in surprise at his answer. "Despite all you've said?"

"The workers are represented by their unions and the unions have lobbyists too," he says.

"But many of these workers aren't unionized," I counter.

"Ah! That's where they're getting screwed," he says.

Vine is momentarily triumphant, but then a look of perplexed concern settles over his brow, as if something troubling has just occurred to him. "I'd love your advice on something," he says, hunching forward. "My fiancée is a nurse. She was trained to be a nurse. That's all she knows how to do. She's paid fourteen dollars an hour. Her sister is a schoolteacher and she gets fifteen dollars an hour. Nothing more than that. You know, it's just . . ." He searches for the words. The tone of his voice has softened, even his posture. "You have someone who's a garbage collector who is unionized earning eighteen dollars an hour. I mean . . . I mean a salesman makes $80,000 a year to a teacher's $25,000. My question is: How do people get unstuck from that situation?"

I am taken aback by his change of tack. Until now, Vine had been the model of K Street self-assurance, recounting for me tales of his conquests as a lobbyist. Now he seems to want assurance from me. I deflect his question into a broader one and cobble together an answer of sorts. "This is a society that does not value nursing and teaching," I say. "It forces people who want to go into the caring professions to make a choice between doing a job that is meaningful to them, and doing something for the money. There's a big loss to society right there. They are devalued jobs."

"It's tragic," says Vine, shoulders slumping. "It's upside down. I don't know the answer. I think there is a disenfranchisement of the poor, of the less well-heeled, the less organized. The disenfranchisement of the have-nots in Washington is very evident. There's no question in my mind about that."

When I first arrived in Washington, I had asked David Broder and numerous other informants which lobbyists they thought I ought to speak to. I was steered toward the large colony of people who had once been part of the Democratic Party machine but were now working the other side of the street. One name that consistently came up was that of Tom Downey, who for eighteen years had been a Democratic congressman from Long Island, New York. "You must speak to Downey," a Republican on one of the congressional committees had pressed me. "He came to Congress when he was twenty-five years old as part of the class of Democrats who arrived just after Watergate. He was bold. He was for the have-nots more than anyone else. Plus he was as effective as hell."

"Where would I find him?" I had asked.

"He's here, on K Street, making a million bucks," came the tart reply.

Downey's lobbying firm, the Downey McGrath Group, is actually situated on I Street, but no matter . . . On a steamy, sweat-drenching day, the kind for which Washington is renowned, I am ushered into his plush air-conditioned conference room.

Shortly Downey arrives, dressed impeccably in an executive dark-gray suit, blue shirt and tie, and accompanied at his elbow by his media man, Tom Scott. Downey seats himself at the head of the table and asks me to summarize my findings. He has a presence about him, a charisma, that I can't quite put my finger on. Maybe it's the way that he asks questions before he talks, or the calm, focused way that he listens, palms placed flat on the table in front of him. I outline the route and rationale of my journey, describe the trend toward greater inequality, say how I have investigated the apparent erosion in some quarters of an attitude that Tocqueville thought was peculiarly American and had dubbed "self-interest properly understood." I explain why I have come to Washington and that I am seeking the perspective of lobbyists, particularly ones familiar with the power games that swirl about Capitol Hill.

When I am finished, he says: "I think you've observed a phenomenon that is getting worse over time, not better. And it's highlighted by easily the most disgraceful vote I've seen since coming to Washington more than twenty years ago." The previous week, the House had overwhelmingly passed a proposal to abolish the federal estate tax. This amounted to a windfall for the very rich, since it is only the wealthiest families who pay estate tax in America.[4] "The fact that this measure was passed is amazing on many levels," says Downey. "It amounts to an estimated $50 billion in lost revenue by the year 2010. If we took that amount of money and diverted it, we could end child poverty in this country next year! On a deeper level, the passing of great estates from generation to generation is contrary to the founding ideas of this country. We did not want to pass on wealth tax-free. We did not want to create inherited classes. That was what they did in England. Our idea was that you made it on your own. What's ultimately fascinating is how many Democrats have abandoned this basic idea of estate tax, an idea that not even Ronald Reagan would have thought to attack. It says volumes about the changing way Americans look at other Americans."

Downey says that when he first came to Washington in 1974, there was a real desire among Democrats to help the poor. But starting in the eighties, when Reagan made the poor undeserving, it came to be that you could not talk about the poor. Downey's comments remind me of the quote by Andrew Cuomo, Clinton's secretary of housing and urban development, who said: "When I took over the department, I talked to one of the sharp political guys in town. He said, 'Look, never say "poverty." It's political suicide for you. The impression is going to be that you're an old-time liberal . . . [part of] the politics of yesterday.' "

"If you look at Congress today, the poor are just less of an issue," continues Downey. "Within the Democrats, the labor movement and African-Americans seem to have less power than they had in the past. It's because of this phenomenon of money and politics. As a politician, your heart may be in one place, but your head may be following more and more the money. That doesn't mean that on some occasions you wouldn't be for . . ." He trails off. Ironically, among the American people, there are large majorities in the right position, he contends. For example, the idea that if you work full-time for a living, you shouldn't be poor resonates with Americans. They support the idea that the minimum wage should be raised, they support giving health insurance to poor children. "But it's when you try and pass legislation along those lines that the powerful moneyed interests come in and say: 'That's real interesting to be for health insurance, and you should be, but let's do it this way.' Then they divert the debate into something else. The ability of powerful moneyed interests to divert attention and to change the subject or redefine the issue cannot be underestimated," he says.

But the powerful moneyed interests Downey refers to are represented in Washington by lobbyists such as himself. "Do you find yourself conflicted between what you believe and what you do as a lobbyist?" I ask.

"Sure I do," he says. "We try not to do . . . We turn down a lot of business."

"You do? Like who?"

"Well, we've turned down the tobacco industry, we turned down the Indian gaming industry. At the end of the day, what I do and who I represent is not that different from when I was in Congress. For instance, we represent the American Foundation for AIDS Research as well as companies like Microsoft. If there are things we don't feel comfortable doing, we don't do them. I don't want to say I'm a saint, because it wouldn't be true. But as we're not owned by anybody, it makes it easier to pick and choose.

"Some of the advocates of the poor—such as the Children's Defense Fund and the Center on Budget and Policy Priorities—are really quite excellent," he adds.

I recall how earlier I had met with Robert Greenstein, the head of the Center on Budget and Policy Priorities, who had told me that advocates for the have-nots were "heavily outgunned." "There are some terrific lobbyists for the have-nots, but on average, the K Street firms representing big business pay much higher salaries than the nonprofit organizations and so they attract the more skilled employees," he had said. The gap in the ability of these two groups to lobby effectively on the Hill is so shockingly wide, and the size of the collection of interests so brutally unbalanced, thought Greenstein, that it is like trying to fight a cannon with a peashooter.

I am about to share Greenstein's analysis with Downey when he says something similar himself. "Overall, the balance of power is such that the poor get a raw deal. They don't have the money to compete with the corporate guys. It's the first rule of politics: He who has the gold wins."

Nevertheless, Downey is an optimist and he sees a silver lining. He believes that politics runs in cycles, and that we are headed out of a cycle of indifference into a cycle of activism. "I think the confluence of this cyclical event and the availability of a lot of money could really make a difference," he says, referring to the huge and growing federal budget surplus. He cites Bush's use of phrases such as "prosperity with a purpose" and "compassionate conservatism" as proof that he has tapped into it. "He has realized he can't continue to take the brass-knuckled conservative approach that he has in the past." America is now generating so much wealth that it has the resources to do what needs to be done, he argues. "The real interesting test for us in the future is that we're going to have the resources to improve everybody's quality of life. The question is: Will we?"

"What do you think?" I ask.

"I think the jury is still out," he says. "What we need is great leadership. A leader who can identify the problems of the working poor and who explains to the people that it's all of our problem and then sets out a bipartisan plan to fix it." Such a leader will need to be able to overcome the powerful moneyed interests, whose aim is to change the subject and prevent things being done, he adds.

I spend much of my week in Washington as a fly on the wall accompanying various other lobbyists on their rounds. I accompany them to private dinners in private dining clubs where they rub shoulders and schmooze with congressmen and key White House staff. I dine with them on lashings of tenderly cooked salmon followed by obscenely large chocolate-covered strawberries, with balls of sorbet to clear our palates between courses and as much red and white wine as we can muster. I ride the subway with them in the network of tunnels below the Capitol connecting the House and the Senate to the adjacent buildings where the congressmen have their offices. I watch while some of them still do the thing after which they were originally named—hanging about in the lobby in the hope that they will bump into congressmen or their staffers and engage them in a little light banter. "Face time," they call it.

Much of it is pretty humdrum stuff.

I discover that on the whole, the K Street crowd are not the grubby villains that newspapers paint them to be, but are instead professionals with the same kind of cold, hard, driven credo you would find in any Wall Street firm. They even talk using the same kind of military and phallic metaphors, boasting about "penetrating through" and the thrill of being "hired guns." And like Wall Street's, their demographic profile is overwhelmingly white and predominantly male. Their apparent crime is that they treat Washington as a profit center, a place where huge amounts of money can be made, and that they are unashamed about it.

"Lobbyists don't give a damn if you're Democrat or Republican," Michael Lewan, a lobbyist who used to be the chief of staff for Democrat Senator Joe Lieberman, tells me. "We're all in this to make money. I've rarely, if ever, had an ideological argument. In fact, that fellow you met on your way up is my partner who looks after the Republicans," he says.

To trace the movements of a lobbyist is to draw a series of vectors that run from K Street to the Capitol, to private clubs, to fund-raisers, occasionally to the White House, but mostly to and from the Hill. Most operate in a bubble seemingly oblivious to the alarming poverty just out of sight of the Mall. In Washington D.C., an astounding 45 percent of children under eighteen are living in poverty. This amounts to a 50 percent increase in the child poverty rate since 1979, an extraordinary statistic especially given the robust state of the economy.[5]

As I move around the capital, I bump into the parents of some of these children working in the usual poverty-wage, service-sector jobs. As in the rest of America, these jobs are disproportionately held by nonwhites who are barely visible to the power brokers. I engage some of them in conversation and discover, for example, that my waiter in a Turkish restaurant on Du Pont Circle is a delightfully refined Tunisian man with a master's degree in English literature who has been unable to find employment commensurate with his education. I meet taxi drivers who are university graduates, some who have masters degrees themselves.

Later in the week, I meet Rick Berman, fifty-seven, a lawyer-lobbyist whose firm, Berman and Company, represents many of the chain hospitality companies—food, beverage, and hotels—that pay minimum wage in America. "We are the biggest lobbyists in America for the hospitality industry," he assures me. Berman eases back in his tan leather chair, his suspenders hanging slack over a blue striped shirt that is open and unbuttoned to his chest. Berman used to be a polo player, and framed photographs of him with his stick and his horse decorate his wall. Chains like Chili's, TGI Friday's, and their trade associations are his clients, he says, as well as coalitions made up of fast-food companies such as Wendy's, the Marriott group of hotels, and restaurant chains like Applebee's and Hooters. Not McDonald's, he adds. They have their own in-house lobbyists.

"Many of our clients are coalitions of companies. That way they can pay us to represent them and retain their anonymity."

"How is that?" I ask.

"We don't have to file reports of which companies we're representing when they're in a coalition," he says. He is referring to the Lobbying Disclosure Act of 1998, which requires lobbyists to disclose their individual clients to the clerk of the Senate.

"One of the most hotly contested issues for my clients is the bid to increase the minimum wage," he says. "It comes up all the time. My job is to jump all over it."

"Do you think the proposed legislation [to increase minimum wage from $5.15 to $6.15] will pass?" I ask.

"My guess is that it will. It has the support of both parties," he says. "The real fight will be over this new thing they call a living wage. It's a bicoastal phenomenon that's spreading like a virus," he says. He hands me a map of the U.S. that shows the dozens of cities that have enacted or have proposed living wage ordinances in the last six years. It began with Baltimore in 1994, and has spread to numerous big cities, including Boston, Hartford, Detroit, Chicago, Denver, Oakland, San Jose, and Los Angeles. Usually, these ordinances require businesses that have contracts with the city council to pay their workers a living wage which, depending on the part of the country, tends to be in the $7- to $10-an hour range. Until now, it has only affected a limited group of businesses, but a few cities are keen to expand the concept so that all businesses within a defined geographical boundary would be expected to pay these rates. This development has Berman hopping mad.

"This is not how America works," he says hotly. "We don't pay people based on need. Maybe the Soviet Union. It's become a mantra: If you work hard and play by the rules, you shouldn't be living in poverty. Well—" he leans forward, wagging his finger— "you know what's also one of the rules? . . . You also have to be able to read English. All these illiterate people . . . Someone should tell them—there's no free lunch here."

But Berman's concerns appear premature. Not one city has enacted a geographically based living wage ordinance, and it's merely a proposal in Santa Monica and in Oakland, California. So why the revved-up response? I ask him as he walks me to the door.

"You know how a fire starts," he says. "It begins out of sight on a tiny spot and soon you've got a fire on the carpet and then the whole building is in flames." Berman smiles and extends his hand. "Sorry to be so combative," he says. "But you see, I'm a lobbyist. And from where I sit, I see fire on the carpet."

The least attractive aspect about the K Street crowd can be their po-faced self-importance and their overinflated egos. "Left to their own devices, politicians would screw everything up," one lobbyist explains to me. "We provide the information that politicians need to make informed decisions."

But at the end of the day, to blame lobbyists for Washington's sullied reputation is to shoot the messenger. Lobbyists do not dance alone. And a question that keeps nagging at me is: How does the unequal balance of forces on K Street impact the way that congressmen go about their business? Is this democracy really for sale to the highest bidder?

It's a tough subject to investigate, because obviously I am unlikely to find a congressman who will admit to being influenced by something as crude as money.

My best bet, I surmise, is to try to speak to the people who know them best.

THE CREEP ON THE HILL

I find myself, one morning, deep underground in the bowels of Capitol Hill, sitting in the Senate Cafeteria, where they sell sandwiches called "Overly Optimistic," "The Great Debate," and "The Filibuster," engaged in private conversation with a man called Jim.

Jim (not his real name) is the chief of staff to a Democratic senator, and he will only allow me to quote him on condition that he remain anonymous. He is a veteran of the Hill, having worked here his whole working life, which has given him, he says, a bird's-eye view of how things have changed in the last three decades.

Jim begins by mounting a defense of the political system in general and of senators in particular. His own boss is "pretty principled," he says. He tells me that the connection between money and power is not a crude one, that it is subtle and complicated. "No good lobbyist will ever ask a politician to do something that will hurt them politically, and congressmen aren't stupid enough to do something that will cost them their seat just for the money." He also says that sometimes the people with the money can be right, that "sometimes we don't know what we're doing."

"But there are some things that worry me," he continues. "I don't have a problem with how much money is spent on politicians. The problem is that the money is all coming from the same people. [As a congressman,] you spend your life going from one group of upper-income people to another. You have to raise so much money that you end up spending most of your time at fund-raisers, and that means less time for the real people who live in your constituency. At first you might resent the trade-off. But over time it becomes easier and easier to spend time with the lobbyists and the corporate guys. Because, you know what? You discover that in many ways, they're just like you—well-educated, high-income young professionals who like to talk about politics, women, sports, and money. They share the same humor and laugh at your jokes. They compliment you and make you feel good about yourself.

"When you do attend a town meeting with your constituents, you end up being harangued for an hour. After a while, what would you rather do? Who do you start feeling better around? So you cut back on the town meetings. And then you know what happens? You start to think like the people you hang around with. You lose your edge. Your sensibility to the problems of real people is dulled. That's the creep on Capitol Hill."

Go to the Ways and Mean Committee, Jim exhorts me, and see how many labor lobbyists are attached there and how many business lobbyists. "When it comes to shaping tax policy, take a guess how many times the business lobbyists outnumber labor lobbyists."

"Twice as many," I estimate.

"Try again," he scoffs.

"I don't know . . . Ten times as many?"

"Fifty to one," he says. "They outnumber them fifty to one."

"Wow!" I gape. "I had no idea it was that—"

But before I can quiz Jim further, he jumps up, checking his watch, and excuses himself. Without a trace of irony, he says: "McDonald's are coming in to see us today—I have to go."

Sarah Walzer, thirty-nine, used to work on the Washington staff of Joe Lieberman, the Democratic senator from Connecticut, early on in the first Clinton administration. Walzer is a lawyer and describes herself as having been "Joe's front line." She would decide which lobbyists he should and shouldn't see. "There were days when I met with a different lobbyist every half hour," she recalls. "It wasn't unusual for me to see eighteen of them in a single day."

She describes her relationship with the lobbyists as a constantly shifting power struggle. "It's an uneasy balance. You're always aware that although they need something from you today, you may need them in two weeks on something else," she says.

"Does that make it hard to say no?" I ask.

"I don't think money affects the vote or the final decision of congressmen directly," she says. "I never saw that in Lieberman's office. I never saw a politician change his mind or amend his vote on something he believed in because of meeting with a lobbyist. But indirectly, it does impact the decision. Money will buy them the opportunity to make their case in person. That has an impact in the long term."

"So it's not a crude case of politicians for hire?"

"Not that I have seen. But I worked for one of the most sincere and moral politicians on the Hill, so the fact that I didn't see it doesn't mean that it doesn't happen. In many cases, the money follows the publicly known position of the senator. People support the people who support their causes and hold their positions. In many ways, lobbyists enhance the process of democracy. It's not all just thwarting democracy. They bring us facts. We have to remember, though, that facts are very malleable. I spent a lot of my time having to look behind the spin on the facts, trying to get past the glossy position papers and the slick videos and the offers of fund-raisers to get to the reality."

Walzer says that lobbyists enjoy most success when a new issue emerges on which the "other side" is not even represented. She recalls the example of the bill brought to the Senate, sponsored by Joe Lieberman and several others, whose aim was to reduce lead levels and do something about the rising number of children who lived in housing estates and who contracted lead poisoning. (Lead poisoning can cause developmental delays and arrested brain-function development, and children under three years of age are particularly susceptible.) "At the time, there were no lobbyists to speak for poor children who suffered lead poisoning, but there was a whole roomful of lobbyists who represented people who used lead in their products and didn't want the law tampered with," she says. "Plumbers, paint manufacturers, even real estate agents—their lobbyists descended on us. They all objected to lead paint abate-ment on account of the cost and that it would interfere with the house sales process. In the end, we managed to get some legislation passed regarding stricter rules of notification [informing prospective tenants that lead paint may exist on the premises and absolving the landlord from liability!]. It was a much-watered-down version of what we had originally hoped for. On the one side, we were as-saulted by a loud, well-funded voice. On the other side, there was virtually no one."

It's a consistent story that I hear, that of the cannon and the pea-shooter. As the relationship between lobbyists and politicians be-comes ever more symbiotic, the have-nots and their advocates risk being crowded out. It's a subtle story too, I am constantly re-minded, but with unsubtle consequences. Because those who frame the debate ultimately draft the laws that impact the lives of ordinary Americans throughout the nation.

It would seem then, like a pessimistic prognosis for the prospects of the have-nots.

But this is not the whole story.

There are at least two offsetting reasons to think that despite the constellation of adverse, entrenched interests, Tom Downey is right and America may be headed out of a cycle of indifference and into a cycle of activism.

The first is that the budget surplus will make it easier to help the have-nots. When new money becomes available, you can give to Peter without taking from Paul. It's less of a zero-sum game. The abundance of resources increases the possibilities of what can be achieved. It allows you to think about helping others without compromising yourself. It allows America to be as magnanimous, generous, and heroic in its prosperity as Tocqueville imagined it would be. President Clinton tapped into this when he told the people: "I believe what a nation does with its prosperity is just as stern a test of judgment, wisdom, and character as what a nation does in adversity."[6]

Many Democrats talk this way, but it is when I start to hear it from the mouths of died-in-the-wool Republicans that I sit up and take note. Which brings me to a second spark of optimism. There is perhaps cause to think that we may be on the brink of a new bipartisan consensus between conservatives and liberals about helping Americans who have been left behind.

In the past, the debate about helping the have-nots got mired in a hopelessly partisan conversation. The core belief of most Republicans (and many conservative Democrats) is that in the open capitalist economy that is America, people progress based on their own merit and effort. The people who got left behind, the poor, the have-nots, whatever we call them, were tarred with the brush of being lazy, immoral, and incompetent. The people, not the government, were held responsible for their own situation. Which meant that government should not interfere unless there was evidence of market failure. Their argument was that if government ended welfare, this would "free up" and motivate those very people who needed to get off their backsides and find a job.

But now that welfare reform has happened, now that the welfare rolls are dramatically down and Americans are working in record numbers, what has become abundantly clear is that many of these working people are nevertheless still living below the poverty line. This is a problem for honest Republicans. Now they begin to perceive the outline of something like a market failure. Now the idea of government doing something to help these people becomes a possibility. Simply put, enacting legislation to help people who are working is much more congruent with American values than help-ing people who are on welfare. Back in 1993, during the first Clin-ton administration, when the Democrat majority pushed to expand the Earned Income Tax Credit into a $30 billion program (this legislation is the most significant antipoverty legislation to come out of the nineties), not a single Republican voted in favor.

The key breakthrough question is: Would legislation to signif-icantly help working poor families attract enough bipartisan support to pass today?

Before I depart Washington, I put this question to Ron Haskins, a veteran Republican, who as the staff director of the House Ways and Means Committee can offer insight into his party's way of thinking.

"I'll be frank—the aftermath of welfare reform has got us con-servatives over a barrel," he says. "Here's why. As long as people sat on their ass, Americans did not want to give them much. That's why liberals were never able to create a generous welfare state—because it wasn't hooked into work. Now we basically said they got to work. And guess what? They did. They went out in massive numbers and started working. So now, okay, they're working, but they're earning between minimum wage and $7.50 an hour on average and they're still on the brink of poverty. What is more, we are starting to see new studies which show that if you supplement the income of these people to a substantial degree—to get them up to $8 an hour—you have a range of incredibly positive social outcomes. You increase marriage, you increase the chances of suc-cess of that marriage, you see positive impacts on the children, both in their behavior and academic achievement, and you reduce do-mestic violence. These are things that Republicans care deeply about. Now you've got their attention."

The effect of this could be profound, Haskins, who is soon to retire from politics, goes on to argue. "Even more interesting than the money itself is the psychological message it sends out," he says, becoming animated. "It's like what Tocqueville said about the hap-piness of Americans being tied to equality of outcomes. It's the understanding that the people will have that if they work, their fellow citizens are willing to help them, and not in a mean-spirited way, but in a generous way. Maybe that's what it is. And that's close to the idea of your book, right? The psychological sort of thing. We're in a very different world in America now and these debates are going to shift. Boy, I hate to be knocking down all these conservative bowling pins, but hey—"

Haskins breaks off in mid-sentence and starts to laugh. "You know what?" He slaps his knee and rocks forward, laughing so much he can hardly get the words out. "I'm thinking about having this discussion with Senator Trent Lott." He gags some more. "I'm just thinking about this conversation, I'm just thinking about what the typical Republican thinks about this topic."

"And what do they think?" I prod.

"Oh, they wouldn't even . . . he wouldn't want to talk about it."

"He wouldn't?"

"Oh, no. He'd deflect it something fierce. That's my guess. He'd say that people have to earn their own money. He'd say that we have set up a society where people are rewarded for work, and for education. He'd say that we are already doing too much to help the poor."

Haskins seems to be contradicting himself—on the one hand suggesting that a new bipartisan conversation is imminent, on the other suggesting that the typical Republican will do his or her utmost to avoid the conversation. It sounds like "compassionate conservatism" might provoke a split in the rank and file. This new conversation, if it ever takes place, is unlikely to be plain sailing.

"Washington is like a bunch of continents," explains Haskins.

"Continents?"

"Yeah. Immovable objects, well established, big and powerful. Soon as you want to change something, you're gonna run into one of them. And when you do, they'll spend a lot of money to oppose you."

His words take me full circle, back to the role lobbyists might be expected to play in easing or stalling this alignment of continents.

I recall how various lobbyists had told me in so many words: lobbyists are most effective when all they have to do is prevent change from happening.

CONCLUSION

Now I am nearing the end. Like Tocqueville, who caught the boat home from New York City, I too must head back north to pack up my things, say my goodbyes, and fly out of Kennedy. It's an easy four-hour cruise up the interstate. Time to download. Time to ramble. Time—I was going to say—to wrap things up.

But summing up is not something I am drawn to do. It strikes me as pat, didactic, repetitive, and boring. The thoughts that swirl within me as I wend my way homeward are much less formal, more stream-of-consciousness. They have to do with the American Dream, and with whether America and its new president will seize the moment. I find myself recalling words from Shakespeare:

> *There is a tide in the affairs of men*
> *which taken at the flood leads on to fortune;*
> *Omitted, all the voyage of their life*
> *is bound in shallows and in miseries.*
> *On such a full sea are we now afloat,*
> *and we must take the current when it serves,*
> *or lose our ventures.*[7]

It's a quote from the tragedy of *Julius Caesar.* I'm thinking: Of course! Click, click, click. America is the modern Roman Empire. And as with all empires, the greatest test of character comes when they're least expecting it, when they're at the absolute height of their powers. On such a full sea is America now afloat. But it seems conflicted—spiritually, politically, and morally—as to which way to go.

On a personal note, I feel a sadness too. Saying goodbye to friends is never easy. But there is something else. I have felt no joy, I reflect, in puncturing the frabjous balloon we call the American Dream. For one thing, it represents more than just a dream for Americans. It's a dream for all of us. For mankind.

But let us at least be honest. The American Dream that Tocqueville described in all its archetypal glory was a dream for whites only. Blacks, mulattos, and Native American Indians were not allowed access. Today America thinks of itself as the ultimate inclusive get-ahead society. It peddles this image both at home and abroad. But according to American social scientists, there is no more social mobility in America today than in other industrialized Western countries. There is not, they say, nearly as much upward social mobility, or inclusiveness, as the American credo would have us believe.

And yet if the credo is out of line with the reality, I wonder, is that a good or a bad thing? It's a bad thing because it's a distortion and because it leads to a state of self-deception. It's a bad thing because people who fall behind tend to blame themselves more than they ought to. It's a bad thing because unless you acknowledge something is broke, no one's gonna try to fix it. But it may be a good thing too. For it motivates people to do the things they need to do to get ahead. It increases personal responsibility and striving.

Tocqueville saw this optimism, and this potential. He called it "the magnificent heritage." But he saw too that in their mad dash to better themselves as individuals, Americans understood a profound concept that would keep them bettering themselves as a society too.

He called that concept "self-interest properly understood."

It was the ultimate unspoken doctrine that gave the country its humanity. It had many elements: a materialism refined by spirituality, a sense of compassion and empathy borne of being in the same boat, which he attributed to the widespread equality of conditions.

Today, in the new economy, the trend is inexorably away from the equality of conditions that Tocqueville saw. Where might it lead? It has become harder and harder to grasp that if you win big, but those around you lose big, you ultimately lose too. The crude equation one wants to avoid—that those who have more money are better and smarter than those who have less—has more currency than ever. It makes for a tougher, more driven, more one-track, but ultimately lonelier America.

Today, while belief in the American Dream is resurgent, self-interest appears not nearly so properly understood.

As I approach the ragged-toothed outline of Manhattan, and drive onto the George Washington Bridge for the last time, I find myself—once again—in conversation with a toll collector, gatekeeper of the city. I roll down my window, stick my neck out.

"This is my last day in America," I tell him. "I've been here three years, two of them traveling around your country, writing a book."

"Wow! That so?" he says, a smile lighting up his dimpled black face. "What's the book about?"

"Chasing the red, white and blue . . . the American Dream," I say. "And it's just struck me. You are my last interviewee."

He reaches out his latex-gloved hand to shake mine. He is tall, well built, handsome, looks in his early thirties. "Pleased to meet you," he says, grasping my hand firmly and giving it a hearty pump. "I've lived here my whole life. My friends call me First Class."

"What?" I shout above the traffic, thinking I must have misheard him.

(The drivers behind me are starting to blow impatiently on their horns.)

"First Class," he repeats, bending closer. "You know, class—that special something about a person money can't buy."

"I like it," I laugh. "First Class, I have one question for you . . ." We're both leaning out of our windows now, our heads almost touching, sweat pouring down his brow in the ninety-five degree heat. "Are you living the American Dream?"

"Not yet—but soon," he says, without missing a beat. "It's gonna happen. It's just around the corner."

He grasps my hand to say goodbye. "Don't forget First Class," he entreats me. "Don't forget me an' I won't forget you."

Then, whoosh!—I'm off, hurtling over the bridge and into the long and the thin of it.

I look back. In my rearview mirror, the toll collector in his airless, cramped booth recedes behind a choking haze of gasoline fumes. But in my mind's eye I can still see his face beaming out at me, against all odds, a luminous, infectious portrait of hope.

NOTES

INTRODUCTION

1. The Harkness Fellowship is administered by the Commonwealth Fund of New York.
2. George Wilson Pierson, *Tocqueville in America,* Johns Hopkins University Press, 1996, p. 129.
3. Ibid., pp. 130–131.
4. Ibid., p. 125.
5. Alexis de Tocqueville, *Democracy in America,* translated by George Lawrence, edited by J. P. Mayer, HarperPerennial, 1988, volume 1, "Author's Introduction," p. 9. (Note that the italics are my emphasis.)
6. See, for example, George Wilson Pierson, p. 7.
7. Tocqueville, volume 2, part 3, chapter 1, p. 561.
8. Ibid., chapter 4, p. 571.
9. "Child Poverty Fact Sheet," National Center for Children in Poverty, Joseph L. Mailman School of Public Health of Columbia University, July 2000. The poverty statistics used apply to the year 1998, being the most recently available statistics relating to the time of my arrival in the United States. In 1998, the poverty threshold was $16,660 for a family of four, and $13,003 for a family of three. The current poverty formula—created in 1965 for President Lyndon B. Johnson to keep tabs on his "War on Poverty"—has remained unchanged since then, except for adjustments for inflation. It is based on a basic food budget that is multiplied by three in order to arrive at the poverty threshold. Families with incomes between 100 and 185 percent of the federal poverty line are deemed near poor because 185 percent is the upper limit used to determine eligibility for a number of government assistance programs for low-income people—such as the School Lunch Program, Medicaid, and the Special Supplemental Nutrition Program for Women, Infants, and Children. Note that the best source for statistics comparing child poverty in the United States to other nations is the Luxembourg Income Study data, a report by UNICEF. This report ranks the U.S. second highest among industrialized nations using a relative poverty measure (i.e., 50 percent of the overall median income).

10. Kathy Larin and Elizabeth C. McNichol, "Pulling Apart: A State-by-State Analysis of Income Trends," Center on Budget and Policy Priorities, December 1997. The report uses "before-tax income for families with at least one child under 18" from the Census Bureau's Current Population Survey. The report compares pooled data from the late 1970s to the mid-1990s (1994, 1995, and 1996).

11. State surpluses alone for the 1999 fiscal year totaled $35 billion, according to the *New York Times*. See Robert Pear, "States Gather Big Surpluses, Benefit of a Strong Economy," *New York Times,* January 5, 2000.

12. See for example: Robert Rector, "America Has the World's Richest Poor People," *Wall Street Journal,* September 24, 1998.

13. Tocqueville, volume 1, part 1, chapter 5, p. 61.

14. See George Wilson Pierson, *Tocqueville and Beaumont in America,* Oxford University Press, New York, 1938. This title, now out of print, was reprinted in paperback in 1996 as *Tocqueville in America* by the Johns Hopkins University Press. Apart from the shortened title, it is an exact reprint of the original. It is to this latter version of the book, therefore—the version still in print and available to readers—that endnote references are directed.

15. For 1830 census population data, see National Censuses tables, Department of Commerce, Bureau of the Census.

16. Pierson, p. 621.

CHAPTER 1: NEW YORK, NEW YORK

1. Official Manhattan apartment prices are taken from the Douglas Elliman Manhattan Market Report for the first quarter of 2000. Official London house prices are for 1999 according to the Land Registry, as reported by the London *Evening Standard*. See Mira Bar-Hillel, "London House Prices Rocket," *Evening Standard,* August 25, 1999, p. 1.

2. Sources of New York City poverty statistics: Mark Levitan, "Poverty in New York City: A CSS Data Brief," Community Service Society of New York, 1999. This report notes that it "provides the most recent measures of poverty in New York City." The tabulations it presents "are calculated from the same source data as that used by the U.S. Bureau of the Census for its annual report on income and poverty nationwide, the March Current Population Survey." The near-poverty statistics for New York City are calculated for me using census data by

demographers at the National Center for Children in Poverty, Columbia University School of Public Health.

3. Jerry J. Salama and Michael H. Schill, "Reducing the Cost of New Housing Construction in New York City: A Report to the New York City Partnership and Chamber of Commerce, the New York City Housing Partnership and the New York City Department of Housing Preservation and Development," published by New York University School of Law, Center for Real Estate and Urban Policy, July 1999.

4. Jared Bernstein, Elizabeth C. McNichol, Lawrence Mishel, Robert Zahradnik, "Pulling Apart: A State-by-State Analysis of Income Trends," a Joint Report of the Center on Budget and Policy Priorities and the Economic Policy Institute, January 2000. Also see S. Anderson, J. Cavanagh, R. Estes, C. Collins, C. Hartman, "A Decade of Executive Excess: The 1990's—Sixth Annual Executive Compensation Survey," January 9, 1991, joint report by the Institute for Policy Studies and United for a Fair Economy. But note, these figures for CEOs are countrywide and not specific to New York City, though they do relate to CEOs in New York City.

5. Pierson, *Tocqueville in America,* p. 67.

6. Ibid., p. 64.

7. Ibid., p. 85.

8. These minutes of the Common Council, New York City, volume 19, dated May 9, 1831, can be viewed at the library of the New-York Historical Society, New York City. I looked them up because I was curious to see what the official city order of business was around the time of Tocqueville's arrival.

9. Pierson, pp. 69–70.

10. Ibid., pp. 152–167.

11. Tocqueville, *Democracy in America,* volume 1, part 2, chapter 10, p. 350. The New York State slavery data is obtained from the 1830 U.S. census.

12. Tocqueville, volume 1, "Author's Introduction," pp. 11 and 12.

13. Pierson, pp. 158–160.

14. Tocqueville, volume 1, part 2, chapter 10, p. 349 and volume 2, part 3, chapter 7, p. 582.

15. Tocqueville, volume 1, part 1, chapter 3, pp. 51–53.

16. Pierson, pp. 23 and 164.

17. Eric Homberger, *The Historical Atlas of New York City,* Henry Holt and Company, 1994, pp. 68–69.

18. H. M. Ranney, "Account of the Terrific and Fatal Riot at the New

York Astor Place Opera House on the Night of May 10th, 1849," published 1849.

19. Homberger, pp. 88–89.

20. Ibid., pp. 110–111; 114; 164. See also: Jacob A. Riis, *How the Other Half Lives,* 1890; Elizabeth Blackmar, *Manhattan for Rent,* 1785–1850, Cornell University Press, 1989; Robert A. Caro, *The Power Broker: Robert Moses and the Fall of New York,* Vintage Books, 1975.

21. Christiane Bird, *New York Handbook,* Moon Publications Inc., 1997, p. 37.

22. The statistics relating to New York City's public housing are from an interview I conducted with Howard Marder, the public information officer of the New York City Housing Authority (NYCHA). The NYCHA is responsible for the administration of the city's public housing.

23. The 1996 Housing and Vacancy Survey.

24. The Chicago Housing Authority has finally admitted defeat with its existing public housing stock and has submitted an ambitious $1.5 billion plan to the federal government to demolish most of their high-rise public housing developments and replace them with new or rehabilitated rental town-house units in mixed-income communities. See William Claiborne, "Chicago Unveils $1.5 Billion Housing Plan," *Washington Post,* October 2, 1999, p. A2.

25. In the 16 years from 1980 to 1996, although the number of households in New York City rose by 120,000, the housing stock only grew by 53,516 units. Demand outstripped supply by a ratio of more than 2 to 1. See report by Jerry J. Salama and Michael H. Schill, July 1999.

26. Statistics quoted are from the New York City Board of Education.

27. Sources: New York State Department of Education; New York City Board of Education; United Federation of Teachers. Also see Anemona Hartocollis, *New York Times,* June 9, 1999, "Citywide Reading and Math Scores Fall Sharply," pp. A1 and B6; June 24, 1999, "Crew to Shake Up 56 Worst Schools," pp. A1 and B6; and September 17, 1999, "Error Shows Risk of a Total Reliance on Standardized Tests," pp. B1–B4.

28. EPP Monitor, A Publication of the Educational Priorities Panel, Inc., volume 3, issue 3, Spring/Summer 1999, p. 18. See also: "Secret Apartheid, A Report on Racial Discrimination Against Black and Latino Parents and Children in the New York City Public Schools," New York ACORN Schools Office, 1996; Noreen Connell, "Beating the Odds: High-Achieving Elementary Schools in High-Poverty Neighborhoods," Educational Priorities Panel, June 1999.

29. City of New York Executive Budget, Fiscal Year 2000, Budget Summary, Rudolph W. Giuliani, mayor; Office of Management and Budget, Robert M. Harding, director, pp. 2 and 18–19.

30. Joanne Wasserman, "Public Lives, Private Schools—Bigwigs Pick Private Ed for Their Kids," *New York Daily News,* April 3, 2000, pp. 1 and 5.

31. Pierson, p. 124.

32. Ibid., p. 113. Also see Tocqueville, volume 1, part 2, chapter 9, pp. 301–303.

33. According to an interview with Denny Fitzpatrick, director of public relations for the New York State Correctional Officers and Police Benevolent Association, the ethnic breakdown of New York State corrections officers is approximately as follows: 70 percent Caucasian; 20 percent African-American; 10 percent Hispanic. The percentage of Caucasians has fallen from 95 percent in the 1970s, and can be as low as 50 percent as you move to prisons situated closer to New York City, he says. In New York City itself, corrections officers are 80 percent of African-American and Hispanic origin, whereas they used to be mainly Italian and Irish. The latter have tended in recent years to prefer jobs in other civil service areas such as the police force, where the pay, benefits, and work environment are regarded as significantly better.

34. Pierson, p. 102.

35. Pierson, p. 105.

36. Paul L. Wachtel, *The Poverty of Affluence: A Psychological Portrait of the American Way of Life,* New Society Publishers, 1989.

37. "Hollow in the Middle: The Rise and Fall of New York City's Middle Class," New York City Council, December 1997, report prepared by Thomas L. McMahon, Larian Angelo, John Mollenkopf.

38. 1996 Housing and Vacancy Survey, Appendix D.

39. Luz Claudio, Leon Tulton, John Doucette, Philip J. Landrigan, "Socioeconomic Factors and Asthma Hospitalization Rates in New York City," Department of Community Medicine, Mount Sinai School of Medicine, New York, *Journal of Asthma* 36 (4), 1999, pp. 343–350.

40. E. B. White, *Essays of E. B. White,* Harper & Row Publishers Inc, 1949.

CHAPTER 2: THE RUST BELT

1. U.S. Bureau of the Census. See also "One in Four: America's Youngest Poor," National Center for Children in Poverty, Columbia University School of Public Health, 1996, p. 70.

2. Pierson, *Tocqueville in America,* pp. 229–241.
3. Also see footnotes by Tocqueville, *Democracy in America,* volume 1, part 2, chapter 10, p. 385.
4. Pierson, p. 241.
5. Ibid., p. 232.
6. Ibid., pp. 258–259.
7. Thomas R. Hammer, "The Once and Future Economy of Metropolitan Flint, Michigan," prepared for the Mott Foundation, 1996–97.
8. Pierson, p. 84.
9. Tocqueville, *Democracy in America,* volume 1, part 1, chapter 1, p. 23.
10. Tocqueville, volume 2, part 2, chapter 8, pp. 525–528.
11. Ibid., volume 1, part 2, chapter 7, p. 260.
12. Ibid., volume 2, part 3, chapter 21, p. 635.
13. Ibid., pp. 636–637.
14. Ibid., p. 639.
15. Ibid., p. 645.
16. For readers interested in a detailed analysis of Flint by the Mott Foundation, and for supporting data and statistics on current trends, see: Thomas R. Hammer, "The Once and Future Economy of Metropolitan Flint, Michigan," prepared for the Mott Foundation, 1996–97; "Survey of Attitudes and Opinions of Residents of Genesee County, Michigan, 1996," prepared for the Mott Foundation by Market Opinion Research, August 1996; "Genesee County FactBook," compiled for the Mott Foundation by Market Opinion Research, January 1997; and "Flint Area Program Plan," Mott Foundation, March 4–5, 1998.

CHAPTER 3: THE OHIO RIVER VALLEY

1. Pierson, *Tocqueville in America,* p. 543.
2. Tocqueville, *Democracy in America,* volume 2, part 3, chapter 14, pp. 605–608.
3. The history of the steamboat on the Ohio is documented by the Ohio River Museum in Marietta, Ohio.
4. Tocqueville, volume 1, part 2, chapter 10, p. 385.
5. Pierson, p. 543.
6. Ibid., p. 552.
7. Tocqueville, volume 1, part 2, chapter 10, pp. 345–346.
8. Ibid., p. 346.
9. Ibid., p. 348.

10. The Quakers held it as an act of faith that no one could be a slave. See R. Douglas Hurt, *The Ohio Frontier: Crucible of the Old Northwest, 1720–1830,* Indiana University Press, 1996, p. 374 (paperback edition).

11. Tocqueville, volume 1, part 2, chapter 10, p. 343.

12. Ibid., p. 354.

13. Ibid., p. 344.

14. See also Hurt, *The Ohio Frontier,* pp. 386–388.

15. Pierson, p. 565.

16. Tocqueville, volume 1, part 2, chapter 10, pp. 317 and 343.

17. Ibid., p. 362.

18. Ibid., volume 1, "Author's Introduction," p. 9.

19. Ibid., volume 1, "Conclusion," p. 412.

20. Ibid., volume 1, part 2, chapter 10, p. 360.

21. President Clinton's State of the Union Address, January 24, 1995, Executive Office of the President.

22. Tocqueville, volume 1, "Author's Introduction," p. 19 and volume 1, part 2, chapter 10, p. 340. Tocqueville refers to the impending publication of Gustave Beaumont's work both in the text of his introduction and in a footnote.

23. For a detailed elucidation of Tocqueville's predictions on the "probable future of the three races," see volume 1, part 2, chapter 10, pp. 316–363.

24. Ibid., volume 1, "Author's Introduction," p. 20.

25. Pierson, pp. 554–555.

26. Ibid., pp. 464–465.

27. Tocqueville, volume 1, part 2, chapter 10, pp. 317–318.

28. For a complete steamship payroll and for descriptive accounts of life aboard a steamship in the early nineteenth century, the traveler is referred to the Ohio River Museum in Marietta, Ohio.

29. Pierson, p. 546. See also the *Nashville Republican and State Gazette,* December 8, 1831, for a newspaper report on the sinking of the steamboat *Fourth of July,* which carries the headline: ANOTHER STEAMBOAT SUNK!

30. See Peter F. Drucker, "Beyond the Information Revolution," *Atlantic Monthly,* October 1999, pp. 47–57.

31. Franklin Toker, *Pittsburgh, An Urban Portrait,* University of Pittsburgh Press, 1994.

32. The reporter in question was Boston journalist James Parton.

33. Heinz History Center, Pittsburgh.

34. Rand-McNally, *Places Rated Almanac,* 1985. Cities are ranked according

to a combination of factors, including climate, housing, health care, crime, education, transportation, arts, recreation, and economics.

35. With one notable exception: Massive and fairly recent Hispanic immigration to the United States has meant that increasingly, Hispanic-Americans are underrepresented in Ohio.

36. Marie Haney, George Vredeveld, Thomas Zinn, "Greater Cincinnati Labor Market Study," Economics Research Group, Center for Economic Education, University of Cincinnati, November 1997, p. 1.

37. "Work Trends: Working Hard But Staying Poor—A National Survey of the Working Poor and Unemployed," a joint project of the John J. Heldrich Center for Workforce Development at Rutgers, the State University of New Jersey, and the Center for Survey Research and Analysis at the University of Connecticut, July 1999.

38. "Working Hard, Earning Less: The Story of Job Growth in America," a publication of the National Priorities Project in collaboration with Jobs With Justice, December 1998. Growth figures quote Bureau of Labor Statistics.

39. Ibid.

40. Haney, Vredeveld, Zinn.

41. "Work Trends."

42. "Working Hard, Earning Less."

43. Tocqueville, volume 2, part 3, chapter 5, pp. 572–580.

44. Ibid.

45. For example, the Haney, Vredeveld, Zinn and "Work Trends" reports mentioned above both point out the increasing primacy of education for securing high-wage employment. However, we need not rely just on these reports—the existence of this trend has become common cause and can be found in almost any modern analysis of the U.S. economy. See also the U.S. Commerce Department, "Falling Through the Net: Defining the Digital Divide," July 8, 1999.

46. Excerpted from David Cohen, "Lord of the Fries," London Evening Standard, July 3, 1995, pp. 27 and 46.

47. Craig Horowitz, "The McCain Mutiny," New York, December 6, 1999, pp. 43–48.

48. Cincinnati, for example, is currently debating a $248 million plan to revitalize its downtown riverfront area. See "Vision for a Busy Riverside Needs $248 Million," Cincinnati Enquirer, October 1, 1999, p. 1.

49. Pierson, pp. 576, 584, 241.

50. Richard Lacayo, "The Sprawl over Brawl," Time, March 22, 1999, pp. 44–48.

51. These tips are published in Kemmons Wilson's autobiography, with Robert Kerr, *Half Luck and Half Brains: The Kemmons Wilson Holiday Inn Story,* Hambleton-Hill Publishing, Inc., 1996.
52. Isaac Shapiro and Robert Greenstein, "The Widening Income Gulf," Center on Budget and Policy Priorities, September 4, 1999. See also Peter T. Kilborn, "Memphis Blacks Find Poverty's Grip Strong—the General Prosperity Fails to Reach All," *New York Times,* October 5, 1999, p. A14.
53. Tocqueville, volume 2, part 3, chapter 7, pp. 582–584.
54. "Working Hard, Earning Less," p. 8. Figures comparing unionized and nonunionized pay use data from the Bureau of National Affairs.
55. Tony Royle, "The Reluctant Bargainers? McDonald's, unions and Pay Determination . . . ," *Industrial Relations Journal,* vol. 30, issue 12, June 1999, p. 135.
56. See U.S. Department of Labor Web site.
57. "Working Hard, Earning Less."
58. Tocqueville, volume 2, part 3, chapter 7, p. 584.

CHAPTER 4: THE MISSISSIPPI DELTA

1. Pierson, *Tocqueville in America,* p. 580.
2. Tocqueville, volume 1, part 1, chapter 1, p. 24.
3. The history and geography of the Mississippi River is documented in the Mississippi River Museum at Mud Island, Memphis, Tenessee. See also the Cottonlandia Museum in Greenwood, Mississippi.
4. Eugene Martin Christiansen, "Gambling and the American Economy," *Annals* of the American Academy of Political and Social Science, volume 556, March 1998, Sage Periodicals Press, pp. 36–51.
5. Figures obtained from World GDP Data.
6. William C. Rivenbark and Don E. Slabach, "Who Pays to Play? Voluntary Tax Incidence and Mississippi Gaming," July 1996, John C. Stennis Institute of Government, Mississippi State University. The 1996 report was based on telephone interviews with 807 Mississippians. See also *Memphis Commercial Appeal,* August 14, 1996, pp. A1 and A9; and the National Gambling Impact Study Commission Executive Summary, report to the President, Congress, Governors, and Tribal Leaders, June 1999, p. 14.
7. Christiansen, pp. 36–51.
8. Tocqueville, volume 2, part 2, chapter 19, p. 553.
9. Mississippi River Museum, Mud Island, Memphis.

10. "The Tunica Miracle," Tunica Convention & Visitors Bureau, Tunica, Mississippi.

11. See also Gary Lee, "Trail of Tears," *Washington Post,* August 1, 1999, p. E9.

12. Maps of Mississippi showing former Indian territory circa 1822–1830 are located at the Cottonlandia Museum, Greenwood. See also Grant Foreman, *Indian Removal,* University of Oklahoma Press, 1972 (originally published 1932 on the one hundredth anniversary of the arrival in Oklahoma of the first Indians as a result of the government's relocation of the Five Civilized Tribes). See also Robert V. Remini, *The Legacy of Andrew Jackson,* Louisiana State University Press, 1988.

13. Pierson, pp. 595–598.

14. See Gary C. Anders, "Indian Gaming: Financial and Regulatory Issues," *Annals* of the American Academy of Political and Social Science, volume 556, March 1998, pp. 98–108. Also see Joel Millman, "Choctaw Chief Leads His Mississippi Tribe Into the Global Market," *Wall Street Journal,* July 23, 1999, p. B1.

15. Mississippi Gaming Commission, January 25, 1999, report to the Mississippi Senate Appropriations Sub-Committee.

16. See note 6, Rivenbark and Slabach.

17. Cindy Wolff, "Bankruptcy Growing as More Live on the Edge," *Memphis Commercial Appeal,* December 12, 1996, p. B5.

18. U.S. Dept. of Commerce, Economics & Statistical Administration Bureau of Economic Analysis, May 1998. See also "The Mississippi Miracle: How the State with the Worst Odds Ended up with the Winning Hand," Harrison County Development Commission, September 1998.

19. The local history of Vicksburg was recounted to me by Gordon Cotton, who for 22 years has been the director of the Old Courthouse Museum, Vicksburg, and is an expert on local history.

20. See also William Raspberry, "Windfall for Segregation," *The Washington Post.*

21. Tocqueville, "Appendix to Volume One," pp. 714–715. (Italics my emphasis.)

22. Executive Summary, The National Gambling Impact Study Commission, June 1999.

CHAPTER 5: ON THROUGH THE DEEP SOUTH

1. I have not disclosed Rhoda B.'s family name even though she gave me permission to use it. I base this judgment on the fact that at this acutely

vulnerable time in her life, she is possibly unable to contemplate the effects of making her situation public.

2. "Southern Style Religion," *PRRC Emerging Trends,* Princeton Religion Research Center, volume 16, number 7, September 1994, p. 3.
3. "British and American Religious Beliefs and Practices Compared," *PRRC Emerging Trends,* Princeton Religion Research Center, volume 15, number 9, November 1993, p. 5. The report notes that "the findings reported for Great Britain are taken from a study conducted by Social Surveys (Gallup) Ltd. in May 1993" and that "the American comparisons are taken from Gallup surveys in recent years."
4. Tocqueville, volume 1, part 2, chapter 9, p. 295.
5. Ibid., volume 2, part 2, chapter 15, p. 542.
6. Pierson, *Tocqueville in America,* p. 69.
7. Tocqueville, volume 1, part 2, chapter 9, p. 279.
8. Pierson, p. 125.
9. Pierson, pp. 153, 158, 220, 500, 649.
10. Tocqueville, volume 1, part 2, chapter 9, p. 295.
11. Ibid., pp. 295–296.
12. Ibid., pp. 297–301.
13. Pierson, p. 500.
14. Tocqueville, volume 1, part 2, chapter 9, p. 293. Tocqueville was quoting a report in the *New York Spectator* of August 23, 1831.
15. "Religion in America—1996 Report," Princeton Religion Research Center, p. 46.
16. Berke, "Religion Center Stage in Presidential Race," *New York Times,* December 15, 1999, p. A20. See also Gustav Niebuhr, "God and Man and the Presidency," *New York Times,* December 19, 1999, section 4, Week in Review, p. 5.
17. David Cohen, "Born-again Husbands—a Promise or a Threat," *Independent,* October 7, 1997, p. 19.
18. Pierson, p. 249.
19. J. Gordon Melton, "The Development of American Religion: An Interpretive View," *Encyclopedia of American Religions,* sixth edition, Gale Research, 1999, pp. 1–18.
20. Tocqueville, volume 2, part 1, chapter 5, p. 448.
21. Ibid., volume 1, part 2, chapter 9, p. 288.
22. J. Gordon Melton, *National Directory of Churches, Synagogues, and Other Houses of Worship,* volume 3, Southern States.
23. Sourced from the "Slavery in Mobile" exhibit, Museum of Mobile.
24. "Gallup Religion Data," *PRRC Emerging Trends,* Princeton Religion

Research Center, 1997. Also see *Yearbook of American and Canadian Churches,* sixty-sixth edition, edited by Eileen W. Lindner, Abingdon Press, 1998, pp. 5–6.

25. Tocqueville, volume 1, part 2, chapter 9, p. 295.

26. Fredrick Douglas Richardson Jr., "The Birth of a Church: Stone Street Baptist, Alabama's First," unpublished manuscript.

27. Fredrick Douglas Richardson Jr. *The Genesis and Exodus of NOW,* Futura Publishing Inc., 1996.

28. For statistics on child poverty, see also *Alabama Kids Count 1998 Data Book.*

29. Andrew Billingsley, *Mighty Like a River: The Black Church and Social Reform,* Oxford University Press, 1999.

30. See also Leo Rosten, *Religions of America,* Simon & Schuster, 1975, pp. 26–38.

31. Note, though, that not all Southern Baptists are conservative. Bill Clinton, for example, is Southern Baptist. Progressive Baptist churches tend to affiliate to conventions other than the Southern Baptist Convention.

32. *Unmasked—Exposing the Secrets of Deception* was shown on December 5, 1999, at 10:10 P.M. on channel TLC.

33. Laurie Goodstein, "Coalition's Woes May Hinder Goals of Christian Right," *New York Times,* August 2 1999, p. A1.

34. "Sharp Rise in Evangelical Christians," *PRRC Emerging Trends,* Princeton Religion Research Center, March 1998, volume 20, number 3.

35. Excerpt from George W. Bush's speech delivered in Indianapolis on July 22, 1999. See also Adam Clymer, "Filter Aid to Poor Through Churches, Bush Urges," *New York Times,* July 23, 1999, pp. A1 and A12.

36. Marvin Olasky, *The Tragedy of American Compassion,* Regnery Publishing, Inc., 1992, p. 219.

37. Tocqueville, volume 2, part 3, chapter 1, p. 565.

38. Oscar H. Lipscomb, archbishop of Mobile, and Raymond J. Boland, bishop of Birmingham, "Make Justice Your Aim: A Pastoral Letter on Poverty in Alabama," December 8, 1990.

39. Pierson, p. 298.

40. Alabama Health Data Sheet, produced jointly by the Alabama Department of Public Health and the Center for Demographic and Cultural Research, Auburn University, Montgomery, May 1999. For poverty statistics, see Alabama Population Data Sheet, Center for Demographic and Cultural Research, Auburn University, Montgomery, November 1995.

41. Alabama Health Data Sheet.
42. New York Times Poll, *New York Times,* December 18, 1999, p. B7. See also Diana Jean Schemo with Marjorie Connelly, "In Poll, New York Catholics Call Poverty a Top Concern," *New York Times,* December 18, 1999, pp. A1, B7.
43. CNN/USA Today/Gallup Poll, May 1996, *PRRC Emerging Trends,* Princeton Religion Research Center, volume 20, number 10, December 1998, p. 5.
44. *Yearbook of American and Canadian Churches,* 1998, Church Finances Statistics, pp. 14 and 321–324.
45. Gallup Poll, "Which Groups Have the Greatest Responsibility for Helping the Poor?" *PRRC Emerging Trends,* Princeton Religion Research Center, volume 20, number 10, December 1998, p. 3.

CHAPTER 6: CALIFORNIA

1. Tocqueville, volume 1, "Author's Introduction," p. 9.
2. According to the U.S. Census Bureau, the 1830 population of the U.S. was 12.8 million. According to the U.S. Census Bureau, Population Division, the population estimate for California as of July 1, 1998, was 32.7 million.
3. For accounts of early life in California, see: Kevin Starr, *Americans and the California Dream,* Oxford University Press, 1973; Earl Pomeroy, *The Pacific Slope: A History of California, Oregon, Washington, Idaho, Utah and Nevada,* Alfred A Knopf, 1965; and Malcolm E. Barker, *San Francisco Memoirs, 1835–1851: Eyewitness Accounts of the Birth of a City,* London-born Publications, 1994.
4. Philip Martin, Elizabeth Midgley, *Population Bulletin,* volume 54, number 2, June 1999.
5. Ibid.
6. Tocqueville, volume 1, part 2, chapter 10, p. 405.
7. "Population Estimates for States by Race and Hispanic Origin: July 1, 1998," Population Estimates Program, Population Division, U.S. Census Bureau.
8. "2000 Index of Silicon Valley," Joint Venture: Silicon Valley Network, January 10, 2000. See also "A Majority of None—Silicon Valley Faces a New Ethnic Mix," special report, *San Jose Mercury News,* April 14–19, 1999, p. 3, for population shift tables sourced from the California Department of Finance.

9. U.S. Bureau of the Census, Current Population Reports, Series P23–194, "Population Profile of the United States: 1997," U.S. Government Printing Office, Washington, D.C., 1998, p. 8.

10. Steven Greenhouse, "Guess Who's Embracing Immigrants Now," *New York Times,* March 5, 2000, Week in Review, p. 4.

11. Tocqueville, p. 55.

12. Pierson, pp. 242–243.

13. Martin and Midgley.

14. Greenhouse.

15. Martin and Midgley. The legislation mentioned is the Immigration Reform and Control Act of 1986 (IRCA). For the work of the commissions, see Select Commission on Immigration and Refugee Policy (SCIRP), "U.S. Immigration Policy and the National Interest," Washington, D.C., 1981.

16. See the Personal Responsibilities and Work Opportunities Reconciliation Act (PRWORA) of 1996.

17. For a quick reference to further details, see Evelyn Nieves, "California Calls Off Effort to Carry Out Immigrant Measure," *New York Times,* July 30, 1999, p. A1.

18. Tocqueville, volume 1, part 2, chapter 8, p. 270.

19. Tocqueville died in 1859. Alexander Graham Bell invented the telephone in 1876.

20. Statistics obtained from the archives of the Seventh-Day Adventist Headquarters in Washington, D.C.

21. U.S. Bureau of the Census, Current Population Reports, Series P23–194, "Population Profile of the United States: 1997," pp. 20–21.

22. Ibid, p. 21.

23. See for example: Patricia Leigh Brown, "Teaching Jonny Values Where Money is King," *New York Times,* March 10, 2000, p. A1. and Evelyn Nieves, "In Man-Rich Silicon Valley, It Seems Like Strikeout.com," *New York Times,* April 10, 2000, p. A1.

24. Nieves, p. A1.

25. See for example: Michael Lewis, *The New New Thing,* W. W. Norton & Company, 2000; Po Bronson, *The Nudist on the Late Shift,* Random House, 1999.

26. "2000 Index of Silicon Valley," Joint Venture: Silicon Valley Network, January 10, 2000.

27. The average price for a single-family home in Santa Clara County in April 2000 is $702,000, according to the local Santa Clara Association

of Realtors. See also Dennis Hevesi, "Average Cost of Apartments Hits $700,000," *New York Times,* May 19, 2000, pp. B1 and B7.

28. Pierson, p. 239.

29. "2000 Index of Silicon Valley." Data from this report was supplemented by an interview with Ruben Barrales, president and CEO of Joint Venture: Silicon Valley Network. Also see John Markoff, "Influx of New Immigrants Found in Silicon Valley," *New York Times,* January 10, 2000, p. C2.

30. Ibid.

31. Ibid. See also Aaron Bernstein, "Down and Out in Silicon Valley," *Business Week,* March 27, 2000, pp. 76–88.

32. Thomas J. Stanley, *The Millionaire Mind,* Andrews McMeel Publishing, 2000.

33. Martin and Midgley.

34. Jared Bernstein and Liz McNichol, "State by State Income Trends," combined report of the Center on Budget and Policy Priorities and the Economic Policy Institute, January 18, 2000.

35. Evelyn Nieves, "Many in Silicon Valley Cannot Afford Housing, Even at $50,000 a Year," *New York Times,* February 20, 2000, p. A16. See also: Aaron Bernstein, pp. 76–88; and Edward Iwata, "Troubles in Silicon Valley," *USA Today,* April 14, 2000, p. 1B.

36. Tocqueville, volume 1, part 2, chapter 7, pp. 246–261.

37. Statistics are furnished by Lois Salisbury, president of Children Now. See also Kids Count data book for a report card of all fifty states.

38. Sam Howe Verhovek, "Internet's Rich Are Giving It Away, Their Way," *New York Times,* February 11, 2000, p. A1.

CHAPTER 7: WASHINGTON, D.C.

1. Pierson, *Tocqueville in America,* pp. 639 and 641.

2. Ibid., p. 667.

3. Ibid., p. 671.

4. The proposal to repeal the federal estate tax passed in the House of Representatives by a vote of 279 to 136. The same bill later passed in the Senate by a vote of 59 to 39. See Richard W. Stevenson, "Congress Clears a Bill to Repeal the Estate Tax," *New York Times,* July 15, 2000, p. A1. Note that estate tax is levied on estates worth more than $675,000, or $1.3 million in the case of family-owned farms and businesses.

5. "Child Poverty in the States: Levels and Trends from 1979 to 1998,"

Research Brief 2, National Center for Children in Poverty, Mailman School of Public Health, Columbia University, 2000.

6. Herb Jackson, "Raising Funds for Corzine, Gore—Clinton Sees Easy Times as a Test," *Record,* July 1, 2000, p. 1.

7. William Shakespeare, *Julius Caesar,* act 4, scene 3, lines 218–224.

ACKNOWLEDGMENTS

I always say, to anyone who asks, that I had three guardian angels in America. The first was my host at Columbia University, Professor Larry Aber; the second was my agent, Jim Levine; and the third was a fellow journalist, Ponchitta Pierce.

It was in conversation with Larry Aber that the idea of this book was first conceived. Meeting in coffee shops, sidewalk cafes, and bodegas in Washington Heights and on the Upper West Side of Manhattan, we began the free-flow, creative process of carving up Tocqueville's journey into manageable chunks and putting together a book proposal. When a publisher had been secured, Larry waved me off on my journeys, offering initial contacts for many of my destinations. He secured for me an infrastructure at Columbia University, which gave me a base from which to operate, and he was an ear for me to express my doubts and insecurities over the enormity of the journey I had undertaken. Later he provided critical input on early drafts of the chapters, offering his time and his energy, while in no way ever seeking to inhibit either my process of discovery or my conclusions. More than all of this, he offered me the greatest gift of all—his friendship.

Jim Levine, my agent, has been the straightest of straight shooters, guiding this book with a wise and steady hand, and hauling me off the rocks on at least one occasion. He too has become a close and dear friend.

Ponchitta Pierce was an early believer and a penetrating reader of early drafts of chapters. Ponchitta's questions helped me to clarify and solidify my thinking, and to justify the conclusions that I reached. She has been a tireless champion of the whole enterprise from very near the beginning of the process to the end. She has offered me her time, her insights, and her friendship. I can scarcely imagine I will ever be able to repay her generosity.

My gratitude goes also to George Witte, my editor at Picador, whose vision of what this book might be gelled with my own, and whose encouragement provided just the right support at critical times.

It is thanks to the Commonwealth Fund, and the generous stipend that goes with a Harkness Fellowship, that I came to America in the first place. Karen Davis, Robin Osborn, and Beth Lowe all bent over backwards to help me stay on and write this book, and for that, and for the immense creative freedom afforded by the Harkness Fellowship, I will be forever grateful.

The initial phases of the book, as well as the cost of travel, were made possible by the generous funding of Columbia University. The staff at the National Center for Children in Poverty, Joseph L. Mailman School of Public Health, Columbia University, where I was based, accommodated me for three years in the most welcoming way and offered friendship, practical assistance, and engaging conversation. My appreciation goes to Jane Knitzer, Barbara Blum, Julian Palmer, Stanley Bernard, Ernesto Diaz, Edie Miller, Lee Kreader, Carmela Smith, Elvis Delahoz, Martha Garvey, Neil Bennett, and Carole Oshinsky.

A special thank-you to Jackie Vine, who helped with some of the early demographic research and who contributed creative ideas regarding my travels to the rust belt and the Mississippi Delta. Thanks are also due to Betty Miles for her close reading of the manuscript.

I owe an enormous debt of thanks to the many Americans who shared with me their time and life stories during the reporting of this book. Without their cooperation and trust, there would have been no meat to this bone.

In addition, I would like to thank the following people, who in their unique way contributed either to the realization of the book, to the well-being of my family in Sparkill, Rockland County, New York, or to the serendipitous coincidence of events that led to my arrival in America. These people include: Jack O'Sullivan, Erica Benner, Michael Watts, Andrew Samuels, Richard Coker, Helen Hogan, Jonathan Broomberg, Bradley Arden, Andrew Nash, Mary O'Reilly, Betty Miles, Richard Korman, Neria Cohen, Aviva Nash, Larry Nash, Yoni Davimes, Yisroel Davimes, Debbie Fox,

Norman Kramer, Anita Kramer, Yuval Cohen, Shira Cohen, Claudia Judelman, Barry Judelman, Vivienne Kramer, Ryan Kramer, Simon Jacobson, Tom McDonnell, and Nora Johnson. For support from my friends across the channel who stayed patient, loyal, and encouraging despite our extended absence, my thanks to Jonathan Wilson, Gilla Gelberg, Jacob Zelinger, Jill Sim, Sandi Sharkey, Karen Lubner, Gary Lubner, Jeremy Krikler, Eliza Kentridge, Anthony Berendt, Dudley Yeo, Dorian Yeo, Lora Wignall, Patrick Tobin, Gavin Evans, Pat Devereaux, Gillian Paul, and David Paul.

For permission to reproduce select quotes from Tocqueville's original diaries and letters as translated and published in George Wilson Pierson's excellent book *Tocqueville in America* (Johns Hopkins University Press, 1996 edition), my appreciation goes to Norah Pierson and Loueva Pierson, respectively the daughter and widow of the late Yale professor George Wilson Pierson. I found the George Lawrence translation of Alexis de Tocqueville's *Democracy in America* (edited by J. P. Mayer, Harper & Row) a pleasure to read and far superior to every other edition. Permission to quote selectively from it has been gratefully received from HarperCollins.

Though the responsibility for the shortcomings and errors of this book are, of course, mine and mine alone, I want to appropriate the sentiments of Tocqueville, who in his introduction asked of his readers: "I realize that despite the trouble taken, nothing will be easier than to criticize this book, if anyone thinks of doing so. Those who look closely into the whole work will, I think, find one pregnant thought which binds all its parts together. But the diversity of subjects treated is very great, and whoever chooses can easily cite an isolated fact to contradict the facts I have assembled, or an isolated opinion against my opinions. I would therefore ask for my book to be read in the spirit in which it was written and would wish it to be judged by the general impression it leaves, just as I have formed my own judgments not for any particular reason, but in conformity with a mass of evidence."

Lastly, I want to thank those closest to me. To my parents, Maurice and Jeanette: Dad, you are a mensch and an enduring inspiration as to how a man should live his life; Mom, your capacity to give in a thoughtful and insightful way has been a gift of inestimable value to me. As a team, you have given me more wise support than any son could ask for. You have allowed me, simply, to be who I am.

To my two daughters, Jessie (ten) and Kayla (six), you have been charming and delightful companions. I am grateful for the positive way you accepted displacement from London and grasped your three years in America with both hands.

Finally, to my wife, Pamela, my partner, my soul mate, and my first reader. You have helped me in both visible and silent ways on more occasions than I can mention. You not only endured my extended absences in a new country with great courage, but built a life and a community in the vibrant, stylish way that only you know how. Thank you for your love and support.

It remains for me to acknowledge the principal musicians that I listened to as I wrote, and who surely eased and oiled the writing process, namely the Buena Vista Social Club, the Afro-Cuban All Stars, and Santana.

David Cohen
London, April 2001